ST. FRANCIS AND THE THIRD ORDER

The Franciscan and pre-Franciscan Penitential Movement

RAFFAELE PAZZELLI, T.O.R.

Franciscan Herald Press
1434 West 51st Street
Chicago, Illinois 60609

ST. FRANCIS AND THE THIRD ORDER: The Franciscan and pre-Franciscan Penitential Movement by Raffaele Pazzelli, TOR. Originally published in Italian as *San Francesco e il Terz'Ordine: Il movimento penitenziale pre-francescano e francescano.* Copyright ©1982 Prov. Pad. F.M.C. Editrice Grafiche Messagero di S. Antonio—Padua. Copyright ©1989 Franciscan Herald Press, 1434 West 51st Street, Chicago, Illinois 60609. ALL RIGHTS RESERVED.

Library of Congress Cataloging-in-Publication Data

Pazzelli, Raffaele.
    [San Francesco e il Terz'ordine. English]
    St. Francis and the third order : the Franciscan and pre-Franciscan Penitential movement / Raffaele Pazzelli.
        p. cm.
    Translation of: San Francesco e il Terz'ordine.
    Bibliography: p.
    Includes index.
    ISBN 0-8199-0953-X
    1. Francis, of Assisi, Saint, 1182-1226. 2. Penitents—History.
3. Secular Franciscans. 4. Third Order Regular of St. Francis—History.   I. Title.
BX4700.F6P3513   1989
271'.3—dc20   89-1433
                                                                             CIP

Cover picture: Sister Kay Francis Berger, O.S.F., Canticle Studio, Joliet, Illinois

PRINTED IN THE UNITED STATES OF AMERICA

"Heirs of that great movement of evangelical life which the *poenitentes de Assisio* embraced, learn to live your vocation . . . as brothers and sisters of penance with an enlightened sense of conversion and of continuous renewal."

Pope John Paul II

TABLE OF CONTENTS

FOREWORD ix

INTRODUCTION xii

ABBREVIATIONS xv

Chapter 1: THE BIBLICAL AND FRANCISCAN UNDERSTANDING OF PENANCE 1
1. THE BIBLICAL SENSE: A. THE PROPHETS; B. THE POST-EXILIC PERIOD; C. THE TEACHING OF CHRIST; D. THE TEACHING OF THE APOSTLES; E. THE TEACHING OF ST. JOHN, 1-4. 2. THE FRANCISCAN SENSE, 4.

Chapter 2: THE ORIGINS OF THE PENITENTS (III-VI CENTURIES) 7
PENANCE IN THE PRIMITIVE CHURCH, 7.— THE GRAVE IMPOSITIONS PLACED UPON THE PENITENTS—THE BEGINNING OF VOLUNTARY PENANCE, 9.—NEW METHODS OF OBTAINING PARDON-MONASTIC PROFESSION AND "CONVERSION," 11.—THE INFLUENCE OF THE EAST, 12.—EVOLUTION OF PENANCE IN THE FIFTH AND SIXTH CENTURIES, 13.—PENITENTIAL COMMUTATION OR SUBSTITUTION, 15.—THE SPREAD OF "PRIVATE PENANCE," 16.—THE SPIRITUALITY OF THE PENITENTS, 17.

Chapter 3: THE DEVELOPMENT OF THE PENITENTIAL MOVEMENT (VII-XI CENTURIES) 20
OVERVIEW: THE EFFECTS OF THE BARBARIAN INVASION, 20.—PENITENTIAL LEGISLATION AFTER THE YEAR 700, 21.—FASTING AND LENT, 22.—CORPORAL PENANCE, 23.—THE PENITENTIAL PILGRIMAGE, 24.—THE EREMITICAL LIFE, 26.—PENITENTIAL ELEMENTS IN THE CAROLINGIAN REFORM, 27.—THE "DONATI" AND "OBLATES," 30.—THE DARK AGES, 30.—THE REFORM OF MONASTICISM AND ITS INFLUENCE ON THE PENITENTIAL MOVEMENT, 32.—CHARITABLE FOUNDATIONS, 35.—THE PENITENTIAL MEANING OF THE TAU, 36.—THE "CONVERSI," 37.—THE CHARACTER OF THE CONVERSI OR PENITENTS, 39.—FURTHER PENITENTIAL TEACHINGS: RATHERIUS OF VERONA (CA. 887-974), 41.

Chapter 4: GREGORIAN REFORM AND THE ITINERANT PREACHERS 43
THE GREGORIAN REFORM AND RELIGIOUS REAWAKENING, 44.—THE APOSTOLIC OR EVANGELICAL LIFE, 44.—THE ITINERANT PREACHERS, 46.—THE PREACHERS OF THE FIRST PERIOD (1090-1150), 46.—A. ROBERT OF ARBRISSEL (CA. 1060-1117), 47.—B. BERNARD OF THIRON (+1117), 48;—C. VITALIS OF SAVIGNY (+1122), 48;—D. GERARD OF SALLES (+1120), 48;—E. NORBERT OF XANTEN (CA. 1082-1134), 48.—CONCLUSIONS, 49.

Chapter 5: ANTI-ECCLESIASTICAL AND HETERODOX MOVEMENTS 51
PETER DE BRUYS, 53.—ARNOLD OF BRESCIA AND THE ARNOLDISTS, 54.—THE PATARIA AND THE PATARINES, 55.—THE CATHARI, 55.—PETER WALDO AND THE WALDENSIANS, 57.—THE HUMILIATI, 59.—DURANDUS OF HUESCA AND THE POOR CATHOLICS, 61.—BERNARD PRIMUS AND THE POOR LOMBARDS, 62.—THE GROUPS OF PENITENTS, 63.—THE

ATMOSPHERE IN THE PENITENTIAL
MOVEMENT, 65.

Chapter 6: FRANCIS OF ASSISI **67**
THE POLITICAL SITUATION, 67.—THE
SOCIAL SITUATION, 71.—THE KNIGHTLY
ELEMENT, 72.—POLITICAL, RELIGIOUS,
AND SOCIAL EVENTS IN THE EARLY YOUTH OF
FRANCIS, 73.—ASSISI, A FREE CITY, 76.—THE
COMMUNAL STRUCTURE OF ASSISI, 78.—
THE WAR WITH PERUGIA, 78.

Chapter 7: THE CONVERSION OF FRANCIS **80**
PRISON IN PERUGIA, 80.—HOME TO
ASSISI, 82.—SPOLETO: GETTING AWAY FROM
IT ALL, 83.—THE EXPERIENCE OF POVERTY,
85.—MEETING THE LEPER, 86.

Chapter 8: FRANCIS BECOMES A PENITENT **87**
FRANCIS, "BROTHER OF PENANCE," 89.—
FRANCIS' THEOLOGICAL AND BIBLICAL
PREPARATION, 90.—FRANCIS AND BISHOP
GUIDO, 92.—THE POSITION OF INNOCENT
III, 94.

Chapter 9: FRANCIS AND THE PENITENTS **100**
THE RAPID INCREASE IN THE NUMBER OF
PENITENTS, 100.—FRANCIS IMMEDIATELY
IS INTERESTED IN THE PENITENTS, 102.—
FRANCIS GIVES A NORMA DI VITA TO HIS
PENITENTS, 106.

**Chapter 10: FRANCIS' DIRECTIVES FOR
HIS PENITENTS** **109**
THE "RECENSIO PRIOR" OR FIRST LETTER
TO ALL THE FAITHFUL (1 LF), 109.—ITS
CHARACTERISTICS AND DOCTRINE, 110.—
THE LETTER TO ALL THE FAITHFUL, 113.—
THE BASIC IDEAS OF THE "LETTERA AI
FEDELI" (2 LF), 114.

**Chapter 11: THE SPIRITUALITY OF
FRANCISCAN PENITENTS** **118**
CHARACTERISTICS OF THE FRANCISCAN
PENITENTS: ADHERENCE TO CATHOLICISM
AND FIDELITY TO THE CHURCH, 118.—

EUCHARIST AND PRIESTHOOD, 119.—THE NEW MAN: A) THE STATE OF PENANCE IS A JOURNEY TO GOD; B) THE SPIRIT OF LOVE, 120.—OTHER VIRTUES OF THE PENITENT, 122. —THE SUBLIME SPIRITUALITY OF THIS "FORMA VITAE," 124.—COROLLARY: "PENANCE" AS THE FUNDAMENTAL CHARACTERISTIC OF THE THIRD ORDER, 125.

Chapter 12: THE "MEMORIALE PROPOSITI" OF 1221-1228 128
THE NUMERICAL GROWTH OF THE PENITENTS AND NECESSITY OF LEGISLATION, 128.— CARDINAL UGOLINO, 130.—CARDINAL UGOLINO AND THE "MEMORIALE PROPOSITI," 132.—THE "MEMORIALE PROPOSITI," 133.— THE APPROVAL OF THE MEMORIALE PROPOSITI, 135.

Chapter 13: THE PENITENTS FROM 1221 TO 1289 138
THE "FRANCISCAN" SENSE OF SOME PAPAL DOCUMENTS, 1220-1230, 138.—THE INTERNAL LIFE OF THE FRATERNITIES AND THE "FRANCISCAN EVOLUTION," 141.—THE "VIR RELIGIOSUS" AND THE VISITATOR, 144. —THE PENITENTS AND THE CIVIL AUTHORITIES, 145.—RELATIONS BETWEEN THE PENITENTS AND THE FRIARS MINOR, 147.—FRIAR CARO OF AREZZO, 150.—THE RULE OF NICHOLAS IV (1289), 150.— TOWARDS A "RELIGIOUS LIFE," 152.

NOTES 155

BIBLIOGRAPHY 213
    1. PRIMARY SOURCES, 213
    2. STUDIES, 217

INDEX OF PERSONS AND PLACES 225

FOREWORD

The publication of Father Raphael Pazzelli's book, *St. Francis and the Third Order*, is a major step in a twenty-year odyssey of rediscovery for the members of the Third Order Regular and the Secular Franciscan Order. These two branches of that part of the Franciscan family known in earlier times as the "Order of Penance" share an ancient heritage and a contemporary quest to recover their shared story. The appearance of this work marks the first time that we English-speaking Franciscans will have access to a comprehensive and well-documented history of the Third Order.

The past two decades have seen not only major programs of renewal among the modern day penitents, but also the completion of two thoroughly revised rule texts promulgated with papal approbation. Paul VI, shortly before his death in 1978, approved the text of the Rule of the Secular Franciscan Order with the apostolic letter "Seraphicus Patriarca." In 1982, John Paul II affixed his signature of approval to a renewed rule and life for the Brothers and Sisters of the Third Order Regular and issued it with the apostolic letter "Franciscanum Vitae Propositum." Both new texts were the result of international consultation. Both texts launched intensive efforts in many parts of the world to give specific expression to the Franciscan penitential tradition in our time. These processes continue into the present.

Participants and leaders alike discovered that these programs of education were filled with surprises. We discovered that while we shared the gospel vision of Francis and Clare with the Order of Friars Minor and the Poor Clares, we, within the Third Order, possessed a distinctive filter for that charism. We found ourselves attending to the way in which Francis communicated that charism to our ancestors, the penitents of his day, as "true faith and conversion of heart" (Rule of 1221: 23,7). We began to explore the implications of this charism in terms of a summons to a biblical life of conversion of heart expressed in works of charity and a commitment to be messengers of peace. We also realized that many of our fraternities and congregations have drawn historic identity and spiritual direction from their affiliation with a branch of the First Order. Enriched as we were by these bonds we came to see that we had yet to fully appreciate our own particular tradition and spirituality. When we asked ourselves why this was so, it was not long before we realized that the scarcity of materials regarding Third Order history in the English language had deprived us of an adequate grasp of the richness of Franciscan diversity and the values of Franciscan unity.

Both of us enjoyed our part in the formation process developed by the Franciscan Federation to promote the new TOR rule that was known as "Roots and Wings." This series of workshops took us across the United States over a three year period. Looking back we can affirm that we were blessed by participating in this time of proclamation and prophetic word. Now we share the conviction that further explanation, study, and development are needed to strengthen our Franciscan living into the future. We welcome this book as the product of years of research and teaching on the part of our brother, Raphael Pazzelli, T.O.R., who takes us back to the Scriptures to examine the biblical foundations of penitential spirituality. He examines the rich ecclesiastical tradition of the "Order of Penitents" as it unfolded from post-Apostolic times into the Middle Ages. He reviews the biographies of Francis of Assisi and the historical evidence of his relationship to the penitential movement and the new direction he gave to it. He painstakingly documents his materials, thus enabling the reader to expand research and knowledge of this vast field of Franciscan study. From this scholarly presentation we can gain a new appreciation of our distinctive call to be followers of Christ after the example of Francis and Clare. But Father Pazzelli does not stop there. Neither should we.

What St. Francis taught our forebearers in the Order of Penance we too have to learn. Walking in Christ's footprints has to be a lived experience, a matter of the heart and not the head alone. The rules of the Third Order Regular and of the Secular Franciscans state the guidance of Francis. Only we can enflesh that. We are called to live the gospel by being obedient to the first public preaching of Christ (Mk 1:15), "Believe the good news and be turned to God. . . ." The manner of our life of conversion based on true faith is expressed through those gospel values that Francis was inspired to see in Christ of the gospel, namely, prayerfulness, evangelical poverty and littleness, obedience to God's will, and the ministry and service of peacemaking. In this book Father Pazzelli roots us well. Our response to God's call to live the gospel as Francis did will have "wings" to the extent that we assimilate and make our own the values of Christ's life.

MARGARET CARNEY, O.S.F.
THADDEUS HORGAN, S.A.

Sister Margaret and Father Thaddeus were members of the seven-person work group of the International Franciscan Commission (1979-1982) that prepared the text of the revised Rule of the Third Order Regular of St. Francis. Presently Sister Margaret is the general superior of the Franciscan Sisters of the Providence of God (Whitehall) and lives in Pittsburgh, PA. Father Thaddeus is presently associate director of the Bishops' Committee for Ecumenical and Interfaith Relations of the National Conference of Catholic Bishops and lives in Washington, D.C.

INTRODUCTION

In response to the question "Who is St. Francis?" the renowned Franciscanist Raoul Manselli responded: "He is a precious stone with many facets and innumerable reflections. The various images of St. Francis are reflections of that one mysterious light, the man and saint, Francis."[1]

This book seeks to illustrate a particular facet, one which has enlightened us from the earliest self-description of the saint and his companions. It is recorded both in the *Legend of the Three Companions* and the *Anonymous Perusinus*, narrating the friars' very first preaching mission, when the small band had not yet received the oral approval of Pope Innocent III, that to whoever asked who they were or where they came from, "they confessed with simplicity to being penitents from Assisi."[2]

The first Franciscan sources also attest to the fact that St. Francis established his own Order of Penance. Julian of Speyer, in his *Vita S. Francisci*, written between the years of 1232-1235 and based on the *Vita Prima* of Celano, clarifying the somewhat obscure statement found in Celano, says that in fact, he organized three orders; "the third is called the Order of Penitents."[3] St. Bonaventure in his turn affirmed: "He then instituted a third order, called the Order of Penitents, those who are called the Brothers and Sisters of Continence."[4]

Franciscan historiography today admits that those brothers and sisters of the Order of Penitents who followed Francis, towards the end of the thirteenth century began to call themselves, or were so named by others, the Brothers and Sisters of the Third Order of Saint Francis, an expression which has prevailed to our own day.[5] In the same order there rather quickly developed a twofold way of life, one strictly lay, the other more properly "religious" or regular. This later brought about two distinct branches: the Third Order Secular and the Third Order Regular of St. Francis.

The Brothers and Sisters of the Third Order of Francis of today, secular and regular alike, are the direct descendents of those "Brothers and Sisters of Penance" who followed Francis and were inspired by him for their own spiritual life. Anyone who closely examines the many congregations of Franciscan Sisters and Brothers following the Rule of the Third Order Regular of St. Francis today will find that very few are able to trace an uninterrupted descent from the "Penitents of Blessed Francis." Nevertheless, in the thought, directives, and legislation of the Church, all of them are heirs of the spirituality that Francis gave to "his" penitents.

In the search for their own identity which currently involves many individual members and entire institutes, the recognition of the identity of the penitents before St. Francis and with him, and the knowledge of what new or renewed ideas Francis gave to "his" penitents, would be of the greatest help. This is the goal to which this book is dedicated.

In recent years the attention of Franciscan scholars of all the orders has increasingly turned toward the penitential movement, that is, to the penitents of the twelfth and thirteenth centuries. This has, in fact, been the topic of many publications throughout the world, as well as the theme of four congresses of Franciscan studies: 1972, Assisi; 1976, Rome; 1979, Padua; 1981, Assisi.[6]

In our opinion, the reasons for the renewed interest are primarily two: first is the desire for a "return to the sources," that is, to the true origins, spiritual and historical, of the institutions, following the advice of the Second Vatican Council.[7] The entire Franciscan movement has, in fact, its historical foundation or initial rationale in the penitential beginnings of Francis. As we have already noted his first followers, before calling themselves *minores*, were called *poenitentes*. Secondly, there is the fact that nearly all other aspects of Franciscanism had been abundantly exhausted (or so it was believed), so that at this time the question of the origins seemed to be a discussion still not taken up and therefore worthy of particular attention.

However that may be, for the followers of Francis in the Franciscan Third Order Secular, as well as for all the tertiary congregations, male and female, who profess the rule of the Third Order Regular, there is still another motive for being interested in the pre-Franciscan and Franciscan penitential movement. Understanding the subject in its origins and development gives us a better possibility of gaining a clearer idea of the charism and identity of the Franciscan Third Order, secular and regular, of today. Therefore, it will help those interested to understand the implications derived from this identity as heirs of the "Penitents of St. Francis," in order to outline the mode of thought and life necessary for an effective renewal of the order in modern times.

ABBREVIATIONS

AFH   *Archivum Franciscanum Historicum*, Quaracchi, 1908 ff.
Anal. Franc. *Analecta Franciscana*, Quaracchi, 1885 ff.
Anal. T.O.R. *Analecta Tertii Ordinis Regularis Sancti Francisci*, Rome, General Curia T.O.R., 1933 ff.
An. P.   *Anonimo Perugino*
Bull. Franc. *Bullarium Franciscanum.* Vol. I-IV, ed. I.H. Sbaraglea, Rome, 1759-1768.
CCh. SL   *Corpus Christianorum. Series latina*, Turnholt, 1953 ff.
1 Cel.   *Vita Prima santi Francisci* by Thomas of Celano.
2 Cel.   *Vita Seconda santi Francisci* by Thomas of Celano.
3 Comp.   *Legend of the three Companions.*
DIP   *Dizionario degli Istituti di Perfezione* (directed by G. Pelliccia and G. Rocca), Rome, 1975 ff.
DS   *Dictionnaire de Spiritualité, ascetique et mystique*, Paris, 1933 ff.
DTC   *Dictionnaire de Théologie Catholique*, Paris, 1903-1970.
E.C.   *Enciclopedia Cattolica.* Vatican City, 1949-1954.
Leg. M   *Legenda Maior* of St. Bonaventure.
1 Lf   Letter to all the Faithful (First edition or *Recensio prior*).
2 Lf   Letter to all the Faithful (Second edition).
Mansi   *Sacrorum Conciliorum nova et amplissima collectio.*
MGH Script *Monumenta Germaniae Historica.* Scriptores. Hannoverae-Lipsiae, 1826 ff.
PL   *Patroligiae cursus completus. Series latina*, J. P. Migne, General editor, Parisiis, 1841-1864.

1

THE BIBLICAL AND FRANCISCAN UNDERSTANDING OF PENANCE

The word "penance" in its more common use in almost all modern languages commonly connotes external acts of mortification such as fasting, vigils, abstinence from certain foods or other pleasurable things, as well as the positive self-infliction of corporal punishment through a physical means, such as a hairshirt or "discipline."[1]

This is not, however, the principal meaning of the term, in either its biblical or its Franciscan context. It is merely a derivative, restricted, and secondary meaning.

It would be difficult, if not impossible, to restore the original biblical and Franciscan meaning to the penitential terminology in common usage, the praiseworthy efforts of the ordinary magisterium of the Church notwithstanding.[2] For a thorough understanding of the spirit and ideals of Francis of Assisi and those who followed him throughout the centuries, especially in the order of "the Brothers and Sisters of Penance," later called the "Third Order Franciscans," it is absolutely necessary to understand this meaning completely.

THE BIBLICAL SENSE[3]

In the Septuagint or Greek version of the Old Testament, as well as in the New Testament books written in Greek, the subjective attitude required for the forgiveness of sin is mainly expressed in the word *metànoia*. The Vulgate or Latin version generally translates this with the words *paenitentia* or *conversio*. The three words have much the same meaning and may be used interchangeably.

In the Greek language the term *metànoia*, even outside the

sphere of religion, indicates a change of persuasion, attitude, or interior plan, either for good or evil. Secondarily, it indicates displeasure or regret for previous behavior. In its biblical notion this meaning is preserved and enriched by the nuances of various writers. In order to understand the full meaning of Christ's invitation to "Repent, for the kingdom of heaven is at hand," (Mt 4:17) we will give a quick overview of the use of the word in the development of biblical penitential teaching.

A. THE PROPHETS

In prophetic preaching *metànoia* (conversion, penance) connotes and requires an attitude which corrects the previous one in relation to God. To repent or convert means to return to the Lord (1 Sam 7:3), lift up one's eyes to heaven (Dan 4:34), turn one's face to God (Dan 9:3). It clearly shows that the return to God is not sincere if it does not effect a change of habit, that is, the resolution to fulfil the will of God. This is clearly expressed by Amos, who says that to seek God (Am 5:4) means to seek good, not evil. (Am 5:14)

Conversion to God means to turn one's back on sin (Sir 17:21-23). Penance signifies a return to a previous state, namely, friendship with God (Hos chapter 3). The prophets tell us that the conditions for pardon are to wash, purifying oneself, and ultimately to behave differently, learning to do good (cf. Is 1:16-17; Jer 7:3 and 4:14). While the earliest prophets emphasize the necessity of the pure monotheistic cult, those nearer to the fall of Jerusalem (587 B.C.) begin to insist on the necessity of personal, interior conversion (cf. Jer 3:10; 4:3-4). Finally, during the exile the call is concretized in conversion of heart (cf. Ez 33:14-15; Mal 3:7-8).

This affective, internal attitude is also expressed exteriorly, using the traditional Israelite signs of mourning—rending the garments, wearing sackcloth and ashes, fasting, etc. (cf. 1 Kgs 21:27-29; Jon 3:5-9).

B. THE POST-EXILIC PERIOD

After the Babylonian exile (587-539 B.C.) the biblical texts more clearly express the need for a true interior conversion in order to enter into the graces of the Lord. It is expressly said that whoever does not abandon sin hopes in vain for the Lord's mercy (Sir 5:1-8); that his sacrifices and fasts are useless (Sir 34:21-31). As the messianic time draws near, the idea becomes clearer and more common that it is essential to refrain from sin and, in sorrow and mortification, to deplore one's past behavior. The charge of hypocrisy which Jesus levels at the Pharisees is not against penitential theory and practice, but only against the improper use of them.

On the threshold of the New Testament John the Baptizer resumes the penitential preaching with his invitation: *"Metanòeite."* (Repent! Convert! Do penance!) (Mt 3:2); he demands a change of practice, producing "worthy fruits of penance" (cf. Lk 3:10-14).

C. THE TEACHING OF CHRIST

Christ's preaching, as described by the synoptics, emphasizing the value of faith and charity, stresses the importance of the motivation of filial love over that of fear. The evangelists further attribute to Christ the same words calling people to conversion as they had placed on the lips of the Baptizer—*"Metanòeite!"* (Repent! Convert! Do penance!); that is, they saw no difference in the *metànoia* preached by Christ, his precursor, and the prophets.

For Christ, conversion is not purely ethical; it will be complete only if one belongs totally to God. Concretely, one must become a disciple of Christ, believing in the gospel (Mk 16:16). This adherence to the Father through Christ fundamentally demands that the individual recognize his sinfulness, be not satisfied with that condition, and desire pardon. These elements are synthesized in the parable of the Prodigal Son. "Christ's teaching interiorizes the idea of sin. The evil of sin comes from the heart, from the interior orientation of the will" (Mt 15:17). Christ's reminder that, according to the natural law, a bad tree bears defective fruit while a healthy tree yields good fruit, (cf. Mt 7:17-20) tells us that "bad deeds are condemned, because their evil stems from the fact that they are 'fruits,' that is, consequences and ultimate manifestations of an evil deeper than the deeds for which, however, the person is fully responsible. Inasmuch as conversion is interiorized, it consists first of all in a change in evaluating things (*metànoia*) from which, if it is sincere, new behavior will inevitably follow."[4]

D. THE TEACHING OF THE APOSTLES

The concept of *metànoia* according to the Apostles "is identical to that of Christ. The evil from which a person must turn is above all the separation from God and Christ. For the Jews this consisted of not having accepted the testimony of Jesus (Acts 3:15-19); for the pagan it means failing to recognize God, the creator and ruler of the world (Acts 17:30). Paul sums up his whole activity as 'testifying to both Jews and Greeks of repentance to God and belief in our Lord Jesus Christ' (Acts 20:21). To indicate the initial conversion to Christ,[5] Paul does not use the term *metànoia* (except in Rom 2:4-5), perhaps because in Hellenistic Judaism the term already had a precise meaning, an active and moral aspect, while Paul saw initial conversion in the perspective of rebirth and liberation effected by the grace of God (cf. Tit 3:5-7; Rom 7:24). St. Paul usually describes this total belonging to Christ with the word 'faith' (*pistis*), which signifies not only an intellectual assent, but also a change of heart, of which good works are a natural consequence."[6]

Paul uses the expression *metànoia* and its derivatives to express the conversion of baptized sinners, that two-fold element necessary for salvation: sorrow (*lùpe*) and the intention to avoid sin (*metànoia*).

E. THE TEACHING OF ST. JOHN

In his Gospel, John does not use the term *metànoia*, probably for reasons similar to that of Paul. In the phenomenon of conversion (especially initial conversion, which is usually the one spoken of in the Gospel), he sees above all adherence to Christ, which he most often calls "faith" and which he describes as "believing" and, most of all, "loving."

The concept of *metànoia*, however, has a special function in chapters two and three of Revelations where the "Spirit" demands of the seven churches the conversion from post-baptismal sin; conversion leads to a change of behavior (Rev 2:5; 2:21).

In conclusion, we can say that, in the Bible, the term *metànoia* (penance) indicates a constant yet developing idea; it is a conversion that is theocentric (turn to God), ethical (flee evil and do good), and affective (love God).

2. THE FRANCISCAN SENSE

This biblical sense of *metànoia*—penance—was fully rediscovered,[7] accepted, and lived by St. Francis:

a. From the phraseology used by Francis in the first lines of his Testament, it is evident that for him penance signified the "conversion of man from a life centered on the personal 'I' to a life which is completely under the will and sovereign lordship of God."⁸ In fact, giving a brief synthesis of his own life, Francis distinguishes two radically different phases of it—that of his own self-centeredness, disobeying or ignoring God, as contradistinguished from that of "doing penance," that is, being directed by the inspirations of God.

Having turned to *penance*, Francis was very soon led to *leave the world*, the *saeculum*. In mediaeval usage, this expression meant to join religious life or to enter into one of the many official forms of the Order of Penitents recognized by the Church of that day. "Thus, penance is the same as *metànoia* in the biblical sense."⁹

b. This meaning of *penance* is also found in the *Vita Prima* of Celano every time the term is used:

1. Francis, having heard the Gospel of the *mission of the apostles* and the comments of the priest that "the disciples of Christ . . . should . . . preach the kingdom of God and penance, immediately cried out exultingly, 'This is what I wish, this is what I seek, this I long to do with all my heart' " (*1 Cel* 23, *Omnibus*, 247). The term, "to preach the gospel and penance" evidently recalls the terms "Repent (*metanòeite*) and believe in the gospel" (Mt 3:2). Penance is conversion and acceptance of the kingdom of God.

2. "From then on he began to preach penance to all with great fervor of spirit and joy of mind" (*1 Cel* 23, *Omnibus*, 247). This step, which immediately follows the preceding event and is closely connected to it both in time and thought, preserves the same meaning of "penance" as in that narrative.

3. When the number of friars had risen to eight, "Francis called them all together, and telling them many things about the kingdom of God, contempt of the world, the renunciation of their will, and the subduing of their own body, he separated them into four groups of two each and said to them: 'Go, my dearest brothers, two by two into the various parts of the world, announcing to men peace and repentance' " (*1 Cel* 29, *Omnibus*, 251-252). Evidently, the "penance" that they were to preach meant the things which "he told them."

4. Pope Innocent III, in approving the proto-rule in the spring of 1210, exhorted "them concerning many things, . . . he blessed (them) and said to them, 'Go with the Lord, brothers, and as the Lord will deign to inspire you, preach penance to all' " (*1 Cel* 33, *Omnibus*, 255). The same Celano, in the *Vita Seconda*, elaborating on this episode affirms that "Francis, therefore, by reason of the authority granted him, began to scatter the seeds of virtue" (*2 Cel* 17, *Omnibus*, 378).

5. This "most valiant knight of Christ went about the towns and villages, announcing the kingdom of God, preaching peace, teaching salvation and penance unto the remission of sins" (*1 Cel* 36, *Omnibus*, 258). "But here, too, the exhortation to penance appears closely linked to the proclamation of the Kingdom of God to which man must be converted."[10]

c. Saint Clare, also, the faithful disciple and interpreter of the thought of Francis, used the word "penance" in the same sense as her teacher. Besides narrating the essence of her conversion in almost the very same words, she encapsulates the meaning of "doing penance" in the same sense brought out by Francis in his Testament: a person finds "great joy in what he otherwise fears," which effects an intimate availability to the will of God.[11]

"From this testimony of the primary sources it is clearly evident that for Francis 'doing penance' in the spirit of the gospel was the God-given beginning of his new life, that he expected his followers to have this as their basic attitude, and that he desired its preservation for all time. With this beginning of his God-centered life, Francis became an integral part of the penitential movement of his day and was, to a certain extent, its culmination. His real objective was man's total conversion to God in absolute, self-transcending obedience. In this sense, 'doing penance' was for him the way to the kingdom of God, which he then wanted to proclaim to all men.

"In conclusion, it may be pointed out once more that, on contemporary evidence, the process which Francis describes as 'doing penance' could be rendered equally well—to correspond to the biblical term *metànoia*—by 'conversion to God'; ... the essence of the concept suffered no change at all."[12] " 'Doing penance' remains the central concept for beginning a truly Christian life which demands an actual break with the 'world' and total conversion to God."[13]

This basic idea of "penance" becomes better clarified, enriched, and deepened, in the two writings which Francis addressed to "The Brothers and Sisters of Penance," that is, the *Recensio prior* (1 Lf) and the *Recensio posterior* (2 Lf), the earlier and later editions of the *Letter to All the Faithful*. In treating these works in greater detail later, we shall discover the penitential instruction that Francis gave to those who followed him in the Order of Penance.

2

THE ORIGINS OF THE PENITENTS

III-VI CENTURIES

The birth of the penitential movement in the West is connected with the evolution of the penitential disciple in the Church in the first centuries, to the evolution, that is, of the ecclesiastical legislation relative to the manner of obtaining pardon for sin after baptism. The penitential movement was also influenced and characterized from its beginning by ascetical forms already recognized and practiced in the East, forms which the hierarchy accepted and adapted to canonical penance.

PENANCE IN THE PRIMITIVE CHURCH

From the dawn of Christianity, in the post-Apostolic age, and in particular after Tertullian (+ after 220) and St. Cyprian the bishop (+258), a penitential doctrine began to be delineated which can be synthesized in these terms: the Christian, even after having committed a grave sin, is not irretrievably lost, neither in the eyes of God nor of the Church. This doctrine finds its explicit scriptural foundation in the first Letter of John who "already faces the problem of post-baptismal conversion: Christians sin (1 Jn 8:10), but their sins may be forgiven through Christ (2:1-2), always presupposing that they abandon these sinful acts, incompatible with union with God."[1]

With baptism, usually administered to adults, there should begin a life of sanctity, of estrangement from sin. In fact, however, even Christians can and do sin. From the writings of the fathers and apologists we also have lists of sins which were considered serious. Listed in decreasing order of gravity, they are: impurity (adultery and other acts), murder, idolatry, magic, avarice, and theft.

For all these sins the Christian could "do penance" and obtain pardon. "Doing penance" was identified as one of the basic signs of *metànoia*, of biblical conversion—changing direction, turning away from sin and redirecting one's life to God. Conversion, primarily an interior movement, should be accompanied by external signs, namely, prayers, tears, fasting, and almsgiving.

The sinner was excluded from participating in the Eucharist. This same assembly, the Eucharistic one, decided the nature and duration of expiation. Once the expiation had been completed, the sinner was readmitted into Eucharistic participation. If the sinner refused to do penance, that is, the prescribed expiation, he was excommunicated; that meant that he was not only cut off from the cultic life of the community, but from its social life as well. This separation lasted as long as the sinner did not agree to perform the prescribed penance; in the meantime, the community prayed for him.

Tertullian described for us the development of ancient penance: the sinner was required to recognize his guilt before God and to admit his fault. This internal attitude would "manifest itself" externally as well, not by public confession in the sense of a detailed confession in front of the community,[2] but by acts of mortification destined to humiliate the penitent, acts which could not fail to draw the attention of his brothers to the sinner. Some typical examples were the wearing of a hairshirt (originally a garment made of goatskin), covering one's head with ashes, rigorous fasting, wearing worn and dirty clothing, prolonged periods of prayers, prostrations, recourse to the priests, recommendations to the friends of God (martyrs and confessors), and, finally, appeals to the prayers of the community.[3]

According to these first witnesses, it was clearly the Church who regulated penance. She intervened through her ministers who fixed the adequate time of expiation, overseeing and guiding the penitents. Without the ministers there was no valid reconciliation; in practice, it was the bishop who reconciled the penitents and who granted the pardon.[4]

In the ancient Church all serious faults, without exception, were pardonable. Only the Montanist heretics (into whose ranks Tertullian later fell) held that grave sins were not able to be forgiven.[5]

The Shepherd of Hermas, a short tract written in Rome around 155 A.D., is a testimony of the growth of a particular concept related to the forgiveness of sins. This pardon was and ought to be, in the opinion of the unknown author, so exceptional that it is possible to receive it only once: "For the servants of God penance is given only once" (*Prec.* IV, 1, 8).⁶ It is this new element which had important consequences. The other writers of the post-Apostolic period were not so categorial in this matter; even if "they had not written . . . explicitly that the sinner could expiate his sins and reenter into grace at his pleasure."⁷ The principle of a single opportunity for remission of sin after baptism continued to be asserted, influencing the evolution of all ancient penitential practice. Penance, with its subsequent forgiveness of sin, became a "second baptism" in a very strict sense; just as baptism of water could not be repeated, neither could penance.

The religious peace brought about by the Edict of Milan in 313 did not essentially change penitential discipline; certain characteristics were merely better delineated. Thus, once admitted into the discipline of penance by the bishop, the sinner became part of a group or special order, called the Order of Penitents, analogous in practice to a religious state, except for its shameful character.

"One entered into the category of penitents in a liturgical ceremony whose essential part was the imposition of hands. This signified the blessing of God upon the penitential exercises which the penitent was required to perform, and was an exterior sign of admission into the order."⁸

During the time in which a person was in the Order of Penitents, he was not prohibited from attending the assembly. On the contrary, the penitents had a special section in the building used for worship where they were allowed to assist in the Eucharistic celebration but did not bring their offering or receive Eucharist.⁹

**THE GRAVE IMPOSITIONS PLACED UPON THE PENITENTS—
THE BEGINNINGS OF VOLUNTARY PENANCE**

From the fourth century on, ancient penance continued to evolve in a more rigid fashion. There is growing documentation of the "interdicts," things which the penitents were not able to do during the period of penance. The concept soon developed that these interdicts were imposed upon the penitent, even after the period of penance, that is, for the rest of his life. Thus the penitent, even the one formally reconciled by the bishop, was forbidden to resume military service. He could no longer serve in the profession of merchant, for it was too closely associated with the danger of dishonest earnings;[10] nor could the penitent assume any public office.

The delicate problem of marital relations for the married penitent was treated in various texts. Most of all, the married penitent was to refrain from conjugal relations during the period of penance. It soon developed, however, as with the other interdicts, that total continence was obligatory even after the reconciliation. The widowed penitent could not contract another marriage, even after the reconciliation. The celibate penitent could not be married before the reconciliation. St. Leo the Great (440-461) allowed celibates to marry after reconciliation, but there is evidence that in the same period in Gaul this permission was already denied.

Thus in practice, due to the severity and permanence of the interdicts, the faithful, even after their reconciliation, continued to belong to the Order of Penitents until death. "The condition of the reconciled penitents could be likened to that of a monk living in the world."[11]

The growing severity of this legislation brought about two consequences: on the one hand, the bishops proceeded with the maximum caution in the administration of penance. They would not admit as penitents those sinners who, in their judgment, would probably not fulfil their obligations. Thus, the Councils of Adge (506) and Orleans (538) prohibited the conferral of penance upon young people, or on married people, except if the married person was of advanced age and acted with the consent of the spouse.[12] Sinners entered ever more rarely into the class or Order of Penitents, waiting until the end of their days to avail themselves of it.

In this very same period, a new phenomenon began and rapidly spread. Some of the faithful, although not guilty of grave sin and therefore not obliged to "do penance," willingly took on the interdicts and entered into the Order of Penance because of their own desire, piety, or love of perfection. They were willing to stay in the "order" for their entire lives, as the practice more or less prescribed. These were the first of the "voluntary penitents," or simply, *the* penitents.[13]

From that time on the penitents seem to have always been present in the Church, up to and beyond the time of St. Francis. After St. Francis, however, the vast majority of them followed his spiritual direction, which was spread by his friars, and came to be known, therefore, as *Poenitentes beati Francisci* (the Penitents of St. Francis), even though in their official documents they continued to refer to themselves as the *Fratres et Sorores de Poenitentia*

(Brothers and Sisters of Penance); not until the end of the thirteenth century did the name Third Order of St. Francis (Tertius Ordo b. Francisci) begin to prevail.

NEW METHODS OF OBTAINING PARDON—
MONASTIC PROFESSION AND "CONVERSION"

With the introduction and spread of monasticism in the West, and especially after its "institutionalization" by St. Benedict in 529, two other means of obtaining pardon for sins rapidly developed: monastic profession and conversion.

Monastic profession rapidly became analogous to "penance" and was also considered a second baptism; therefore the professed entered anew, by his profession, into the Mystical Body of Christ and consequently could be readmitted to Eucharist without any other formality. Gennadius of Marseilles (+495 ca.) affirmed that religious life is considered a form of private penance and was therefore a substitute for the public penance of the Church.[14]

"Conversion," with its many nuances, came to assume the greatest importance in the history and spirituality of the penitents and therefore merits a more thorough treatment in our study.

By the term "conversion" is meant the decision to make a more or less radical break with one's previous lifestyle, that is the world (*saeculum*); the person, who was not necessarily a public or habitual sinner, pledged to live a new kind of life, a "life of penance." This commitment was realized by the person's entrance into one of the many forms of penitential life which were developing within the Church from the fourth to eighth centuries.

Those who chose this "conversion" and manifested it publicly by living it out in one of those forms were commonly called "conversi"—the most common name for the penitents throughout their history. Whether or not all "conversi" were penitents will be the subject of scholarly debate for years to come; however, it is certain that all penitents were, from this time onward, considered "conversi."

These conversi did not necessarily live in a monastery with a determined rule, nor in hermitages or *ritiros*. Many of them lived "in the world," involved in various occupations, with the exceptions of those commonly restricted by interdict for the penitents. Essential to their life, however, were mortification and continency.

Conversion soon came to be considered as having the same spiritual effects associated with entrance into the primitive "official" order of penance—the one established in the early Church for public sinners who desired to be reconciled—as well as entrance into monastic life by means of profession.[15] In effect, conversion brought about the remission of sins.

THE INFLUENCE OF THE EAST

We have previously noted that the penitential movement was influenced from its very beginnings by ascetical forms recognized and practiced in the East. It is historically documented that from the first centuries of the Church there was a continual influx of people, and therefore, of ideas, from the East to the West, via the consular roads of the Roman Empire. Monasticism was already present in the West—imported from the East—before the time of St. Benedict (480-543). *The Life of St. Anthony*, written by St. Athanasius (296-373), spread rapidly and brought the monastic concept to the West. Pilgrimages to the holy places of Palestine began to be practiced in the West as early as the fourth century, and contributed to the knowledge of Eastern spirituality.[16] The transmigration of the monks from East to West, which began in that same period, continued and intensified, even after the institution of western monasticism; there is evidence that it continued until the end of the twelfth century.[17]

In the East, before the fourth century, "conversio" was also called "abrenuntiatio," that is, renunciation. In Egypt, from the time of St. Anthony the Abbot (251-356) those Christians who bound themselves to the twofold ideal of renunciation and chastity were called *apotaktikoi*, a term which Cassian translated in his *Institutiones* (1. IV) by the word *abrenuntiantes*, that is, those who renounce (the world).

As early as the fourth century groups of "abrenuntiantes" could be found in Alexandria of Egypt; this group formed, as it were, an intermediate group between clerics and laity. They publicly manifested to the bishop their intention to embrace the ascetical life; they lived in small groups near the churches, or in individual houses. The virgins were under the authority and direction of a deaconess. Both groups, men and women, provided for their livelihood by work and placed the fruit of their labor in common. They took an active part in the liturgy.[18]

In the third century the theologians of Alexandria elaborated a theological concept of "conversion-renunciation" in both its ascetical and practical aspects of renunciation of sin. "Conversio" could, in this way, be developed into a program of life applicable to ascetics and penitents alike.

For Dionysius of Alexandria (+264 ca.) conversio was a gift of God, which the person accepted as a response to the divine initiative. Punishments of God (life's misfortunes) which could lead to conversion were viewed in the light of divine teaching or as manifestations of his love.[19]

This theological concept is naturally connected with the eastern theology of sin and its cure, which was the foundation of monasticism. In this concept, the fundamental remedy for sin is "flight from the world," understood in a literal sense, whenever possible. Those who could not literally "flee" into the desert, should avoid the world. There were prescriptions and counsels about fasting, sexual continence, a certain distancing from "negotia" (trafficking with the world), and most especially about reading the Scriptures.

Other characteristics that can be seen in the conversi (abrenuntiantes-poenitentes) from the beginning was an insistence upon a particular mode of dress which would indicate externally the interior phenomenon of conversion. This concept always remained present in the spirituality of the penitential movement—the interior obligation should be exteriorly visible by means of a form of dress, that is a distinctive sign, and by means of a new life-style, a new modus vivendi, that of "conversatio."[20] Such an historical reality should perhaps invite supporters of differing opinions to a greater reflection.

These ideas accompanied the transmigration of the monks and came to blend with those of the great masters of western spirituality followed by the penitents.

EVOLUTION OF PENANCE IN THE
FIFTH AND SIXTH CENTURIES

The documents from the fifth and sixth centuries allow us to see how the difficult requirements and interdicts to which the penitents had to submit, mostly for the rest of their lives, quickly discouraged the majority of sinners from partaking in the reconciliation process, even though those sinners were of good will; the practice of "official penance" almost disappeared. Historians now speak openly of a "penitential vacuum."[21] It is symptomatic, for example, that Cesarius of Arles (+542) no longer invited sinners to seek canonical penance, well recognizing the more or less hopeless situation; he counseled them that, "with works of mortification and an authentic penitential spirit they (should) prepare themselves for the grace of reconciliation which they would receive 'in extremis' that is, when they were gravely ill or dying."[22] "From the middle of the fifth century to the beginning of the seventh, there is a progressive erosion of the primitive penitential discipline, even though there was not yet a clear image of what future developments would bring. This period, preparing for the new order of things, marked the end of the ancient era and the beginning of the mediaeval one, although no one can fix an exact date to mark the dividing line between the two."[23]

In the meantime, the beginning of the fifth century saw the growth of a new penitential practice which had begun and developed in the Celtic and Anglo-Saxon monasteries. These nations seem to have never practiced the "ancient penance." The missionaries who came to the European continent from these islands introduced a form of penance practiced there, which has also been called "insular penance"; Saint Columbanus (540-615) and his disciples were the leaders in its diffusion. According to this new practice, sinners, clerics and laymen and women alike, were able to be reconciled as often as they needed. The sinner had recourse in private to a priest, who would in turn impose a "penitential tax" (from which comes the name "tariff penance"), usually consisting of fasts, almsgiving, and other bodily mortifications. When the "tax" had been paid, that is, when the specified work was completed, the sinner would present himself a second time to the priest to receive "reconciliation."

Every sin was assigned a precise penance. These penitential tariffs are still preserved for us in collections called "penitential books," or simply "penitentials." The penitential tariff consisted of mortifications of varying length and degree of difficulty, such as bodily mortification, prolonged vigils, recitation of prayers, especially the psalms. Most of all there were fasts of various types and lengths. Thus, the expression "to do penance" developed a meaning previously not connected with it. In the terminology of the penitentials, it often meant to fast.

Among the penances imposed, in addition to fasting, there were the payment of monetary fines to a church or monastery, pilgrimages to the tomb of some saint, and the temporary prohibition of conjugal relations. Note these last two examples of penance, which we find again later among the "voluntary penitents": the first takes a noteworthy development; the second gives us an explanation of how this particular form of penance developed diverse forms of legislation from that absolute legislation already seemingly required in the ancient form of penance.[24]

Reconciliation was normally granted after the "tax" for sin had been settled; even the oldest penitentials, however, show that from the very beginning, in exceptional cases, primarily due to illness of the penitent, difficulties in travel, or severity of weather, the priest confessor could recite the prayer of reconciliation immediately after the confession. With the passage of time this became common practice.

Tariff penance is the direct ancestor of penance as it is still practiced in the Latin Church, although with some notable changes of no great consequence to this study.[25]

PENITENTIAL COMMUTATION OR SUBSTITUTION

From the very beginning of the so-called tariff penance there was seen the phenomenon of "redemption" or penitential commutation. A person who received a "penance," such as a long period of fasting, was allowed to substitute acts of shorter duration or of lesser difficulty, such as prayer, almsgiving, and the offering of Masses. He could even contract with a third person, a pious person, monk or layman, or a "voluntary penitent" to perform the "tariff" in his place. The Penitential of pseudo-Theodore (ca. 830-847) bears clear testimony to this phenomenon: "He who does not know the psalms, or who is not able to remain awake or to perform the genuflections or to remain with arms outstretched in the form of a cross, or to prostrate himself upon the ground, may select another to take his place, because it is written: 'one carries the burden of the other' (Gal 6:2)."[26]

This system of commutation was often used for the "non-solemn public penance," that is, the penitential pilgrimage. We will later see the development of the phenomenon whereby voluntary penitents, those of the Order of Penance, go on penitential pilgrimages for others; this practice lasted until the fifteenth century. We have documentation which shows that, around the years 1440-1450, in the beginning of the month of August, that is, at the time of the "Porziuncola indulgence," Assisi was filled with penitents. There were those who made a penitential pilgrimage for others and were remunerated, even with money, for this work.

Private penance—what later became known as private sacramental penance—was at first imposed for hidden sins of any nature. This type continued to spread, until it eventually became the only form of reconciliation of sinners.

THE SPREAD OF "PRIVATE PENANCE"

Towards the second half of the sixth century, when the use of private penance began to spread on the European continent, a noteworthy reaction took place. An example of the reaction of the local churches can be found in the canons of the great Council of Toledo (the third) in 589: "There are those persons who do penance for their sins, not according to the canons, but in a disgusting manner; every time they sin they go to ask pardon from ordinary priests. In order to stop such abominable audacity, this Council orders that penance shall be given according to the canonical forms of antiquity, that is: if the sinner repents of his fault, he is first suspended from communion and, having taken his place among the penitents, he should often return for the imposition of hands. When his time of expiation is over, if the bishop, having examined him, finds him worthy, [the bishop] readmits him to communion. Whoever returns to his old sins, either during the time of penance or after his reconciliation, will be condemned according to the force of the ancient canons."[27]

Despite the tough language of this decree, the "abusive" method of private penance was rapidly spreading in the nearby regions as well, and was acknowledged in conciliar decisions only a short time later. For example, the Council of Chalon-sur-Saone (650) approved a new method of penance, which had been brought to eastern Gaul by St. Columbanus and his disciples: "Let it be known that all we priests agree that priests may tell the penitents what penance they should do after the confession of their sins."[28]

There is no longer any doubt that the rapid spread of "private penance" was due in large part to the preaching of the Celtic monks, and this took place primarily because "canonical penance" had fallen into disuse because of the difficulties previously mentioned. After the forced evacuation by Rome and the occupation of these islands by the barbarians, the administration of penance in the Celtic Christian centers of Ireland and Great Britain passed primarily into the hands of the monks, mostly because there were no or few secular priests in those centers. The monastic practice known as "revelation of conscience," by which, at day's end a monk would confess his faults to the Abbot and receive pardon for them "had played a considerable role in the development of religious life; it is easy to understand how the monks, convinced of the value of such a practice, had spread it."[29] They encouraged it among the simple faithful. "The Celtic monks were untiring missionaries. It could be said that nearly all the regions of the Latin West . . . heard them preach. From the second half of the sixth century, throughout all of the seventh, and for a good part of the Carolingian period, Irish monks travelled throughout Gaul. The most famous of these monks was, of course, St. Columbanus, founder of the monastery of Luxeil, which exercised its influence over a great number of other monasteries. Taking into account the disciples of the saint and other lesser-known Irish missionaries, one can account for the spread of the Celtic penitential discipline not only in a large part of Gaul, but also in Bavaria, the Germanic language area, in Switzerland and Alsace, and as far as Thuringia. Bearing in mind that St. Columbanus died in Bobbio (Italy), we can understand the vastness of the area in which his influence, either direct or indirect, was felt."[30]

During the time of the Carolingian reform, which we shall treat later, the two methods, both public penance and private penance, were still in use; the second, that is, private penance, was "burying the first."[31] It is an historically documented fact that, as can be proven by the existence of the penitential books throughout these areas, by the seventh and at the beginning of the eighth century, private penance was in use throughout Europe except in Spain, where the many councils of Toledo[32] tried to discourage it, and in Italy, where Rome kept a closer eye on the ecclesial life of the country.

With the growth of private penance, there was a clear distinction between the public penitents and the voluntary penitents. These first made expiation for their sins in the manner prescribed for days, months, and years as established by the penitentials; the second group remained in the *Ordo Poenitentium* for the rest of their lives. "These are the two aspects of the *Ordo Poenitentium* throughout the middle ages."[33]

THE SPIRITUALITY OF THE PENITENTS

The same concept of conversion as an internal and external act by which the Christian, not weighed down by serious sin, and therefore not obliged to do so, publicly decided to abandon the way of life which he had formerly led and to devote himself to God in one of the various forms of penitential life, reveals that the ultimate goal of such a choice was to make God one's point of reference and very reason for life; this end was obviously very spiritual. This interior decision, however, was also externally visible by means of the penitential habit.

We have already seen how eastern theology had influenced

one line of thinking in this regard. It must have spread with the diffusion of "conversio" already found in the Orient. This same term "abrenuntiantes," that is, those who renounced the life-style of the world, is indicative of this. When the use of private penance later proceeded to spread, as has been seen, there began a series of teachings which explicitly insisted upon the necessity of "interior conversion," of sorrow for sins. This is evidently owing to the fact that the penitential legislation resulting from the proliferation of the penitentials continued to develop the concepts of real or personal commutation;[34] this caused the practice of official penance to become a rather mechanical process. Each sin was assigned a corresponding external penance; it is evident that there was always the danger that interior conversion could be neglected.

Among the loftier teachings concerning penance are those of Isidore of Seville, bishop of that city from 601-636. In his various works[35] he "has collected and synthesized the best of the penitential spirituality, drawn from St. Augustine and St. Gregory. He does not so much speak about canonical penance, even though he certainly knows about it, but of conversion of the heart,[36] explaining and emphasizing the interior dimension which should make penance a Christian 'way of life.' St. Isidore clearly taught that penance is not only an act or rite, nor is it either a temporary internal disposition. It is and should remain a constant disposition of the religious spirit, a permanent consecration to a new style of life, interior as well as exterior, but most of all interior."[37] "One could say that St. Isidore presented a complete psychology and pastoral outline of 'conversion.' The noblest aspect of this is the penitent's intention to uproot from the soul that type of complacency which could invade it after repentance. . . . He therefore insisted upon those constructive and mystical aspects of perfect sorrow which focus one's entire interior attention upon the contemplation of God and sighs with desire for eternal life in him."[38]

This teaching represented the age-old inspiration of those who consecrated themselves voluntarily to the penitential life. However, among the great Christian masses who began to make use of private penance for the remission of sins, the tariff system already mentioned, and the almost mechanical process which characterized it, soon caused a progressively degenerative process in the biblical concept of penance. In the terminology of the penitentials, penance mostly meant fasting. This and other prescribed works, most of them external, slowly obscured the meaning of conversion. The two components of the concept of penance—interior and exterior—will, throughout the ages, have alternating times of prevalence. According to the fervor of the period, and varying from place to place, each of these concepts was emphasized. We shall find it necessary to return to this topic when treating the penitential milieu in which Francis found himself at the time of his conversion.

3

THE DEVELOPMENT OF THE PENITENTIAL MOVEMENT

(VII - XI CENTURIES)

OVERVIEW: THE EFFECTS OF THE BARBARIAN INVASION

It is extremely difficult to re-create a precise outline of the situation which clearly describes the social and religious milieu of the period from the seventh through the eleventh centuries; it was during this period that the voluntary penitential movement continued to develop and to take on its own physiognomy, often the result of various external influences.

We must first of all remember the immense social transformation that took place following the great migrations of new people, referred to in history books by the rather negative term of "the barbarian invasions." These people began moving toward the West in the fourth century, upsetting secular institutions and, at times, creating a chaotic vacuum in civil life. The Church, the only institution able to maintain the old order of things, was thus in a position to initiate a reconstruction which began at different times in various countries through the fusion of the new peoples with the old. This process was more rapid in those regions where the newly-arrived, for the most part Arians, were converted to Christianity. Where, instead, the conquerors remained Arians, two distinct groups were discernible for a longer period. Such is the case, for example, in the south of France, in Spain, and above all in Africa. The peninsular part of Italy, although conquered, was less absorbed and, beginning with the Byzantine conquest in the middle of the sixth century, seems to take on again some of the external traits of the ancient period."[1]

Among the ecclesiastical institutions which substantially survived, we must mention the voluntary penitential movement. The so-called "canonical collections" which were gathered from conciliar canons and pontifical decrees bear undeniable witness of this. Synodal activity, which was very great in various areas of the West during the fifth and sixth centuries, was particularly intense in Spain after the conversion of the Visigoth King Recadero in 589. It suffices to recall the numerous Councils of Toledo held during the seventh century.[2] France was the land of Councils *par excellence* during this period. From 506 (Council of Adge) to 585 (the Second Council of Macon) a total of thirty councils took place there. In all of the legislative documents emanating from provincial and national councils, there is a considerable treatment of the penitential discipline. One of the more famous collections of canons is the *Hispania*, possibly the work of St. Isidore of Seville, and contemporary to the Council of Toledo in 633.[3] A simple examination of the titles of this collection tells us that penance, both voluntary and public, occupied the attention of the bishops. The entire second part of Book II "De institutionem monasteriorum et monachorum atque ordinibus poenitentium" is dedicated *ex professo* to penance. Examples of this are the following: title XIV—The good to be sought from penance; title XV—What penance can do; title XVII—The administration of penance and the times for penitence; title XVIII—The rules for penitents; title XIX—The times of remission for penitents; title XX—Concerning the non-reception of penitents; title XXI—Concerning those who die in penance.[4]

PENITENTIAL LEGISLATION AFTER THE YEAR 700

With the encounter and partial coexistence of the two types of penance, namely, Roman (public) and insular (private), the latter used in the West for granting pardon from sin and thus readmission into the ecclesial community after grave and public sin, penitential legislation took on diverse characteristics from one nation to another, depending upon the predominance of either of the two modes. In Italy and Spain the "old penance" prevailed, while in the north of Europe private penance was more in vogue. There are, however, at the same time new and common characteristics, rather uniform, relating particularly to what the penitents could or could not do. Since the voluntary penitents spontaneously associated themselves to the legislation regarding public penance, these new characteristics became a part of their life as well.

One of the more constant prescriptions found among the penitential decrees of the national and regional councils of this period is the obligation of the penitent to disassociate himself from the secular militia. Even the public penitent was not permitted to return to it at the end of his prescribed period of penance. What is meant by this secular militia? A distinction must be made between the two categories of this group: the "togata" and the "paludata." The former regards certain occupations and public offices; the latter concerns bearing arms and participating in wars.[5]

a. The "militia saecularis togata": The penitent was prohibited from holding those offices, duties, and occupations which of themselves cannot be exercised without sin, or only with great difficulty. Among these offices were always included those of judge, lawyer, and magistrate.[6] The occupation of "merchant" was also commonly listed because of the negative understanding of the morality of that profession, growing out of a long history.[7] Nevertheless, in the seventh century, certain distinctions were made in regard to this point. The restriction concerning merchants came to exclude farmers, artisans, and shopkeepers.[8] In regard to trade, just and unjust profit had to be taken into consideration.[9]

In regard to the administration of justice, one consequence was immediately seen, namely, that when the penitent found it absolutely necessary to turn to the courts to redress wrongs that he has suffered, he was required to appeal to the ecclesiastical courts rather than to the civil ones.[10]

b. The "militia saecularis paludata": Belonging to the penitential order excluded one from bearing arms, military life, and participating in wars. On this point there is a constant tradition in the council decrees.[11] Only with reluctance did the bishops grant permission for penitents to join the "militia paludata"; usually only professional soldiers who had no other means of support were allowed to return to the "militia" after their period of penance.[12]

FASTING AND LENT

After the seventh century more precise prescriptions regarding the penalties or "penitential medicine" already present in the Western churches began to appear in the legislation. Notable among these are the regulations concerning fasting and Lent.

a. Fasting is one of the characteristics that appear from the very beginning in penitential legislation, and thus was carried over into the life of the voluntary penitents. It is, however, only in this period that are first found the minute regulations that continued for centuries in the practice of Christian life. The week was divided into two parts, each composed of three days. The first part (Monday, Wednesday, and Friday) was popularly called "legitimate week-days"; they were mostly considered "esuriales," or days of strict fast, from which one was not readily dispensed during the period of penance, except for sickness or travel. The other week days were not marked by such strict fasting, and, except when the penance had been imposed as a "gravissima," dispensation was more easily granted. Sunday was, following ancient tradition, exempt from fast.

b. Lent. Around the year 700 there appeared in the West the observance of three lents. A canon of the year 730 exhorted the clergy to remind the faithful to "make three legitimate fasts during the year," that is forty days each before Christmas, Easter, and after Pentecost. The canon, however, appears to be spurious. In reality this custom, like many others, came from the Eastern Church.[13] A certain Theodorus Graecus seems to have introduced this practice into England and from there it may have passed into other regions. The two minor lents (the ones not in practice today) were not always of forty days, but at times were only assigned for twenty or fifteen days, with a possible dispensation from the bishops in consideration of the lesser gravity of sin or in consideration of the person. Other lenten periods were also mentioned at times.[14]

Knowing of the multiple lents that St. Francis observed,[15] we are able to realize the source of such penitential practices. One must also remember that at times, after the reconciliation of a penitent, either because of the gravity of the sin or for other reasons, "he was given the obligation to fast on a certain day, and especially on Friday for the rest of his life, or at least to abstain from meat and wine for that day."[16]

CORPORAL PENANCE

The term corporal penance, as it is used here, means the voluntary flagellation of one's own body for reasons of penance. This kind of discipline was unknown in the West, not only until the eighth century, but for a further two hundred years. Evidence shows that it was introduced into Italy around the years 950-960 and was practiced by seculars as well as monks. In the beginning there was some discussion about the licitness of flagellation;

later it was accepted as a means of exchange for the monks to compensate for other penances.

The system of penitential commutation was in full vigor, and allowed the exchange or redemption of penalty through money or alms-giving.[17] The monks, who could not freely dispose of money, were cut off from this exchange. Thus the question was raised: "Could the monks not be allowed this redemption through voluntary corporal punishment?" This later gave rise to a further principle: "Anyone who could not pay in money could satisfy their penalty with corporal punishment."[18] In consequence of such reasoning, public penance admitted public flagellation, which up until this time was allowed only for servants and settlers, clerics and monks. The act of flagellation was later called discipline; this term soon came to be applied for the instrument of corporal penance as well.

THE PENITENTIAL PILGRIMAGE

The penitential book of Robert of Flamesbury, dating from 1207-1215, is a sure witness to the three ways in which the reorganization of penitential discipline began to develop at the end of the twelfth century and the early part of the thirteenth: solemn public penance, public non-solemn penance, and private penance.

"Solemn public penance is that which is had at the beginning of lent when one solemnly takes upon himself the sack-cloth and ashes. This is also called public penance because it takes place publicly.

"Non-solemn public penance takes place without the lenten solemnity and is also called a penitential pilgrimage.

"Private penance is that which is done before the confessor."[19]

The elements or penitential forms described and accepted in this late document had really developed through long centuries even if the third element, private penance, was only sanctioned for the first time at the Fourth Lateran Council in 1215.

What concerns our study is the second form mentioned by Robert of Flamesbury, namely, the *penitential pilgrimage*.

a. The voluntary pilgrimage was one of the more constant forms of the penitential movement. It can be found in the very beginnings of the movement and became even more note-worthy over a long period of time extending beyond the time of St. Francis and lasting until the end of the Middle Ages. St. Jerome had previously recommended it as a means conducive to true penance.[20] We have already made mention of the idea of pilgrimage to the holy places of Palestine which spread in the West as early as the fourth century. The pilgrimage later had the Celtic monks among its supporters, the very same ones who diffused the "tariff penance." A common name for pilgrimage was service of God in penance. Pilgrimage became almost second nature for the Irish people.[21] Leaving one's relatives was a high form of renunciation in a land where family bonds were strong. In the biographies of the Irish saints there are frequent references such as "make a pilgrimage in the name of the Lord" or "for the cure of the soul," or "to gain the heavenly fatherland." Leaving meant to go in search of solitude, as well as to face the dangers and hardships of a long voyage, the penitential nature of which was emphasized by fasting and prayer. Penitential pilgrimages were a way of fulfilling an imposed or voluntary penance; in addition, it was a way of bringing Christ to people who as yet did not know him. At the origin of monastic activity and expansion of medieval Ireland we thus find mortification through voluntary exile,"[22] that is, pilgrimage.

Pilgrimage was considered an expiatory work of great ascetic or devotional value. Later, in a more monastic environment, it would be held that, in order for the pilgrimage to be truly valid, it should lead a person to the regular monastic life.

In order to understand the high level of spirituality attributed to pilgrimage, we must keep in mind that the pilgrimage of the Middle Ages (especially before the year 1000) was very different from that which we understand today, both in custom and practice. We take for granted that, if proper caution is taken, one's home and other properties will be well guarded during the period of absence and will be in order when the pilgrim returns home. In the period of which we are speaking, the pilgrim left everything behind, with no hope of finding anything upon his return. The return itself was, moreover, entirely hypothetical. He departed, leaving everything, choosing to live outside his own environment, often outside his own country, as a stranger and an unknown. He faced, unarmed and poor, a journey shrouded in mystery and uncertainty, in search of grace and pardon. He was a wandering hermit who, like Abraham, "a pilgrim and nomad of the one God," answered the command of the one who had invited him to leave his own country and to go toward that land which had been shown to him (cf. Gen 12:1).[23]

In later years the Crusades also assumed the penitential significance already present in the concept of pilgrimage to the holy places. Assuming the obligation to join in the attempt to liberate the Sepulchre of Christ was, for many, an opportunity to gain a bigger or richer fief, or to further trade at the expense of the infidels; for others it was an adventure for which they had nothing to lose but their lives. For the penitent, however, sewing upon one's shoulder the cross of the Crusades was equivalent to dedicating oneself completely to the following of Christ in answer to the call of God—"God wishes it"—and to participate in an undertaking conducted by God himself.

Undertaking the journey for the sake of piety alone was considered a penitential act and was of such value that it obtained the remission of any other form of penance that had been imposed for sins committed. Conquering the holy land was seen as collaborating in the spread of Christianity, the kingdom of God. To reach and dwell in that land was to see and touch personally the places sanctified by Christ and his Mother. From the Crusades the cult of sacred relics developed; from it there was also an increase in devotion to the humanity of Christ and the divine and human maternity of the Virgin.[24]

b. The imposed pilgrimage. This was properly the non-solemn public penance. It could be imposed by any pastor in a rather simple ceremony: at the door of the church the priest publicly consigned to the departing ones the distinctive signs of their status—the knapsack and walking-stick.

This penitential pilgrimage, which could be repeated, was given for less scandalous public sins. It became a common phenomenon in medieval Christianity, but sometimes was less than edifying. Although the pilgrimage had been imposed upon them, the penitents did not always enter into it with the spirit that should have characterized them. The groups of apparently devout pilgrims passing through the countryside and reciting psalms during the day were often something quite different during their nightly stopovers.[25] This caused attitudes of diffidence and even of hostility toward pilgrims in some areas; these attitudes affected the voluntary pilgrims, those who were intent only on their own sanctification. There are examples of holy pilgrims, such as St. Roch of Montpellier, being persecuted and imprisoned as spies or vagabonds.

THE EREMITICAL LIFE

It would seem almost a contradiction, but it is a fact that, in the very same period in which pilgrimage spread as a practical form of penitential life, another form of life diametrically opposed to it also flourished—the eremitical life.

Originating in the cenobitical life in the East, it easily spread to the West, reaching its highest point when the conditions of civil and ecclesiastical life were characterized by great confusion and uncertainty. The eremitical life meant saying farewell to the "world," a separation from it in order to seek God alone. Dal Pino writes that "the greater part of the hermits sought in solitude the *eremetica puritas*, the anchorite liberty of total detachment, recollection, and prayer." Some lived for a long time in one place; others migrated frequently, often to avoid people who came to visit them. In some cases the hermit accepted companions and, without founding a monastery, set them up in small groups or in separate cells, placing them under a common discipline. There were also recluses, particularly women, who lived near churches or monasteries; these became known as "conversi." The eremitical way of life was adopted as either a permanent or a temporary way of life, and one could come to it from the monastic or lay state. The influence of some of these men is noteworthy. In constant contact with the people from whom they are not separated by monastic walls, they periodically leave their solitude in order to invite the people to penance, to establish peace, to reform decadent monasteries. They then return to solitude. In the south of Italy, the eremitical life, because of its ties with the Greek monasteries, assumed a decidedly oriental character. Here their lives were characterized by independence, the practice of the ascetical life, that is, by contemplation in peace and quiet, by work and absolute silence. At times they lived in caves hewn in rock near a church, which itself resembled a cave.[26]

We will speak later of the importance which the eremitical ideal assumed contemporary with the reform of monasticism.

PENITENTIAL ELEMENTS IN THE CAROLINGIAN REFORM

"The Carolingian reform" refers to the period in church history, from the time that the sons of Charles Martel took possession of Merovingian France (741) until the middle of the following century, as well as the powerful reform movement which characterized it and which found its highest point in Charlemagne, Holy Roman Emperor from 768 until his death in 814. "The two inscriptions placed on the coins of Charlemagne synthesize his entire program: one side reads *Religio christiana* and on the other side is inscribed *Renovatio romani imperii,"* observes Leclercq, a noted scholar of the period.[27] It involved restoring an empire fallen under the invasion of different peoples, which required a unity of government and organization. But the new order was to be Christian, dominated by the Church and established by means of a return to Rome and its Christian past. On the more spiritual side of this return, St. Boniface was the promoter (672-754), commissioned for this task directly by the Holy See.[28] Charlemagne imprinted upon the period as well as on the reform a particular character, corresponding to his political and ecclesial vision which was not always in perfect harmony with the universal ecclesiastical ideal of the popes.[29] Under his successor, Louis the Pious (814-840) the Church sought to liberate itself from the "Protectorate" of the state and asked of the state only that it respect the measures that the Church intended to adopt. The unification of Western Christianity in the Holy Roman Empire was certainly a positive factor that permitted the rapid expansion of the measures decided at the center into the various regions.[30]

Penance, the only factor that demands our consideration in the wide-reaching Carolingian reform, was generally favored by the movement. Leclercq affirms that, "among the laity, groups of penitents, oblates, and fervent Christians were developing, organizing themselves and multiplying, especially around the monasteries. We know of the existence of these groups in the preceding period."[31] In the area of doctrine and praxis in penitential legislation, the reformers sought a better coordination of the two modes that were then in practice, that is, public and private penance. Because of the many preceding conciliar norms, things were in a chaotic state. Trying to achieve some order, the legislators accepted as a solution the principle already widely in effect that "for a public sin there was to be public penance and for a hidden sin (even a serious one) there was to be private penance."[32] This distinction which ultimately became law was partially the result of an intense reaction to the penitential manuals and the discipline that they represented. The reaction was particularly against the laxism which the manuals introduced (when two manuals disagreed, the lesser penalty was given) and the abuses brought about by the practice of commutation. This practice, as we have already stated, allowed the penitent to substitute almsgiving for fasting or have others (pious persons or penitents) fast, offering them a monetary compensation. The rich, however, who were able to buy the persons who performed their penitential works, were thus in practice exempted from performing any penance.³³ The Carolingian reformers of the ninth century would have wanted a pure and simple return to the penitential discipline of the fifth century, but it was obvious that that was not possible.³⁴ They contented themselves in giving a more organic order to the principle: to a public offense there was to be a corresponding public penance; to a private offense, a private confession.

The more important aspect for our consideration here, however, is that the spiritual writers of this period insist upon the interior aspect of penance. A letter, probably written by Rabanus Maurus to Queen Judith, the second wife of Louis the Pious "gives us a vision of the program of prayer and austerity which consisted in the way of doing penance" (*modus paenitentiae*), for a woman of the world. This text . . . allows us to catch a glimpse of what was probably the spiritual exercises of many fervent Christians, penitents of whom we have no traces in history or literature.³⁵

Unfortunately, the greater part of the spiritual works that have come down to us are addressed to important personages.³⁶ However, the teaching contained in them is probably the same that was given to the simple penitents. We here present some examples: the penitent should practice justice, mercy, and moderation; he should maintain detachment from goods, preserve peace in the family; he should place his trust in God in times of peace as well as war; he should always be on guard and maintain a right intention, a pure heart; he should nourish love for Christ and for Sacred Scripture; he should be recollected, make the examen, and be receptive to the inspiration of God.³⁷

"Of the princes and all the laity, Jonas of Orleans asks a true conversion. . . . He advises the laity to receive Holy Communion more frequently, not only on the three major feasts, even normally at every Mass, not out of habit, but devotion."³⁸ Together with Holy Scripture, frequent prayer was to be the other great nourishment of their spiritual life, preferably to be done in a consecrated church.³⁹ The treatise of Rabanus Maurus *de modo paenitentiae* bears witness to an attempt to interiorize the penitential practices. In it are found not only the immediate sanctions, but an entire theory, a true and proper theology of repentance, of trust in divine forgiveness and a serene expectation of the last judgment."⁴⁰

These and similar instructions permeated the life of the penitents in this period, and, in our opinion, were the only lights to which they could turn in the immediate turbulent future.

THE "DONATI" AND "OBLATES"

During the Carolingian reform we witness the diffusion of a new form of penitential life, that of the "donati" or oblates. They were people who, seeking to fulfil their own conversion, placed themselves in the service of God by putting themselves at the disposal of a church, monastery, or episcopacy. This is what St. Francis did at the Church of San Damiano, immediately following his inspiration-encounter with Christ crucified.

This practice was gradually established with the rise of the system of commutation, beginning with the offering of one's goods. Those who had no money to offer for the commutation of their penance offered part of their immovable goods to new hospitals, churches, and monasteries or donated them to already existing institutions, thus sharing in the spiritual benefits granted to such institutes and participating in the merits which flowed from the life of prayer and works of charity of the monks and priests who lived in them.[41] The donors generally retained the interest from these goods during their life-time.

We know of cases, as early as the end of the eighth century, in which Christians offered themselves and their own goods before death so that they might benefit from spiritual suffrages.[42] This practice gave rise to the "oblates," although this phenomenon later became more closely connected to the Benedictine Rule and to their monasteries.[43] With the passage of time even this penitential practice created abuses. Common law ever more often granted an exemption from taxes and other obligations on the goods donated to the above-mentioned types of institutions, as well as for the people who entered the Order of Penance, even as oblates. Less scrupulous persons "offered themselves" to churches and monasteries in order to benefit from these privileges without really practicing the corresponding form of life. Charlemagne himself took measures against these abuses as we can see in certain decisions of the Chapter of Aquisgrana.[44]

THE DARK AGES

With the final decline of the Carolingian Empire (which, according to historians coincided with the deposition of Charles the Fat at the Diet of Tribur in 887) and the ensuing political-social dissolution,[45] there begins a period of anarchy and confusion in the West that reaches the point of desolation which does not spare any nation, nor even the Church. This is very evident in Italy and in the Roman curia as well. There are examples of great abuses, schisms, and scandals in the papacy, the meddling of the laity in the churches and monasteries, simony, and lay investiture.[46] The papacy practically became the prize in the struggles among the powerful Roman families. Distinguishing themselves for baseness among these were the families of the Teofilatto and, later, the Crescenzi and Tuscolo.[47] In the twenty centuries of the history of the Church this period was the bleakest, to such an extent that it is often referred to as "the dark ages"—*saeculum obscurum*. It lasted until the imperial crown finally passed into the hands of the German princes (the first of which was Otto I in 961) and even longer.

Historians generally agree to credit Otto and his successors with the restoration of order in civil and religious life. Ecclesiastical and institutional surroundings began to function somewhat; churches and monasteries regained their liberty.[48] However, certain imperial provisions also caused later ecclesiastical evils. To dispel the possibility of competition among lay princes, Otto strengthened the power of bishops through investiture and the concession of public rights, along with ever increasing goods.

Such temporal goods returned to the crown at the death of the bishop. Since the bishop was a prince of the empire, the emperor was responsible for nominating him. The combination of these elements effected the lessening of the religious presence in the ecclesiastical ministry, its dependence upon the state, the secularization of the episcopacy, and, probably worst of all, the introduction of simony into the religious office of the bishops. The imperial authority who was to select the new prince-servant-bishop was obviously more interested in his fidelity to the crown and his administrative ability than in the moral qualities so necessary for that role. Thus there was a multiplication of bishops who were more princes than pastors. The unworthy bishops were followed by, as cause and effect, the growth of an unworthy clergy and the spread of simony, that is, the buying and selling of ecclesiastical benefits connected with the episcopacy and parishes, and concubinage of the clergy, that is, the very evils which the Gregorian reform will set about to correct.

For the sake of objectivity, we must recall the few bright spots that come from those torches of vitality conserved in some monasteries and bishoprics not affected by the above-mentioned evils. In Germany, for example, the internal life of the Church grew and intellectual life regained its vigor.[49]

In all this what is most noteworthy is the fact that the Christian people became aware of the conditions into which they had fallen and from here began the reaction which will reach its highest point in the Gregorian reform of the succeeding century. More time is needed, however, before the above-mentioned bright spots can be found in Rome, that is, in the papacy itself, and the favorable conditions become strong enough to once again illuminate and transform the entire Latin West. The reform will have a beneficial influence, as we shall see, for the ancient institution of penance and for the penitents as well.[50]

**THE REFORM OF MONASTICISM AND
ITS INFLUENCE ON THE PENITENTIAL MOVEMENT.**

Western monasticism contained within itself the strength for reaction and self reform; it was the first and most influential factor of renewal during and immediately after the dark ages that followed the Carolingian fall. This probably remains as the most noteworthy merit of monasticism in its first thousand years of existence.

In the beginning of the tenth century reformed monasteries were already spreading in Burgundy, Lorraine, England, and Italy. In this last nation, there immediately arose eremitical tendencies that brought the work of reform to more radical positions. It was monasticism that eventually assured unity to the entire historical development of the reform. "It will be the abbots who will take the initiative for the movement and, most of all, those monks who, having become popes or cardinals in the second half of the eleventh century, will bring about its triumph.[51] "The monks were the first to organize an action of defense and mutual help . . . to fight against the interference of the laity for the spiritual liberty to attend to the works of the Church. They formed associations among the abbeys which, up until this time, had been isolated. These were the federations whose juridical bonds were very tenuous and which often arose from the fact that one monastery had received their reform influence from another. Little by little these formed true 'congregations' of monasteries and later, the first of the religious orders, that of Cluny—*Ordo Cluniacensis*. On the continent, three names dominated this movement—Cluny and Gorze to which must be added Monte Cassino in Italy. Cluny was founded in Burgundy in 910, Gorze in Lorraine in 933."[52] Gorze exercised its influence toward the north and east of Europe; Cluny in France and later in Spain, Italy, and England. Between Cluny and Gorze there existed certain differences that became evident within their respective spheres of influence. While Cluny was purely a monastic reform, that is, it concerned itself with the internal affairs of the monastery, under the influence of Gorze, especially in Germany, the abbeys continued to play a role in the evangelization already begun by St. Boniface. In England also, where many of the abbey churches were cathedrals, the care of souls (*cura animarum*) occupied a certain part of the monks' life.[53]

One can understand that the persons who had the greatest influence on the penitential movement in this period and the entire eleventh century as well, those who can be called the inspirators of penitential spirituality, were the very same reformers of monasticism, especially the great masters of the eremitical life such as Saints Romuald and Peter Damian, educated in the spirituality of Cluny. Another influence was that of the Orient because of its close connections with the Greek monasteries in the south of Italy.

Let us treat each of these, underlining certain fundamental ideas of spirituality which we find repeated in the penitential movement, and through it, in St. Francis.

Cluny: The monastery of Cluny, founded in Burgundy (France) in 910, soon gave expression, especially through the writings of the Abbot Odo (924-932), to the theological and ecclesial meaning of monastic life. It developed the cult of the humanity of Christ and the maternity of the Blessed Virgin; it popularized the added offices of the dead, of all saints, and the *penitential psalms*. It developed some of its own Marian devotions; through Abbot Odilio (994-1049) it gave us the first known example of a specific act of spiritual vassalage or a *commendatio sui*, expressed in a special service to the Blessed Virgin, *who became the model and protectress of the whole Cluny congregation*.[54]

St. Romuald:[55] Dependent upon the spirituality of Cluny and a great propagator of it, he indicated the lines of development of the later medieval piety, directed toward the emphasis of the *mystery of the Incarnation of the Word of God and the divine and human maternity of the Blessed Virgin*, his mother, expressed in suitable devotional formulas that constituted the source from which many Christian people drew.[56]

St. Peter Damian (1007-1072):[57] In common with Cluny he also manifested a *profound devotion to the humanity of Christ*; he poetically expressed his praise of the Mother of God, of whom he considered himself a servant; he supported the spread of the Marian Saturday devotion, and of the little office of the Blessed

Virgin; he made acts of consecration to the service of Mary, already found in the tradition of Cluny as well.[58]

The oriental tradition continued to make its influence felt, especially in the field of Marian piety. The formulas associated with the *devoted service* to the Virgin, very much alive in the West during the twelfth and thirteenth centuries, found their first expressions in the places where there was an influx of the Byzantine world, as well as by the migration of Sicilian monastic colonies into the Italian regions of Calabria, Lucania, and Puglia, brought about by the Arab occupation of Sicily in the ninth and tenth centuries.

The eremitical life of the penitents was thus, above all, under the influence of the great masters of the eleventh century.

Toward the end of that century and at the beginning of the next, the eremitical ideal became an expression of an alternative to monastic life. Known in the West since the Gregorian reform, it later assumed such fame and vitality that it gave rise to numerous institutions and contributed to affirm religious ideals among the people. In fact, almost immediately, the preaching of the gospel undertaken by some of the hermits involved the laity more and more in the work of renewal.

The eremitical life developed as a search for evangelical life, not because of a crisis in monasticism, which remained vital. Perhaps it was in some way brought about because of the fact that the monastic institutions remained "very capitalistic and feudal, humanly too powerful to respond to the demands of a society in full demographic, economical, and social development which sought in the Gospels an alternative to the diffused thirst for wealth and a solution to the new religious demands of the common people and the artisans of the city."[59]

In contrast to monastic prosperity which consisted of imposing buildings, a moderate and tranquil life, administrative duties, and worries connected with the large possessions and the acquisition of private churches, there arose a desire for poverty in daily life and in buildings, the need for hard manual labor, life in solitude, penance, and prayer.

These were all elements that formed a part of the spiritual package of the penitential movement, elements which Francis found in the movement and which were assumed by him and conserved in great part, not only for the penitents, but also for the Friars Minor, as is seen from the prescriptions of the *Regula non bullata* (ER).

From this spiritual richness resulted more than a simple return to the past. It was more directly a return to the origins, to the gospel, to Christ himself, a desire to make his poverty of life real, and to announce it to the poor.

CHARITABLE FOUNDATIONS

In connection with the growth of the penitential pilgrimages, both voluntary (devotional) and imposed, various charitable institutions arose—hospices, hostels, and hospitals, promoted by the laity or clergy, where penitents could practice their ideal of charity.

The first important example that we have is that of the "Brothers of St. Jacopo d'Altopascio," a charitable hospital association, reportedly dating from the year 746.[60] The hospital of Altopascio, constructed along the "Via Romea or Francesca"[61] "for the accommodation of pilgrims" is mentioned for the first time in a document of 1056. The association obtained a new rule from Gregory IX with the bull *Solet annuere* of April 5, 1239.[62] The religious of this order were "simple lay-brothers or brother-priests, deacons and other clerics, or knight-brothers: the priests were not many. . . . The brothers were mendicants; the habit was gray or brown; they wore as a sign on their mantles or their cowl a gimlet or hammer which had the shape of the Tau."[63]

Another charitable institution which also had the Tau as its symbol was the "Hospital Brothers of St. Anthony the Hermit," called simply the "Antonines." Founded in France in 1095, their principal activity was the care of the sick, especially lepers. One of their specialties was the "fire of St. Anthony," also called "the burning sickness."[64] "As testimony of their relationship to the order, and also as a symbol of their charitable vocation, they used to carry in their hands a stick at the end of which was a Tau. Likewise, they sewed a large Tau on their habits."[65] In the beginning of the thirteenth century they had 369 foundations, one of which was in Rome.[66]

With the movement of great masses of people toward Jerusalem for the Crusades, this phenomenon of charitable institutions grew into the institution of religious-knight orders, whose specific purpose was to attend to the needs of the Crusaders.

The first of these were the Hospitalers of St. John of Jerusalem, who had their origin in a hospital for "pilgrims and for the sick" at Jerusalem, begun in the commercial section of the city by the merchants from Amalfi, a maritime city from which many Crusaders set sail. The hospital was near the Church of St. John the

Baptist, from which it took its name. Later followed the Order of the Knights-Templar, founded in 1118 with the purpose of "keeping the road that led along the coast of Palestine to Jerusalem free of bandits."[67]

Independently of the Crusades, although connected with the aforementioned foundations, there arose between 1170 and 1180, in a climate of evangelical reform and as an expression of charitable works, the Hospital Brothers of the Holy Spirit.[68]

These institutions greatly influenced the development of a humanitarian Christian sensitivity among the laity, especially among the penitents, and equally influenced St. Francis, as can be seen from the *Regula bullata* (LR).[69]

The increase of pilgrimages and the intensification of charitable activity was certainly connected to the Crusades.[70] Among the first to participate in all these movements were the penitents.

THE PENITENTIAL MEANING OF THE TAU

We have seen that certain charitable-penitential associations took the Tau as a distinctive symbol. Historians and students of anthropological phenomena have shed some light on the various meanings that the Tau had during the centuries of its greatest spread.[71] Among these we cannot neglect the penitential meaning that the symbol had in the period immediately prior to St. Francis. A clear witness to this can be found in the spiritual tract, *Liber de poenitentia* of the Anonymous Benedictine of the twelfth century.[72]

This work, evidently of Cistercian derivation, was written at the end of the century, in the year 1189,[73] and addressed to the segment of Cistercian monks who favored taking an active part in the Crusades as diplomats, organizers, chaplains, preachers, and even as combatants.[74]

In mentioning various ways of deploring sin, the author says: "Examine your thoughts, words, and works accurately and see if you have sinned in these things. If you believe that you have gravely sinned, take upon yourself the sign of the Tau, the sign of those who weep and lament their faults. The Tau represents the figure of the Cross, a sign of the passion of Christ. Imitate, therefore, the passion of Christ and fulfil in your flesh whatever is lacking in the passion of Christ. If you do this, the judge will pass by without striking you; that is, he will pardon you."[75]

In the Latin text the word *poenitentia* is understood either in the biblical sense of *metànoia* or *conversio* (to detest evil and return to God), or in the sense of the grace of conversion; thus penance is both an emanation from man and a gift of God. In fact, defending the possibility of obtaining pardon from God every time there is in man true penance, the Anonymous writer affirms: "When there is the return to God (*poenitentia*), there is also pardon. The (grace of) conversion (*poenitentia*) comes to the sinner from God, from whom also comes pardon. Thus each time God grants the grace of conversion, he also gives pardon."[76]

This text also shows us the interior aspect, the spirituality of the Tau. It does not have the power to take away the wrath of God *sic et simpliciter*, that is, by the fact that it is worn on the habit of the penitent, but only insofar as it is an exterior sign of metànoia, of internal conversion. "If you will have acknowledged your sins and liberated yourself from them and you will have taken upon yourself the Tau, that is, if you will have the sorrow of a true penance (*si amaritudinem verae paenitentiae . . . habueris"*), the angel of the Lord will not strike you, that is, the chastisement of the Lord will not come upon you."[77] The sorrow is not an exterior penance but signifies a sentiment of the soul, an interior sorrow of which the Tau is an external sign.

In the Rule of Altopascio there are two prescriptions concerning the Tau. Chapter XXV states: "All the friars . . . shall wear the Tau on their cape or cowl or on their mantles; that is, on their breast, so that God, through that sign and our faith, works, and obedience might guard us and, for the wearing of that sign he might defend us together with all our benefactors both in soul and in body, in this life and in the future life."[78] In chapter LI, in the ceremony of investure and reception into the order, it is prescribed: "The master or the prior shall take the mantle or the cowl and show to him the sign of the Tau which is upon the mantle. Then the master or the prior shall place the above-mentioned mantle on his neck, saying: 'Through this sign of the Tau which we give you, may God save you and guard you now and in the future and lead you to eternal life.'"[79]

Here also, as in the teaching of the Anonymous Benedictine, we see that the Tau was not considered salvific of itself, but had to be accompanied by faith and charitable works, performed for the love of God "so that God, through that sign and our faith and our works and our obedience . . . might guard us . . . and defend us both in soul and in body."

THE "CONVERSI"

It has already been stated that "conversi" was the more common name for the penitents throughout their history. They were the ones who had decided upon a *conversio*, that biblical *metànoia*, who had shown, often publicly, their desire for a break, more or less radical, with their previous form of secular life and who, in fact, had entered into one of the various forms of penitential life that was developing in the Church.[80]

From all the phraseology that is found in the medieval documents, it seems that we are unable to reconstruct a guideline that establishes a clear distinction between voluntary penitents and non-monastic conversi.[81] On the contrary, it seems that the two terms are synonymous and were used interchangeably; thus we find "conversi" who have chosen one of the many forms of penitential life.

The only exception in which we can speak of conversi who are not penitents is suggested by the canons of certain councils held from the fifth century on, which demand that the candidates or aspirants to the priesthood undergo a time of preparation in the state of "conversion"; this state is also called "*religio*." Distinct from the voluntary penitents, these "conversi" did not remain in that state for the rest of their lives, but only for that period of their preparation.[82] This regulation also serves as a witness of the high esteem in which the hierarchical Church held the state of the "conversi."

It would be well to recall at this point the principal groups or types of *conversi* or penitents found during this period in the Church:

a. The *married conversi* are persons who continued to live in their own families; their life of penance included abstinence from marital relations, at least periodically.

b. The *voluntary pilgrims* were those who went on pilgrimages to the Holy Land or to the tombs of the Apostles. The pilgrimage became a wide-spread ascetical, penitential, or devotional work.

c. The *hermits* lived alone or with one or two companions in grottos or caves. This element became very wide-spread in the tenth and eleventh centuries, during and after the reform of monasticism.

d. The *donati* or *oblates*, who gave themselves to the service of God (*Domino servire*), placing themselves at the disposal of a church, monastery, or episcopacy, generally with the characteristic of stability.

e. The *virgins* (not liturgically consecrated) lived with their families; they were frequently called *religious virgins*, the handmaids of God, or the devoted ones.

f. The *recluses* were women who consecrated themselves to God without entering traditional institutions. Their names varied according to time and place—they were known as the *incarcerated, penitent sisters, vested ones, pinzochere,* and later, especially as *Beghines.* Their support was assured either by work or by the charity of the faithful.[83]

THE CHARACTER OF THE CONVERSI OR PENITENTS

a. All the sources indicate that the characteristic dress, the habit of penance or eremitical habit, consisted of a tunic, walking-stick, cincture, knapsack, and sandals; at times the Tau was sewn or drawn on the mantle or cowl.

b. The penitents dedicated themselves to charitable works, mostly in hospitals, hospices for pilgrims, and in leprosaria.[84] Certain groups of penitents were identified with the establishment of a hospital or an association (today we would speak of a chain) of hospices. Among the activities of the individual penitents were their work in restoring churches, gratuitously helping in the construction of cathedrals or hospitals[85] as well as burying the dead, especially during the times of epidemics and plagues which were frequent throughout the Middle Ages.[86]

c. The penitents dedicated themselves to a life of prayer. The oldest extant *Propositum* contains detailed prescriptions on this point, which vary according to place and century. Such prescriptions generally require more of the penitents than is asked of the ordinary faithful. Examples of this are in the norms for reception of Communion and the sacrament of penance.[87]

d. With the spread of private penance there appears a noteworthy variety of dispositions, again according to time and place, in the dispositions regarding continency. In general, the norms ranged from absolute continency for the single penitents or widows to a periodic continency for the married.

e. The penitents were usually required to abstain from popular feasts, shows, dances, and noisy banquets because of the evident danger of indecent language, drunkenness, and their consequences.

f. They were usually required to abstain from public offices, especially from judiciary functions, that is, of judges and lawyers.

g. Conversi were ineligible for military careers, bearing arms, and participating in wars. From this prohibition, which was more or less constant, there derived the refusal to take an oath of fealty, first to the feudal lords and later to the communal (civil) authorities.[88] It was this situation which brought about the first serious conflicts between the penitents and the civil rulers at the beginning of the twelfth century.

h. In certain areas there was also a prescription against riding horses. In case of sickness or other necessity, the penitent was to prefer another mount; the horse was considered the prerogative of the rich and of nobility.

It is important to note that the basic dispositions relating to the practical life of the penitents, whether voluntary or imposed, were already defined by the middle of the fifth century and remained practically unchanged until the thirteenth century. These were found codified in a wonderful way in the *Memoriale Propositi* of 1221-1228.[89]

In regard to a classification or juridical position of the penitents in the Church, we observe that in the seventh century the Council of Toledo (633) had called the voluntary penitents *religiosi viri qui nec inter clericos nec inter monachos habentur*, that is, religious men who are not considered clerics or monks, and, since some of these are inclined to wander about (that is, had no fixed residence) the Council, in canon 53, "ordered the bishops to gather them into the clergy or assign them a fixed residence near a monastery, provided they were not sick or old. In certain monasteries these affiliated penitents were called brothers of penance (*fratres poenitentes*) to distinguish them from the cenobitic monks who were called simply brothers."[90] Because of this and similar steps taken by regional councils, the membership of the penitents in the ecclesiastical state, that is the clergy, became a common doctrine, even granting them clerical exemptions and privileges. The great jurist Gratian, wishing to justify the prohibition against the penitents regarding the bearing of arms, used the phrase "because the penitents live under ecclesiastical rule."[91] In the same manner, a gloss on canon 21 of the *quaestio* 4 of *causa* 17 clarified the juristic thought of the day regarding the penitents. In explaining what is to be understood by the expression "*Deo devotis*" *omnibusque ecclesiastic personis*, that is, all ecclesiastical persons devoted to God, used in that canon, Gratian explained: "by the expression 'devoted to God' we understand the conversi, the penitents, templars, hospitalers, all of whom enjoy the clerical privilege; wherefore they are part of the clergy."[92] This doctrine gradually became accepted universally, and thus it was in the time of St. Francis.

FURTHER PENITENTIAL TEACHINGS:
RATHERIUS OF VERONA (CA. 887-974)

Among the more notable teachings concerning penance in the post-Carolingian period are those found in the works of Ratherius of Verona.[93] Even though they do not attain the spiritual level of St. Isidore of Seville,[94] they are texts of a tradition belonging to a continuous line of penitential thought. Ratherius seems to be the faithful and natural follower of St. Isidore of Seville.[95]

Most of all, Ratherius witnesses to the history of the existence of the two-fold manner of penance in his time and area: one, the imposed penance that lasted for a certain period of time; the other, the voluntary penance which one entered into for life.[96]

Ratherius first called the attention of the penitent to the fact that there must be a perfect correspondence between his external penitential dress and his interior sentiments of humility: "If you are converted to God with a sincere heart, have in your soul that humility which you show externally by your habit. If this correspondence is lacking, you will be liars who show men a conversion with a false heart; and fakes provoke the wrath of God."[97]

In effect, then, for Ratherius "to do penance" means "to perform worthy fruits of penance," that is, charitable works for one's neighbor: "Are you a penitent or do you desire to become one? Remember above all the rule of penance given by the Baptizer of the Lord: Produce fruits worthy of penance. The penitent must put this into practice with generosity if he desires to obtain the mercy of the Lord."[98] As an example of this, he immediately listed the spiritual motive for each of the works of mercy, both spiritual and corporal, to which the penitent should dedicate himself.[99]

Furthermore, the penitent should be particularly attentive to the command of Christ concerning pardon: "Besides all these ways of meriting the pardon of God, there is another way that was instituted by the Lord himself and defined by him as to order, nature, and utility in many passages of the gospel: 'Forgive and you shall be forgiven.' " Ratherius then cited all of the gospel passages relating to pardon.[100]

"To produce worthy fruits of penance, it is necessary to know how to abstain cautiously from things that are licit."[101]

Ratherius' teaching regarding perseverance in the "life of penance" is both interesting and significant. "The way of penance and perseverance in it is a difficult thing. Who can pretend to remain there by his strength alone? Invoke, then, every day, or rather every moment, divine help; whether in silence or in whatsoever thing you do, ask for it seriously from the Lord: 'O God, create in me a pure heart.' And if you see that because of bad habits of the past it is difficult for you to remain in such a life, I beseech you, do not abandon it. . . ."[102] Later, continuing in the same line of thought, Ratherius wrote: "It is difficult to carry a large stone uphill; it is easier to go downhill with it. Equally so, no one can be perfect from the beginning. . . . Attach yourself to Christ and exclaim: 'Draw me after thee' " (Cant 1:4).[103]

In Ratherius we must recognize one of the great masters of the penitential life. He is also a further witness that the two elements of penitential life, perseverance in penance or continuous conversion and works of charity, were already considered essential in his day. They remained the stronghold in the life and spirituality of the penitents, including those who followed Francis of Assisi.

4

GREGORIAN REFORM AND ITINERANT PREACHERS

Beginning with Cluny, propagated and strengthened by its own abbots and those of monasteries following its reform, as well as by such great masters as Saints Romuald, Peter Damien, and John Gualbert, the spirit of reform spread from the monastic world—primarily through the influence of the penitents—to the Christian masses, to the more sensitive clergy, and ultimately to the papacy with the election of Clement II (1046).

When Leo IX (1049-1054), who had surrounded himself with pillars of the reform such as Umbert of Silva Candida, Frederich of Lorena, and Hildebrand (Gregory VII), embraced the reform, the papacy became the promoter of the moral renewal of the clergy. Thus the spirit of the reform changed its focus from the continuous condemnation of simony and nicolaitism to the rebuilding of structures and seeking to eliminate "investiture," the cause of the introduction of unworthy elements in the clergy and frequently of the subjection of the Church to secular powers.

Principal successors of Leo IX, namely, Stephen IX (1057-1058), Nicholas II (1059-1061),[1] and Alexander II (1061-1073), are all linked, either by origin or education, to the monastic reform centers. With the election of Gregory VII (1073-1086) the reform reached its peak, so much so that history has bound this period to his name—the Gregorian reform. It was intensified even more after Gregory until the time of the First Lateran Council (1123) by means of more austere monastic and canonical foundations. The laity became increasingly involved in the reform because of the itinerant preachers. At this point, however, the movement was not properly directed, mainly because of the lack of guidance at the lower levels and, as a result, it became the victim of the most heterodox forms.

In order to understand the substance of Francis' contribution to the history of the Church and of his influence especially on the penitential movement, it is necessary to have a deeper understanding of the complex period which immediately preceded him.

THE GREGORIAN REFORM AND RELIGIOUS REAWAKENING

It would be simplistic and anti-historic to try to find a single common denominator capable of explaining the various religious movements, orthodox as well as heterodox, which made the eleventh and twelfth centuries one of the most vital and active periods in the two-thousand year history of Christianity. Some see different motivations in these two centuries.[2] Others discover one or another common element.[3] Partially following Morghen's opinion on this point, it seems legitimate to affirm that the dominant element always present in the various religious movements of the twelfth century was the continuation and diffusion of the desire—already present in the second half of the eleventh century—to return to the gospel life of the apostles, considered as the norm and model of poverty and of evangelization for the whole Church.

In synthesis we may say that the Gregorian reform proposed a double aim: to free the Church from the interference of the secular government (the Holy Roman Empire) and to reestablish the regular life among the monks and diocesan clergy. Although these aims were partially reached, still to the majority of Christians, those more deeply committed, it was not so apparent. The official Church—bishops and priests—still appeared to be an organism surrounded by wealth rather than by an evangelical aura.

THE APOSTOLIC OR EVANGELICAL LIFE

The expression "evangelical life" or *vita apostolica* is an expression that we meet repeatedly in the period from the pre-Gregorian reform through the beginning of Franciscanism and beyond. It represents the ideal and the battle cry around which all the reformers rally; it is the cry of orthodoxy and heterodoxy alike. Let us try to clarify our ideas on this subject.

The realization of the Gregorian reform had the effect—which we can call collateral— of spreading the ideals of the *evangelical life of the apostles*, i.e., the desire for a return to Christian origins in the observance of gospel virtues; this is also called the *vita apostolica*. The life of the apostles is considered the model of Christian life, and therefore the model for all. This is a fundamental point for an understanding of the "new penitential climate" of the twelfth century. While in the past only monks had been considered the followers of the apostolic life, during the reform the conviction spread that this life was identified with the Christian life and must be followed by all believers.[4]

In its first important appearance, at the Roman Synod of 1059, the expression *vita apostolica* merely implied some elements of the common life (refectory and dormitory) for the clergy and a certain sharing of goods. Canon four of this Synod states: "We have decided that ecclesiastics (priests, deacons, and subdeacons) of the above-mentioned orders must have near the Church for which they were ordained a refectory and a common dormitory as befits truly pious ecclesiastics; they shall also administer in common all the revenues of the churches. We ask them with insistence to live a true apostolic life, that is, in common."[5] The aim of this legislation was clear; the common life was to protect celibacy. Apostolic poverty, in the sense of abandoning all goods, is not asked by the Roman Synod as an indispensable element of the apostolic life.

The canonical chapters, i.e., the canons regular, which emerged following this decree of the Roman Synod quickly discovered, however, that their common life did not satisfy the spiritual needs of their more committed members. These felt that, for their common life to be a truly apostolic life, a deeper commitment to poverty was necessary. By the end of the eleventh century, therefore, the expression *vita apostolica* already implied a true, lived poverty.

At the same time, especially in the first fifth of the twelfth century, the concept of the apostolic life acquired a new element in addition to that of poverty, namely, preaching, especially in an itinerant lifestyle.

The first itinerant preachers, canons regular, were the most significant example of this. They left the canonical life first to become hermits and later to begin their itinerant preaching in strictest poverty, precisely because at that point they felt that these two elements—a life of poverty and preaching—were the essential components of a truly apostolic life. For example, "In this way, before the foundation of the Premonstratensians in 1119, Norbert of Xanten spoke of his life as 'both evangelical and apostolic' and designated the followers of his ideal as 'imitatores apostolorum'" (PL 170, 1292).[6] The same two elements—poverty and preaching—remained characteristics not only among the so-called itinerant preachers, but also among the Cathari and Waldensians. They were equally accepted and shared, even though the fundamental principles are different, by St. Francis of Assisi in the last and definitive stage of his conversion.

THE ITINERANT PREACHERS

Once the aims of the Gregorian reform, namely, the renewal of monasteries, the abolition of simony, and of the concubinage of the clergy were reached, the religious forces reawakened by this very reform continued practicing and preaching the ideal of the *vita apostolica* as the norm for every Christian life.

This is what brought about the emergence of the period of itinerant preachers, spontaneous, semi-authorized, and non-authorized alike. Some were monks, others laymen, spontaneous preachers who believed themselves sent by the Spirit to carry out their mission, "men filled with enthusiasm and fervor who felt themselves moved to fill the void left by official preaching."[7] They all tried to make the apostolic life their own characteristic and the basis of their preaching. The most conspicuous and concrete aspect was poverty, to which all the penitential movements, both orthodox and heterodox, adhered.

If we want to consider as itinerant preachers all those involved in this activity from about 1090 until the beginning of the Franciscan itinerant preaching (1210), a period of about 120 years, we must make a clear distinction between the preachers of the first part of this period who were at least semi-authorized and orthodox, and those of the latter portion who, in addition to being unauthorized, were clear critics of ecclesiastical authority (e.g., Peter de Bruys and Arnold of Brescia), initiators of heterodox movements (the Waldensians) or propagators of pre-existing heretical currents such as the Cathari.

While we will immediately deal with the first group, we will speak of those "of the latter period" in the chapter on the anti-ecclesiastical and heterodoxical movements with which they are identified.

THE PREACHERS OF THE FIRST PERIOD (1090-1150)

The itinerant preachers of this period were mostly canons regular or monks who began their preaching spontaneously and only later received authorization, in some cases directly, from the Roman pontiff. Their doctrine orthodox, their life based on poverty, they had an immense following among the Christian people, a phenomenon particularly true in northern France (Normandy) and around the French-German border, with reverberations in the neighboring regions. A characteristic consequence of the phenomenon was that groups of faithful, men and women alike, abandoned their houses and possessions to follow these preachers on their pilgrimages day and night. The spiritual good produced by these preachers was certainly great, and was concretized by a Christian reawakening in those regions where the phenomenon occurred.

"True followers of Christ and the apostles, they went from place to place, proclaiming the kingdom of God. . . . Their preaching planted in the hearts of their hearers a desire to live virtuously, while the example of their ascetical life, clearly evident in their coarse clothing and unshod feet, spurred many to follow their example. Living in complete poverty, these preachers, in effect, adopted the ideals of the apostolic life, not merely as abstract ideas, but as concrete modes of day to day existence."[8]

Let us briefly recall the principal preachers.

A. ROBERT OF ARBRISSEL (ca. 1060-1117)

The first itinerant preacher to receive pontifical authorization, Robert was a diocesan priest and a counselor to the bishop of Rennes in Normandy. In order to dedicate himself to contemplation, he first became a hermit-penitent, later becoming superior of a group of canons regular who wanted to live "according to the manner of the primitive Church."[9] At this time he began to go around barefoot and in poor clothes, preaching in the neighboring dioceses. Seeing that this way of doing things had great results among the people, he left the canons to dedicate himself completely to itinerant preaching. In 1096 Pope Urban II authorized him to lead the life of an itinerant preacher in which activity he spent the rest of his life. His preaching was mainly of a moral rather than theological nature and was directed most of all to the poor. But "people of all classes and states of life, men and women, rich and poor, old and young, struck by his words and example, hastened to follow him." For his followers, called the "Poor of Christ," he established new monasteries which housed men and women, though in strictly separated quarters. Just before his death Robert united these individual monasteries to form the Order of Fontevrault.[10]

B. BERNARD OF THIRON (+1117)

A contemporary and companion of Robert of Arbrissel, Bernard also dedicated himself to itinerant preaching. In 1101 Pope Paschal II approved his way of life, authorizing him to preach, hear confessions, and to do all that a public preacher should do.[11] The characteristic of his life and that of his followers was an extreme poverty. They wore a poor habit made of coarse material, almost without form, much different from the ordinary monastic garb.[12] He had no intention of founding a new religious order, but only of living "as a hermit with a few disciples who followed him." Many people, however, wanted to imitate him; monks and other religious even abandoned their monasteries to follow him. Thus was formed what came to be called the Order of Thiron.

C. VITALIS OF SAVIGNY (+1122)

Another contemporary and companion of Robert of Arbrissel and of Bernard of Thiron, Vitalis also became a penitent-hermit, living in strict poverty and distinguishing himself by special ascetic practices, such as going barefoot, never shaving, and dressed in the roughest clothing.[13] That which distinguished him from the other itinerant preachers was his concern to alleviate and even to attempt to solve the social problems of his day.[14] Thus he promoted the erection of shelters for the homeless and hospitals for lepers, providing even for their food and care. He defended the rights of the poor, becoming their spokesman and defender. He too had followers who eventually formed the Order of Savigny.

D. GERARD OF SALLES (+1120)

Already a secular priest, Gerard became a canon regular on the advice of Robert of Arbrissel. Convinced, however, that the literal observance of the rule of St. Benedict could be realized only in solitude, he left the monastery to become a hermit, later dividing his time between the hermitage and itinerant preaching. He led a life of strictest mortification, so much so that he was compared to St. John the Baptist. He too had numerous followers, who came to form the Order of Cadonin.[15]

E. NORBERT OF XANTEN (ca. 1082-1134)

Norbert was the greatest and best known of the itinerant

preachers and it was he who, for all practical purposes, completed the cycle of this phenomenon. He began his religious life as a canon in Xanten (diocese of Cologne), but he soon devoted himself to the activity of itinerant preaching, first in Germany and later in France. Distributing his riches to the poor, he dressed in a tunic and mantle and went barefoot to Rome to meet Pope Gelasius II (1118-1119). The pope, deeply impressed by Norbert's plans, gave him the permission to preach. He dedicated the rest of his life to itinerant preaching and to the reestablishment of peace. Going from place to place, his greeting was the evangelical "Peace be to this house." He said that he had become a "preacher of peace and imitator of the apostles" only by the grace of God.[16] Preacher of penance and salvation, he became protector of the poor, considering himself a "pilgrim and stranger on this earth." His life was centered on the gospel whose precepts he lived to the letter. "He carried neither purse nor shoes nor two tunics; he was content with a few books and his Mass vestments."[17] He affirmed that his sole concern was that of incarnating the evangelical and apostolic ideals in his own life.[18] He encouraged others, his disciples among them, to follow his example. While some of his companions considered his example and guidance sufficient rule for them, he maintained that a rule and a religious order were necessary to observe perfectly the "evangelical and apostolic counsels." Thus, he adopted the rule of St. Augustine for his followers. His new order took the name of the Premonstratensians.

CONCLUSIONS

"It is striking and significant, for example, that each of these men began his religious career as a member of a traditional ecclesiastical institution, usually as a monk or canon regular. Subsequently, each of them left this structured religious life in search of something else. Each decided to live in strict poverty like a hermit, but at the same time to wander from place to place preaching the gospel of penance. Surely these men in their own lives were reflecting the spiritual restlessness of their age."[19]

It is most important to note that the itinerant preachers—who began their wandering at the beginning of the twelfth century, lived in poverty, preached "as the apostles did," and gathered groups of followers—found themselves immediately faced with the problem of how to insert themselves and their followers into the structure of the Church, which did not envision groups whose members while aiming at the "perfect evangelical life" did not at the same time live according to a rule and in a monastery. Thus there was no place for the groups who roamed about the countryside. This presented a threefold development:

1. Many of the itinerant preachers and their followers entered the pre-existing religious orders or formed new ones. We have already noted that each of the itinerant preachers mentioned above began a new religious order.

2. Many laymen and women who had followed the itinerant preachers joined the penitents; that is, they entered into the canonical penitential state established by the Church for repentant public sinners in the first centuries.[20]

3. Others were incautiously attracted by the growing poverty movements which rebelled against the ecclesiastical orders and which soon even became heterodox.

Unfortunately, what was lacking in the twelfth century was the foundation of a religious order which would have as its ideal not only the apostolic and poor life of the gospel, but also preaching in the midst of the people to encourage, support, and guide those who aspired to an apostolic and evangelical Christianity.[21] The new religious orders already spoken of did not sustain that rapport with the Christians who remained outside the monasteries, a rapport which had characterized the life of many of the early preachers. The pre-existing orders lived their traditional monastic life and did not dedicate themselves to preaching. The secular clergy, even if they were no longer involved in the scandals of simony or concubinage, were usually uneducated; and they certainly did not dedicate themselves to preaching and instructing the faithful.[22]

5
ANTI-ECCLESIASTICAL AND HETERODOX MOVEMENTS

For all practical purposes the period of the great orthodox itinerant preachers came to an end with the death of Norbert of Xanten in 1134. It seems that there has not yet been enough study of why a phenomenon which seemed to cause so much good in the regions where it occurred, did not continue beyond that brief period. Perhaps the organizational failure to bring about lasting change discouraged many. At any rate, it is obvious that, in the end, itinerant preaching brought about "wanderers," frowned upon by the official Church which would have preferred them to enter monasteries. In fact, these preachers were forced, or at least induced by circumstances, to found new branches of monastic orders. At this point the phenomenon ended.

The "enlightened" wisdom of Francis would be the element needed to invite people "to remain in their own homes" and to await his coming and that of his friars, itinerant preachers, who would tell them "what you are to do."

Around the year 1140, because of the loss of the authorized preaching of the itinerants and the persistent—in fact, growing—hunger for the word of God and spiritual direction brought about by the actions of these preachers, the phenomenon of the unauthorized preachers, mostly laymen, emerged; they soon moved into disobedience to the ecclesiastical hierarchy and into heterodoxy.

Actually, the phenomenon of rebel preachers, both religious and laity, had sporadically appeared earlier in various sectors of the Church. The ex-priest Peter de Bruys preached against the hierarchy around 1112-1120. "An anti-ecclesiastical attitude can also be noted in the preaching of Tanchelm in Flanders and Brabant; a similar phenomenon emerged in Florence (1117), in Orvieto (1125), and in the diocese of Treviri (1122.)[1]

Honorius of Autun, who wrote around 1125,[2] in his *Speculum Ecclesiae* openly attributed the phenomenon of the lay preachers to the lack of preaching on the part of the priests: "clero tacente, verbum Dei ab indoctis saepe proferetur," that is, "since the clergy do not preach, the word of God is often announced by the laity," that is, by those who do not know it well.[3] In somewhat coarse phrases he then gave the reason for the clergy's silence: "For this reason, it is said that they (the clerics) are like dumb dogs, unable to bark. They do not dare proclaim the word of God because they are aware of their own unruly lives; that is, they abstain from preaching in order not to be reproached for their perverse lives."[4]

In the opinion of this author, the principal reasons which led these preachers—most of them lay people—and their movements to the heterodoxy life are the following:

    a. The primary reason is the refusal to accept the legislation of the Church in force at that time, i.e., the official preaching of the gospel could be exclusively done by those who had the authority (clerics) or the explicit permission to do so. Until the end of the twelfth century, the Church was not at all inclined to grant permission to preach to anyone who was not a priest or at least a monk.

    b. The insistence in their preaching of contrasting the evangelical, apostolic, and poor lives of their groups with the life of the official Church (bishops, priests, and monks). As a result, the preachers soon explicitly exhorted the people to imitate their way of life and to oppose that of the institutional Church.

    c. The fact that, during the Gregorian reform, in order to combat clerical simony and concubinage, the Church rightly emphasized the need for a moral life in those who administered the sacraments.[5] This fact was then used to spread the idea that those bishops, priests, and monks who did not lead a moral life did not have the right to preach, nor to administer the sacraments. By contrast, those who led a "poor, apostolic, and evangelical" life, even if they were not priests, had the right to preach.

To be more specific, let us consider some propositions—some orthodox and some heterodox—which were taught and spread by these movements in various periods of the twelfth century.

    a. The Christian vocation is a call to live according to the example of Christ and the apostles; every Christian who lives in this way is perfect—a true successor of the apostles.

    b. The life led by some groups and preached by them was in

conformity with the New Testament and was the only valid Christian life; the life of the institutional Church did not correspond to this norm, and should therefore be fought.

c. The validity of the sacraments and the right to preach did not come from priestly ordination, but from the moral and apostolic life of those who administered the sacraments or preached.

It is not surprising that the groups who professed and tried to teach such principles were condemned by the Church. However, the majority of Christians, most of whom had little if any education, were unable to distinguish between true and false doctrine. As Ida Magli observed, we should remember that "the majority of those who joined the popular religious movements of this period, whether heterodox or orthodox, usually belonged to the lower classes of medieval society—farmers and illiterates."[6] They were attracted more by the preacher's moral severity and life of poverty than by his doctrine.

For a more complete treatment of the argument, we now present the principal initiators or preachers of those movements which, like the Cathari, began as heretical, or those that became so later, such as the Patarines, Arnoldists, and Waldensians.[7]

PETER DE BRUYS

Very little is known of the early life of Peter de Bruys. He became a priest but was deprived of his office of pastor. Between 1112 and 1120 he began his heretical preaching in the Delfinato, passing on into the regions of Toulouse, Narbonne, and Arles. Having incited the people against the priests, whom he called impostors, he immediately attracted many followers, whom he formed into a type of troupe which mistreated priests and monks, sometimes even forcing them to marry. Abelard names Peter a subverter of divine and ecclesiastical institutions. According to Peter the Venerable, the principal errors which de Bruys spread were the invalidity of infant baptism, the uselessness of church buildings, and the repudiation of the cross because "it recalled the ignominy" to which Christ was subjected.[8] De Bruys also claimed that prayers and good works could not help the dead; he denied the sacrifice of the Mass and the sacrament of the Eucharist, because, in his interpretation, Christ had effected these once and for all. He also rejected most of Sacred Scripture, keeping only the Gospels and the letters of Paul; these, however, were to be left to the liberal interpretation of the faithful. His connection with Henry the Deacon (of Lausanne) only served to intensify his anti-ecclesiastical tendencies. His followers were called the Petrobrusians.

Peter himself met a tragic end: one Good Friday between the years 1132-1140, while he urged the people to throw their crosses into a fire which he had lit, the angry people turned on him and threw him into the fire. The ideas of Peter de Bruys were spread largely in the regions of Albi, Toulouse, and Carcassonne, preparing the way for the later spread of the Catharist heresy.[9]

ARNOLD OF BRESCIA AND THE ARNOLDISTS

Though Arnold of Brescia (+1155) cannot really be called an itinerant preacher, he often lectured the people on themes pertaining to the church reform. He was a disciple of Abelard[10] in Paris, and spread his ideas in Italy. Arnold took part in the lively dispute between Abelard and St. Bernard, supporting his teacher. Persecuted for his ideas, he had to take refuge with some friends—even ecclesiastics—in Switzerland and Bohemia. Some time around the year 1145 he was in Rome, where in reality, he was more interested in the spiritual than in the political side of the dispute between the papacy and the Roman senate. "The object of his discourses was still only the reform of ecclesiastical dress, the invitation to an ascetical life more in conformity with the evangelical ideals. Nonetheless, it was fatal that he established a connection between his religious movement and the political movement of the Roman senate." This eventually led to his downfall, especially after he proclaimed that ecclesiastics "should not possess earthly goods and that these goods were the property of the laity, and thus of the princes."[11] Adrian IV (1154-1159) demanded his expulsion from Rome. After several incidents, especially after Arnold had caused a riot in which a cardinal was injured, he was captured by the followers of Frederick Barbarossa who, at that time, was interested in getting into the good graces of the pope. Arnold was turned over to Peter, prefect of the city of Rome, who condemned him to death. It is probable that he was hanged and burned.

Arnold's disciples gave rise to a particularly vocal sect in the Church, the Arnoldists. Following Arnold's teachings and often enlarging upon them, particularly his idea that "the clergy who did not lead a poor life were liars and deprived of authority," they considered the evangelical virtues as the basis of the priestly and hierarchical order. The Arnoldists refused to receive the sacraments from any priest they considered unworthy; they taught that it was their duty to resist the exercise of judicial and coercive power by the Church and that a poor and austere life gave the laity the right to preach without ecclesiastical approval. Because of the anti-hierarchical and anti-priestly character of their preaching, the Arnoldists had much influence on the heretical evolution of the Italian Waldensians and the Humiliati. Together with these groups, they were condemned by the Council of Verona in 1184; by the thirteenth century they could no longer be counted as a distinct group.[12]

THE PATARIA AND THE PATARINES

The Pataria was originally a politico-religious movement, begun in Milan in the second half of the eleventh century, during the Gregorian reform and in conformity with it. They represented the reaction of the pure elements of the Ambrosian Church against the corruption spreading in it under the double forms of simony and nicolaitism.[13] Only later did some heretical elements, the Cathari, begin to infiltrate the Milanese Patarine movement. Ever since that time, the terms "Cathari" and "Patarini" were used to indicate the heretics of the Manichaean type for whom there was not yet any specific term. Thus, in common usage in twelfth century Italy, both names indicated those heretics who rebelled against the ecclesiastical authority, and tended more or less to the errors of dualism. Thus, the Patarini, along with the Cathari and the Albigensians were included in papal proscriptions. In the historical field, however, they should be distinguished from the adherents of the original Patarines.

THE CATHARI

"Around 1100 A.D., Landolph the Elder, a chronicler of the time, called the opponents of ecclesiastical matrimony Cathari (the pure) and thus established a point of contact between the heretics of Monforte (near Albi), who were captured and tried in the castle of the same name, and the followers of the Pataria. In the second half of the twelfth century the name Cathari was used to indicate certain heretics (Eckbert of Schönau, *Sermones contra catharos*). From that time onward, the use of the word spread rapidly."[14] The first so-called Cathari missionaries made their appearance in the West around 1140 in Cologne. There is some dispute as to whether their Manichaean dualism was in direct and continued succession with third century Manichaenism, or at least with Bogimilism which flowered in the Balkans at the end of the tenth century. Morghen categorically denies it[15] and attributes the contents of Catharism, and its similarity with Manichaenism, to "tendencies which we could call rationalistic,"[16] to New Testament origins of heretical thought, to the "direct appeal of the gospel, that is, to a continuous and incessant recalling of the words of Christ and the example of the Church of the apostles"[17] as well as to "that vast movement of conscience which, precisely at the beginning of the eleventh century, contradistinguished the start of the great battle for reform *ab imis fundamentis* [from the very foundations] of the whole religious, political, and social life."[18]

It has been established that, in its first appearances, Catharism was presented only "in the context of movements of apostolic life in favor of a poor Church." Abbot Everino of Steinfield spoke of it in his letter of 1143 to St. Bernard, in which he also explained the doctrine of these new heretics:

"They say that the Church exists only among themselves because they alone follow faithfully in the footsteps of Christ and that they alone live the apostolic life, since they do not seek the things of this world, neither houses nor fields, nor even money: as Christ possessed nothing, he did not permit his followers to possess anything. They tell us, 'you instead seize house upon house and field upon field and seek the things of this world so that even those you consider the most perfect such as the monks and the canons regular possess all these things. Even if it is not their private property, they are still owners.' Of themselves, the heretics say: 'We are the poor of Christ, *nos pauperes Christi.*'"[19]

Nonetheless, it is definite that even "from the second half of the twelfth century the Catharist churches in the West were in a relationship of doctrinal and hierarchical dependence with the heads of the various and contrary dualistic communities of the Balkan and oriental countries."[20]

The Cathari spread rapidly, later establishing centers in Languedoc, Champagne, southern France, and Lombardy. In Languedoc they soon organized their church, calling it "the church of the perfect," with its own hierarchy. The Cathari of Cologne had their own bishop. In 1144 the clergy of Liege wrote to Pope Lucian II, telling him that the heretics had "priests and other prelates as we do."[21]

In their work against the clergy, the Catharists were in some way involuntarily helped by conciliar decrees during the period of the pre-Gregorian reform. The aforementioned Roman Synod of 1059, in canon 3, had stated that "no one could assist at the Mass of a priest who publicly kept a concubine or a *subintroducta mulier*; such a priest "could not celebrate Mass, read the gospel and the epistle."[22] The Cathari began to contest more than the Mass of the concubine priests; they denounced the entire Church, "not because of the incontinence of the priests but because of the new criteria represented by the wealth or poverty of the Church. A rich church could not be the church of the apostles. Refusing the sacraments from priests who did not live the apostolic—that is, poor—life, the Cathari consecrated the Eucharist themselves and administered baptism by the imposition of hands."[23] In addition, the Cathari, whatever their origins, openly professed dualistic and docetic ideas, which we can synthesize as follows: there is a good God, creator of spirits; and a bad god, creator of the visible—that is, material—world. The body, therefore, comes from the devil and the soul from God. Our souls are in our bodies as in a prison. Christ was neither God nor man, since matter is impure. He was an angel, the adopted son of God, who took the appearance of man. This Christ, therefore, only apparently became man in the womb of the virgin Mary. He appeared to live, suffer, and die in an apparent body. "In the baptism in the Jordan, the Spirit entered and lived in Christ and remained there until his glorification, descending therefore on the apostles and communicating himself to believers through baptism which, for the Cathari, did not consist in a baptism of (evil) water, but of an exorcism effected through the reading of gospel texts and the imposition of hands; this was called the *consolamentum*. To the 'perfect,' the leading minority, the *consolamentum* granted impeccability; the ordinary faithful could be freed from their sins by means of the *apparellamentum*, a type of penance."[24] The Cathari also denied the Trinity. In spite of these theological errors, "the moral demands of the Cathari were very rigid, their life was austere, and in clear contrast to the laxity of the clergy."[25] This latter point explains their rapid growth and success among the uneducated Catholic lower classes.

PETER WALDO AND THE WALDENSIANS

When the dualistic and docetic doctrines began to seep into their preaching, the Cathari soon found opposition in a new group of itinerant preachers; the new group, headed by Peter

Waldo, seemed to want to defend the orthodoxy of the faith.

Waldo, a rich merchant of Lyons, was seemingly suddenly converted upon hearing the life of St. Alexus; in observance of the *"si vis perfectus esse,"* [if you wish to be perfect], he chose "absolute poverty for himself, intending to follow faithfully all the teachings of the gospel, which he had translated into the "Roman" language. This was around the year 1170. He began to preach and soon had many disciples who followed him, abandoning all their goods, begging and preaching.[26] The phenomenon of the itinerant preachers was repeated, with no significant differences.

Peter Waldo, however, was a layman and soon found opposition to his preaching from the bishop of Lyons, who prohibited him from "begging and preaching." After some years of conflict, Waldo and some of his disciples went to Rome, where they presented themselves to Pope Alexander III and the Third Lateran Council, which was then in session (1179). "After the English lawyer Walter Map had examined their orthodoxy, the pope admitted them into his presence, and was struck by what he saw—they were barefoot, dressed in rough wool, without baggage, having all things in common like the apostles; naked, following the naked Christ.[27] The pope approved their choice of poverty, but ruled that, in the matter of preaching, Peter Waldo and his companions would have to submit to the decision of the local bishop. Returning to Lyons, Waldo was called before the diocesan synod to prove his orthodoxy; the year was 1180. The anonymous chronicler of Lyons has preserved for us the profession of faith which Peter Waldo made on that occasion.[28] The first part of it is a summary of the Catholic faith from the *Statuta Ecclesiae Antiquae*, to which Waldo added an explanation of his choice of life: "Because, according to the apostle James, faith without works is dead (Jas 2:17), we have renounced the world, distributing our goods to the poor, as our Lord advised; we have decided to be poor in the sense of not worrying about tomorrow, and accepting neither gold nor silver nor anything except food and clothing for the day from anyone. It is our plan to observe as precepts even the evangelical counsels."

In exchange for this profession of faith, Waldo received from the papal legate, Cardinal Henri de Marcy, the approval of his *apostolic life*—which now implied not only his life of absolute poverty, but also his begging and itinerant preaching. This permission to preach was, however, still dependent on the condition established by the pope, i.e., that their preaching be allowed by the local bishop.²⁹

Either external circumstances or a false interpretation of the permission obtained from the pope and the synod of Lyons prompted the Waldensians not to ask the permission of the ecclesiastical authority each time they preached. The archbishop of Lyons who had been so hostile to them had died, and the see was vacant for some time. The new archbishop, Jean de Poitiers, a weak man and of dubious moral character, was against the preaching of the laymen and declared them "in error"; he excommunicated the group and expelled them from his diocese.³⁰

Waldo and his followers then emigrated to those regions which were known to be less rigid in applying the laws against heretics, namely, Languedoc and Lombardy. In the former they continued to preach against the Cathari and upheld orthodox doctrine; in Lombardy they mixed with the Arnoldists, and were successful in preaching among the Humiliati. Soon they were identified with the groups among whom they worked. Since they lived among heretics or in suspect environments, church authorities looked askance at them; they naturally no longer bothered to ask permission for their preaching. In 1184 the Council of Verona included them in the same category as the Cathari, the Arnoldists, and the Humiliati in its proscription and condemnation.³¹

THE HUMILIATI

The Humiliati, or Umiliati, as they were known in Italy, represented an evangelical movement of perfect Christian life, which arose among the wool-workers and merchants in the suburbs of Lombardy between 1170 and 1178. Living on the outskirts of the feudal cities and already conditioned by the new industrial and commercial capitalism, they united in a lay association for religious and social purposes. "The first Humiliati lived with their families and took part in their work. They 'humiliated themselves for God,' adopting rough clothing of 'untinted cloth' in sharp contrast to the fine, colored fabrics of the time. They refrained from lying, which, along with smuggling, corrupted the moral sanctity of industry and trade. . . . They kept themselves free from the constrictions of the feudal system and the corporations by abstaining from oaths. Strong in ascetical discipline, they confronted the attacks of the various heretical sects of the second half of the twelfth century with their preaching and public debates."³² However, since preaching was forbidden to the laity, and they disobeyed the restrictions of the hierarchy in the matter, they too were included in the writ of excommunication issued by the Council of Verona against the heretics. This condemnation brought about a schism within the group; part of them tended toward dogmatic error, allying themselves with the Cathari and Waldensians. About 1205, in Lombardy, another group constituted the sect known as the Poor Lombards.

In any case, the majority of the Humiliati adhered to the politics of recovery begun by Innocent III in the early years of his pontificate, which had begun in 1198. In the interim, at the heart of the Humiliati, an evolution took place; it somehow developed into three distinct, but not separate, groups. The clerical element, belonging to the Humiliati formed a group known as the "first order," constituted according to canonical norms; it also included nuns, solemnly consecrated to religious life as it was then understood, that is, "in choir." An association of monastic life—lay brothers and sisters, living in adjoining houses—formed the second order. The religious-worker association of men and women remaining in the married state comprised a third order. "Innocent III approved them in 1201 and authorized them to preach morals. Many of them, clerics as well as laity, men and woman who were educated, distinguished themselves as effective preachers and fierce opponents of the heretics."[33]

Jacques de Vitry, in his first letter written from Genoa in the beginning of October 1216, writes, "It is difficult to find anyone in the whole city (of Milan) who would have the courage to resist the heretics except for some holy men and women religious whom the seculars call, and not without a certain malice, the 'Patarines.' The pope, however, who gave them authority to preach and to combat the heretics and who furthermore approved their congregation, calls them the 'Humiliati.' They renounce all their goods; they gather together in various places, and live by the work of their hands; they often preach the divine word, and willingly listen to it. They are perfect and firm in their faith and effective in their work. This 'religion' is widespread in the diocese of Milan where we can count more than 150 conventual congregations of men and women, each in their separate houses. This does not take into account those who remain in their families."[34]

During the thirteenth century the "Praepositi" of the four principal houses of Como, Viboldone, Pavia, and Fossalto directed, each in its turn, the intense movement of expansion of the Humiliati. The second order emphasized the monastic forms, and grew to be more like the first; the third order became better organized and in 1291 held a general chapter independently of the other two. "The Humiliati were asked by various communes to augment local industry and to help support the economic independence of the cities and towns. The profits from their work were used in charitable acts, most of all in hospitals and leprosaria. Together with the Franciscans, they enjoyed the popular support of the people; they were given public offices, e.g. treasurers of the communes or other tasks, such as collecting taxes.[35] In the fourteenth century their numbers began a slow decline; the order was suppressed by St. Pius V in 1569.

DURANDUS OF HUESCA AND THE POOR CATHOLICS

"The Poor Catholics" was the name given to a group of Franco-Spanish Waldensians who, after the dispute-filled conference of Pamiers in September 1207, separated from the other Waldensians and under the guidance of Durandus of Huesca began negotiations with Pope Innocent III. Within a year, on December 18, 1208, to be exact, they were reunited to the Catholic Church. With the letter *Eius exemplo* of that date, the pontiff notified the archbishop of Tarragon and the suffragan bishops of that archdiocese that he had "kindly accepted Durandus and his companions after having diligently examined them and had ascertained their adhesion to the Catholic truth." The letter refers to their "profession of faith," similar to the one of Peter Waldo, along with the explicit reprobation of certain teachings attributed to the Waldensians. The letter also states that the Poor Catholics were zealous preachers, living in absolute poverty and according to the norms of a propositum of penitential life which the pontiff also approved.[36]

In three additional letters, dated May 12 and 13, 1210, the pope confirms the same approbation and asks the archbishops of Tarragon and Narbonne to be benevolent towards these children who had returned to the fold. The leaders of the Poor Catholics were explicitly named, along with their places of origin. "This is where the principal centers of the Poor Catholics are located: Catalonia, Southern Spain, and Northern Italy; these are areas where the Cathari heresies and the Waldensian movement developed."[37]

From the letter *Dilectus filius Durandus*, dated May 26, 1212, we learn that a group of "penitents" followed the Poor Catholics. In the letter addressed to the bishop of Elne in the Pyrenees, the pontiff speaks of the principal directives of the *propositum vitae,* and asks the bishop to approve it if he finds it in conformity with the Catholic faith (*emanare . . . de fonte catholicae puritatis*). Here we see an example of a lay group dependent on an organization which was more strictly clerical or "religious." "The relationship between future lay groups and the mendicant orders appears clear."[38]

BERNARD PRIMUS AND THE POOR LOMBARDS

From the time of Peter Waldo, groups of his followers had gathered in Lombardy. After the Waldensians and the Humiliati were condemned in 1184, "the extremist form of life of this latter group had an influence on the Waldensians in Lombardy who, for their part, spread their anti-clericalism to the heterodox Humiliati. The two heretical factions in Lombardy joined to form the sect known as the Poor Lombards" around the year 1205.[39] Among their teachings, they denied "that the Catholic priesthood had the power to confer validly the sacraments, to preach, or to have other authority. They asserted that it was licit to rebel against priests and to disobey ecclesiastical precepts. According to them, lay people of upright lives had the faculty to consecrate the Eucharist."[40] They also denied that secular authority had coercive or punitive powers, especially in regard to the death penalty for heretics and the use of oaths.

In 1210 the majority of the Poor Lombards, under the leadership of Bernard Primus and William Arnald, were reconciled with the Church. On June 14 of that year, Innocent III addressed a letter, *Cum inaestimabile pretium,* to all bishops. In it the pontiff informed them that he had reconciled the above-mentioned leaders and their followers to the Church after having received their profession of faith. According to the letter, this profession explicitly stated their adhesion to the Roman Church, to the Catholic hierarchy, and to the sacramental doctrine, particularly that of the Eucharist. "The positions censured by the Church in these new movements had never been stated so clearly as in this document."[41] In it is granted the permission to profess collective poverty and the preaching of a penitential or controversial character.[42]

Only some months before *Cum inaestimabile,* the same pontiff, Innocent III, had orally approved the "fraternity" of Francis of Assisi, based on a life of poverty, and granted him the faculty, which he could delegate to others, to "preach penance to all."

THE GROUPS OF PENITENTS

What was the condition of the penitential movement during this tumultuous period? We lack the documentation necessary to give a complete answer, but we must assume that the penitents who remained orthodox were also unwillingly involved in the prevalent suspicious atmosphere. Lacking directors who could guide them safely, they continued to suffer from a two-fold problem: the ever-increasing desire for "penance" and an uncertainty as to which leaders to follow.

From the twelfth century on, simple penitents had tended to form groups or fraternities which, without living in common, adopted the same "propositum" of penitential life; they bound themselves together and accepted a certain amount of control by the authorities of the group with a pledge or promise that was called a "profession." These members "were distinguished from the surrounding society in whose midst they continued to live by the dress that they wore and the type of life that they professed."[43] Admission to such groups was open to married persons also, who continued to live in the married state, with certain limitations; the celibates who entered the fraternity were generally considered bound to a promise of continency, from which the name by which they were commonly called comes—"The Order of Continents." Some of these were ancient confraternities which had originated under various circumstances, but always animated by the penitential spirit; others were groups of laity who had joined a certain order of knights.

An example of this last category can be found in the military-knightly "Order of St. James" which began in Spain in 1161.[44] This group had three categories of members. "The first was comprised of married knights who were not obliged to continency; the second group were the celibate knights who took a vow of chastity; the third were clerics who served as hospitalers or teachers for the children of the married knights. Pope Alexander III approved this institute and its categories in 1175. In order to recognize this new order as a valid religious order, Alexander III solved the difficulty introduced by the married state of the members of the first group by giving their profession of the vow of obedience the significance of a profession of penance."[45]

This order is also interesting for our study because, except for a certain analogy found in the Premonstratensian Order in 1119, it represents the first time in which the documents clearly speak of a "Third Order." Also, the Humiliati, already mentioned, can be considered an example of a group leading a penitential life. Although this group had evolved into "three orders" during this same period, the documentation does not clearly speak of it until 1201.

Some time after the year 1184 there is mentioned another group of penitents in Vicenza, at the Church of St. Desiderius, some of whose members were married. In the documents these are classified as *conversi* (both men and women) or as *brothers and sisters who do penance*. Each family had its own separate dwelling. Upon entering the community, they offered themselves and gave up the right to all immovable goods, their tools, as well as the fruit of their common labor in the fields, which they cultivated together. In this manner they intended to realize, within the penitential state, the communal ideal of the first Christians. The ideas prevalent in the Gregorian reform probably encouraged them; however, it is interesting to note that it is the penitents themselves who constitute a community, not in virtue of their penitential state, which does not imply a confraternity or communal life *per se*,[46] but because they are brothers and sisters to one another.

The vast movement of the Beghards and Beguines would need a separate study of their many divisions; we know, however, that later many of these groups followed the spirit of the "third rule" or entered directly into the *Penitents of Blessed Francis*.[47]

The development of the penitential movement from a "state of life" into a group or fraternity or non-monastic order did not happen without conflicts or difficulties before it became a reality accepted by the Church and later an institution recognized and approved by the Church.

The enthusiasm and evangelical ideals first spread by the reform of the monastic movement and later by the Gregorian reform found neither support nor leadership among the monastic orders or the secular clergy. Thus those who sought to follow such ideals without entering either of the above states, gravitated to spontaneous or self-made leaders who were often opposed to the disciplinary and eventually doctrinal teachings of the Church, as history has shown us repeatedly.

"Only the movement led by Francis and Dominic and their orders . . . could welcome Christians inspired by evangelical ideals yet wishing to remain in their homes; this movement succeeded in directing their energies and fulfilling their religious needs, finally giving form, consistency, and subsistence to the non-monastic evangelical life in an 'order' of simple penitents."[48]

THE ATMOSPHERE IN THE PENITENTIAL MOVEMENT

It is difficult to precisely define the spiritual atmosphere that dominated the penitential movement of the twelfth century. Certain Conciliar canons urged the bishops to act to keep the movement alive; and although these documents offer proof of the esteem of the institutional Church for the movement and its utility, they do not give an adequate response to our question.

External studies give us some understanding of the meaning of "penance" and the "life of penance" within the penitential movement itself. Foremost among these are the studies that have treated medieval man in the light of anthropological studies, such as those of Professor Ida Magli, who holds the chair of the Anthropological Faculty of the University of Rome.[49] "Medieval man, aware that the acknowledgement of one's humanness is an acknowledgement of God, thereby 'posits' God, and himself in relationship to God. His 'being' in relationship to God seems sufficient to give meaning to his whole life; or rather, it seems that life, all life, is this way of being, this way of knowing oneself, of finding oneself. The journey of medieval man is not a journey to reach God. . . . The man of penance is stationary, he *stands* in God's presence; he is a pilgrim in an 'order' of pilgrims, a penitent in an 'order' of penitents, a 'flagellantus' in a 'confraternity' of flagellanti—that is, he is in a 'state' of life that does not imply progression, transformation, or the attainment of something different, unless it is a progression, transformation, or an ever more certain and deeper conviction of his achievement of his *status* of penitent and pilgrim. In other words, the real question is one of man's true and proper attitude toward life, his cultural *modus vivendi*, his deep psychological and religious roots; it also is seen, most of all, as a total vision of the proper way of *being* which finds its cultural outlets in well-defined historical and social institutions."[50]

If this is true, and we do not have reason to argue against this study, we must acknowledge that the biblical meaning of "metànoia" had either been lost or forgotten throughout the centuries. In the years immediately preceding Francis' period, there was only the external aspect, corporal penance, which existed mainly as a cultural or religious phenomenon, mostly in an ostentatious yet mitigated form.

Was this, then, the atmosphere that Francis found when he entered the penitential movement immediately after the "vision" at San Damiano? In addition to his desire to be a penitent-apostle, was there another element that motivated him—namely, did he begin his itinerant preaching to be a guide and master of "true penance" to those who already belonged to the penitential movement? These are interesting questions that still await a reply.

Nevertheless, it is a fact that, when Francis gave life to "his" penitential movement, he imprinted on it new ideals, new aspirations and characteristics. It was "his" movement that eventually provided the answer to the aspirations of the Christian people.

6

FRANCIS OF ASSISI

Francis was born in Assisi, in the region of Umbria, probably in 1182, of a rich merchant family—that of Pietro di Bernardone and his wife, Lady Pica.

In order to understand the elements which certainly influenced Francis during his formative years, and thus to compose an internal "portrait" of him, it is necessary to try to reconstruct the political, social, and religious milieu of Assisi during his youth.

There is much information to keep in mind—the few items mentioned in the biographies, especially in the *Vita Prima* of Thomas of Celano and the *Legend of the Three Companions*, and the facts touching upon the history of Italy, particularly Umbria and Assisi. They help us reconstruct ordinary life as well as the main events of these years, events which were inevitably etched on the sensibility, development, and personality of Francis, both as child and adolescent.

THE POLITICAL SITUATION

Assisi was one of the many Italian cities in the process of becoming autonomous, even if they were still technically under the jurisdiction of the Holy Roman Empire. Its jurisdiction was, in turn, contested by the papacy, which claimed the rights over central Italy, dating to the times of the Carolingian empire, even if they were unable to exercise it. Within this historical context, since the various cities of Umbria were primarily seeking their own independence, they thus turned to the imperial or papal authorities, according to where they perceived the advantages to lie.[1]

In the second half of the twelfth century Assisi was under

imperial rule, that is, it was part of the empire. However, the reasons for this position are clearly political—not a choice made from conviction or out of love of the German empire. The reasons for this position are shown in a diploma, or imperial rescript, of Frederick Barbarossa, dated November 21, 1160. In substance, he declared Assisi a free city under the protection of the empire.[2] As in every other important imperial city, or one of strategic importance, Assisi had an imperial official who lived in the fortress on the top of the hill.[3] His residence was supposedly a guarantee against war or enemy attacks. However, the presence of a handful of imperial soldiers did not impede the local political situation's evolution towards autonomy, as happened in the majority of the cities of North-central Italy. From 1162-1184 there was a continuous growth and uprising of autonomous city-states, referred to as communes, throughout this part of the peninsula, which the imperial authority was too weak and too far away to prevent. The attempt to restore such authority over the Italian cities brought about some heroic battles, including some historical defeats and victories—but, in effect, it ended with the independence of the communes.

The main reason, however, that Assisi was "imperial" was that its traditional rival, Perugia, was "papal." Only an historical synthesis of the secular situation and particular events can explain the enmity which permeated the very air that people breathed and was passed on from generation to generation. Although Perugia and Assisi were so close geographically, they nevertheless belonged to two different ancient civilizations, divided by the Tiber River.

As in the time of the Romans the Tiber divided Tuscany from Umbria, so in the Middle Ages it had divided the part of the Italian peninsula occupied by the Byzantines—including Perugia— from the part occupied by the Lombards. The Duchy of Spoleto, which included Assisi, originated as a Lombard Duchy. Thus for centuries Perugia and Assisi had formed the "front lines" in the battles between different civilizations and cultures.[4] In addition to the ancient enmity, a more recent problem added to the rivalry. In a period not easily documented—the eleventh century, or possibly earlier—Perugia had occupied a strip of land on the far side of the Tiber and thus in Assisian territory. This "Campagna" lay between Ospedalicchio and Collestrada. The dream of the Assisians had been to win it back. We know how such aspirations incite the young to action, which explains the participation of the twenty-year-old Francis in the battle of Collestrada in 1202.

For centuries imperial and papal diplomats had played on the situation, promising Assisi help in reclaiming the territory, thus hoping to draw the city to their side.

In the interim, in imperial Assisi the popular sentiment was not on the side of the German emperor. On the contrary, in the very year of the imperial diploma (1160) Barbarossa had begun the repression of civil liberties with the destruction of Cremona in northern Italy. "Italian cities, even those which had been loyal to the emperor, had a rude awakening; they realized that it was impossible even to hope to maintain their freedom under the rule of Barbarossa. If they did not want to return to their former slavery, they would have to fight the German, his armies, and his supporters."[5] The emperor's supporters included greater and minor vassals, with their castles spread throughout the countryside and their fortified houses in the cities. They controlled commercial routes, imposed high tariffs, and demanded tolls.[6] The people began to disobey them, contesting and even denying their traditional obligations of service. They deserted the fields and sought refuge among the city walls, thereby increasing the urban populations and the development of the artisans' guilds. The vassals, in their turn, had recourse to imperial authority and demanded that their ancient rights be restored.

This common pattern was certainly the situation in Assisi from 1164-1174. An imperial city, it was, for all practical purposes, marked by "treason."

Christian, the archbishop of Magonza and chancellor of the emperor, was delegated to take care of the restoration of imperial rights in central Italy. More of a soldier than a shepherd, he convened an impressive assembly in Siena in 1172; the principal vassals of Italy were invited to attend and present their case against the cities which were claiming autonomy. A multitude of vassals, captains, counts, and vavasours of the cities of Tuscany, the Marches, the Spoleto Valley, and Lazio attended. Analyzing the situation, Christian began to take repressive action. Excommunicated by the pope, he placed himself at the complete service of the emperor. "He spent all of 1173 fighting in Tuscany. In the beginning of 1174 he went into Umbria where he destroyed Terni and seized Spoleto and Assisi."[7] The devastation of the cities of Umbria was so great that the documents of that day, still preserved in the archives of the cathedral of Assisi,[8] refer to those times as "captio Capitalis," that is, the fatal and ferocious capture.[9]

Assisi, forced to return to imperial protection, alternated its festive days of imperial pomp and splendor with days of ardent desire for liberty. In the winter of 1177-78 the emperor Frederick and his court were installed in "La Rocca" "amid universal homage."[10] The years that followed were marked by a growing desire for liberty, expressed in sporadic acts of a practical nature: many openly refused the "ominicio"[11] and service; others abandoned their lords, breaking the bond of fealty. This was the situation into which Francis was born.

The period from 1174-1210 marks the last and definitive collapse of the feudal structure in Assisi. In 1174 the city was destroyed by imperial forces. In 1198, when Francis was sixteen years old, Assisi was freed once and for all from imperial domination. In 1203 the first social pact was made between the "boni homines" and the "homines populi"; in 1210, the year of the approval of the proto-rule, the second pact between the "maiores" and "minores" in Assisi was recorded. To fail to try to understand these facts would, in the author's opinion, show a lack of desire to know the man Francis, thereby indicating a willingness to accept as good "a human event too often transfigured."[12]

The break-up of the feudal system had begun some time earlier for a variety of complex reasons which historians discuss in weighty volumes. The system had managed to remain more or less stable as long as the armies of the emperor supported or sustained it. With the Peace of Constance between Frederick Barbarossa and the Italian communes (June 25, 1183), a practical compromise had been reached—the communes were assimilated into the imperial fiefs. Free in name, they recognized all authority as coming from the emperor. He reserved for himself all right of appeal through a "nuncio" who had to live in the city or in the bishop's house. The citizens were obliged to swear an oath of fealty every ten years. Even the consuls—a new institution which had begun in the last decade of the twelfth century in the independent or semi-independent cities—were obliged to take the oath. In practice, however, the consuls represented the typical communal magistrate, free in fact if not in name. Under their direction the move toward independence grew where it was not a pre-existent reality. The cities were preparing to fight the last remnants of imperial domination as soon as the occasion presented itself, which meant attacking and destroying the castles of the vassals still faithful to the emperor. Ferrari, describing the condition in Italy after the Peace of Constance states: "The consular city was nothing more than an oasis (of liberty) in the midst of a feudal forest of the regime: the countryside belonged to the noble descendents of the Lombard, Frankish, and German hordes.

Towers, fortresses, and castles rose on every parcel of land. . . . (In the countryside) every man was a servant, every land had a lord, the people obeyed the rural counts, the roads were divided by tolls, the merchants were robbed by the castle owners."[13]

THE SOCIAL SITUATION

In the period immediately preceding the birth of Francis, and even more so during the years of his youth, a deep change took place in the social classes, even in Assisi. For several centuries of the High Middle Ages the principal distinction had been between the "nobili" and the "plebei." At this time, however, there was the growth of the "borghesia," which caused other criteria to become more important than birth. Thus there arose new and different categories which often overlapped and changed rapidly. In Assisi as in other central Italian cities, the most conspicuous new distinction was that between the "boni homines" and the "homines populi."[14] To the first group belonged the traditional "nobili" as well as the new "maggiori" of the free cities, that is, the lesser vassals who had left their country castles to live within the city walls, and the notaries, judges, and rich merchants. In fact, for some time there had been a new force within the Italian cities—the merchants who stressed their growing importance, which soon became supremacy, based on money. They began to build a new class, diverse, turbulent, extremely busy in buying and selling, jealous, vain, factious, whose importance rivaled that of the vassals. There were now two powers struggling, two groups whose pride was hurt. The vassals envied the wealth of the "nouveaux-riches," while the latter wanted to imitate their neighbors in high positions, honors, arms, and even knighthood.[15] A new fever was growing, a new idol, among the merchants— the accumulation of wealth. Fortini, who knew how to make the old documents speak as no one else could, wrote "For this fever which enflamed all in its vast, unheard-of frenzy, they left their homes, risked dangerous roads, travelled for weeks and months . . . paying tolls and ransoms. Every trip was a battle; every return a miracle."[16]

This is the milieu into which Francis was born. His father, Pietro di Bernardone, was one of the richest merchants in town. Fortini states: "The merchants were the most directly interested in the war against the vassals who closed the roads to commerce, attacked the caravans, imposed taxes, demanded tolls. . . ."[17]

In some Italian cities, including Assisi, another division was rapidly establishing itself, that of the "maiores" and "minores." Here, too, the division did not depend exclusively on birth, even though the ancient nobility were, by right, always included among the "maiores." This group was constantly in flux, a changing classification according to power, economic strength, patrimony, etc.[18] There were constant coalitions between upper and lower classes; the "homines populi" against the "boni homines"; the "maiores" against the "minores." From time to time, at least until 1198, there was also distinction and struggle between the men of the free city and the last defenders of the imperial might.

THE KNIGHTLY ELEMENT

Another element played an important part in the psychological development and orientation of the young Francis; the knightly element or "chivalry" remained within the saint, although sublimated, even after his conversion, as it reigned among the nobles and in the aspirations of the new social classes, the wealthy and educated. Today it is not easy to recreate or describe this element which possesses something of the intangible, but we must have some idea of it lest we risk not understanding a very important aspect of the saint of Assisi. Although Francis was not noble by birth, he spent his youth in the company of the sons of nobles, and his aspirations were directed toward nobility. Some particular events touched him so deeply that he decided to go on a knightly expedition—to Apulia—in 1205. This knightly element was incarnated in the Provençal poetry which had spread at that time to the various parts of the Italian peninsula, especially by the jesters or the professional wandering minstrels. This poetry, born in southern France, in Provence, at the beginning of the twelfth century, was based on the atmosphere of the genteel and refined feudal courts and mirrored that world of courteous customs. Basic to it was the sentiment of "courtesy" of the knight towards the feudal lady, the countess, or the princess of the castle. It was the homage of a subject, the praise of the nobility, and the beauty of the lady. She was a type of angelic figure, to whom all the dependents of the fief or castle looked with devotion. The subjects, especially the knights, were ready to "serve" her and to die for her; they were happy if they could declare themselves her "vassals," that is, her dependents, if she recognized and accepted that "vassalage." This concept had nothing to do with paganism or sensuality; we know it had been accepted in the spirituality of Cluny and Citeaux and transmitted through them into the penitential spirituality in a special devotion to Mary. This Provençal element must have grown and taken hold of Francis for any one, if not all, of three reasons: the frequent trips to France by Pietro di Bernardone; the probability that Lady Pica, Francis' mother, came from France, or to be more precise, from Provence itself; Francis himself eventually and possibly repeatedly accompanied his father on business trips to France or that, especially in 1204-1205, he may have travelled there alone. The historical fact that Francis knew Provençal and sang in that language has no other plausible explanation than one or all of these hypotheses.[19]

POLITICAL, RELIGIOUS, AND SOCIAL EVENTS IN THE EARLY YOUTH OF FRANCIS

In 1187, terrible news reached Europe, crushing the hearts of all, nobles and commoners, the great and the small, papists and imperialists alike: on October 2, after eighty-four years of Christian domination, Jerusalem had fallen into the hands of Saladin.[20] So great was the confusion and pain throughout Christendom that the very civil and daily life of even the little towns was upset. Pope Urban III, who had worked so hard for peace among the Christian princes of Palestine who were fighting among themselves (the main cause of the fall of Jerusalem), became ill and died a few days later. A document from the archives of the cathedral of Assisi tells us that the city visibly participated in the general mourning: the people dressed in sackcloth; the name of Jerusalem was on everyone's lips, almost to the point of obsession. It had not been only a spontaneous reaction but the effect, almost commanded, of the first encyclical letter of the new pontiff, Gregory VIII (October 21, 1187-December 17, 1187) signed eight days after his election. The letter "Audita tremendi severitate judicii" of October 29, was written in apocalyptic tones.[21] The people were invited to weep openly and to do penance. The churches remained open night and day. The priests of Assisi continually repeated the mournful psalm of the people of Israel: "Deus, venerunt gentes in hereditatem tuam"—"O Lord, your enemies have invaded your house."[22] "Large paintings were made which depicted the Holy Sepulchre trampled upon by horses and Jesus Christ oppressed by Mohammed. Each person accused himself of having caused the misfortune by his sins. The minstrels abandoned their love songs to weep over the enormous tragedy."[23]

All of this and what followed must have been part and parcel of the earliest impressions and memories of the five-year-old Francis.

On December 17 of that same year, after only fifty-seven days as pontiff, Gregory VIII died, increasing the pain and sorrow of the Church. Two years later, in May of 1189, the emperor Frederick Barbarossa, after many long battles with the popes of Rome, was reconciled with the new pope, Clement III (1187-1191) and left on a Crusade with the largest army that the West had ever assembled for such an expedition. However, on June 9, 1190, Frederick drowned while crossing the River Selef, near Seleucia. Francis was then eight years old.

After the occurrence of all these tragic events, life in Assisi was once again caught up in prosperity and the fervor of autonomy. "It was the period in which the city, freed from the nightmare of imperial threats, concretized its politics of expansion. In 1193 it violated the confines laid out in the diploma of Frederick and occupied Nocera, and the citizens of Assisi established themselves with homes and possessions within its walls."[24]

In 1194, however, there was a revival of imperial fortunes in southern Italy. The new Emperor, Henry VI, son of Frederick Barbarossa, returned to Italy, conquering various cities and reducing Salerno to a heap of rubble. The vassals, lords of the castles and of the countryside, full of hope, resumed their positions and once more let their power be felt by their subjects.

In that same year—Francis was now twelve years old—a new imperial messenger was installed in la Rocca of Assisi: Conrad of Lutzenfeld, an ex-commander of the imperial army, took the title of "Count of Assisi."[25] Conrad had supported the attack of Capua against Tancred in 1191. In 1193 he acquired a certain notoriety "when Monte Rodone was seized; every single inhabitant was killed by his troops."[26] He was now in control of a vast territory comprising Rieti, Spoleto, Foligno, Assisi, and Nocera. He must have been an ill-tempered man of quick mood changes, for the new class of citizens of Assisi immediately gave him a strange nickname, "Mosca-in-cervella," which literally translated means "Flies in the head," but connotes extravagance and unpredictability. One doesn't need much imagination to think of Francis and his peers repeating that nickname, which lent itself to a play on words "Be careful because Conrad may lose his head." However, the people of the area respected and feared him.

The following year, 1195, there were great festivities in Assisi on the occasion of Empress Constance's visit there. The empress, wife of Henry VI, was on her way to join the emperor in Sicily when her son was born in Iesi, in the Marches. The baptism was held in Assisi; Frederick II was baptized in San Rufino's, at the very same font where, thirteen years earlier, Francis had been baptized. It was an uncommon civil event; and the eyes of Francis, always "avid for splendor and magnificence, must have been satisfied by that splendid display, the rich ceremonial and parade of symbols and emblems."[27]

Francis grew up in this rapidly changing environment where contrasting social forces followed one another in rapid succession; seesawing between autonomous citizenship and the re-affirmation of the imperial forces. In the meantime, he continued his intellectual formation in the school annexed to the church of San Giorgio, under the direction of the canons of the cathedral of Assisi. The names of two of the teachers have been preserved for us in the documents; the rector of the school was John of Sasso and Canon Guido was one of the teachers.[28]

In the following year, 1196, at the age of fourteen, Francis would have been assumed by his father into the large shop of imported and domestic cloth. This was the normal age for a young man to begin his occupation. Intelligent and outgoing, Francis quickly learned the art of the business world, knowing how to combine making a profit with earning the trust of his clients. "Those who knew him in that period of his youth describe his happy and lively spirit, his generosity, utter extravagance, and sumptuous elegance."[29] The paternal warehouse was often emptied of rich cloths, soft silks, and flaming velvets. The youth looked to Francis to learn the latest French styles.[30]

Celano himself tells us that Francis excelled in "finesse, beautiful words, songs, and elegant and soft clothes."[31] The critics affirm that he tried to make himself more than his condition allowed. In reality, he never could tolerate being second in anything. Such was his character; his munificence and his ability to spend money freely won him the admiration of the other young men of Assisi, both of his class as well as those superior to him; that is, the sons of those few vassals who lived within the city now, along with the richer members of the new social order of the "boni homines."

In the meantime, after the departure of Empress Constance and her court, the sentiments in Assisi returned to independence and anti-imperialism, not only because of the arrogant behavior of Conrad and his retinue throughout the territory, but most of all because of the news which came from southern Italy and Germany of the mistreatment of and cruelty to the surviving members of the Norman court.[32] The child king, son of Tancred, was blinded then killed by imperial soldiers; Tancred's tomb was profaned; the archbishop of Salerno was killed. Sibyl the wife of Tancred was held prisoner in the abbey of Hoemburg in Alsace, along with her three young daughters. "It is said that the three princesses lived in a mysterious prison, weighted down with chains.... Perhaps one day a knight... would set out to free them."[33] The dreams of young men like Francis, now fifteen years old, were kindled by the knightly legends which came from France; and their spirits were inflamed.

In that same year, September 28, 1197, Emperor Henry VI died of a "malignant fever" in Messina while he prepared to join his army for the new Crusade.[34] Many Italian cities, taking advantage of the confusion in the imperial quarters, made their move to become independent.

ASSISI, A FREE CITY

For Assisi, the right occasion for its final liberation from imperial rule presented itself a few months later, at the beginning of 1198, when, upon the death of Pope Celestine III (+January 18, 1198) Lotario dei Conti di Segni was elected pope and took the name Innocent III.

The new pope's first important action was to attempt to reclaim the lost territories of central Italy, beginning with the duchy of Spoleto. Taking advantage of the disputes about the succession of Henry VI, Innocent first reached an agreement with the marquis of the March of Ancona. He then invited Conrad of Lutzenfeld, Count of Assisi, to meet with his delegates in the nearby city of Narni.[35] As soon as they learned of Conrad's departure from the Rocca with a part of his escort, the Assisians "rose up and took possession of the fortress. They refused to accept the messengers of the duke of Spoleto who asked that the fortress be handed over to the representatives of the pope. They took the citadel by force as the bells rang out and, as the imperial and pontifical legates looked on, destroyed it."[36]

Francis was sixteen years old at the time. Although no biographer tells us whether or not he participated in this action, knowing his vivacity and total insertion into city life, we can presume that he did; he probably also participated in the events that followed, the logical consequences of the libertarian fervor which animated the townspeople. By now the only obstacle to full freedom for the whole territory were the last traces of the imperial powers represented by the large and small castles of the vassals which still rose menacingly throughout the countryside. The citizens' army, expanded by young volunteers, began to tear them down systematically, a practice which continued until the following year, 1199. Fortunate indeed were the castle owners who had stopped demanding services and tolls and had moved into the city. The great castle of the lords of Sassorosso, just above Spello,[37] the most important of all the fortresses, was destroyed.[38] Minor castles such as those of Montemore, Poggio San Damiano, all within a few kilometers of the city, were torn down. They had dominated the important intersections where, for years, their owners had collected tolls. It was truly the end of the great feudal system, and it was all watched by the astonished and dreamy-eyed Francis, a seventeen-year-old.

In that same year, May 28, 1198, Innocent III sent to Guido I, Bishop of Assisi,[39] the bull *"In eminenti Apostolicae Sedis"*[40] by which he granted Assisi "apostolic protection" of the Holy See, with all the juridical consequences affirmed in other bulls.[41] He confirmed many other clauses of the "ecclesiastical liberties,"[42] even against the eventual reclaim of rights on the part of the "free communes." Although the bull did not produce immediate changes in ecclesiastical jurisdiction or in relations with the empire, it is of great importance to our study because it was precisely the knowledge of these firm pontifical prescriptions which convinced the two consuls of Assisi, in the autumn of 1206, "not to proceed" in the "case of" young Francis, "oblatus" of San Damiano, as his father, Pietro di Bernardone, had requested. By that date they must have known well the firmness of Innocent III and Guido, the new bishop of Assisi, in defending their own rights.

During this period of bitter fighting, Assisi lived another life, varied and feverish, made up of feasts, banquets, and song;[43] Francis was king of the feasts. The "Three Companions," contrasting the greediness of Pietro, tell us that Francis was taken up with *joi de vivre* and was extremely generous; they add that he associated with others like himself, devoting himself to games and song, going around the city day and night. All his earnings were immediately turned into banquets and feasts.[44] Yet the critics did not cease their complaining, grumbling that the son of the merchant went around buying things for himself and others as if he were the son of a prince. They would run to his parents and tell them their envious complaints. These, however, loving their son deeply, in reality were proud to see him so popular and admired. In the end Francis always had his way.

THE COMMUNAL STRUCTURE OF ASSISI

Soon after the storming of the Rocca, Assisi formulated its own communal statues. In fact, in that very year, 1198, the documents first mention the "consuls." Their numbers varied; at times they were two, at other times three. Elected by citizens chosen by the people for a term of one year, they had executive power and judged civil and penal matters. In general, however, the administration of justice was in the hands of judges; administration of the public treasury was entrusted to a "camerarius" or steward.

In the system of government in Assisi the consuls appear only in the years of 1198-1212. After that date we no longer find consuls, but only a mayor, (podestà) who was, at first, an extraordinary officer with almost dictatorial powers, elected in times of particular crisis which demanded unity of command, as was the case from 1202-1204. In such cases there was an interruption of the power of the consuls, who later resumed their office. However, there are only brief periods in which the consuls and the mayor can be found contemporaneously.[45]

The first mayor recorded in the Assisi documents is Gerard of Filibert in 1203, an excommunicate. It is not clear if he was included in excommunication because he was a member of the Cathari or for some other reasons during the time that he was mayor of Spoleto in 1201. The fact remains that, because of Gerard's election, Innocent III placed Assisi under interdict. Since the Assisians refused to submit to the pope and impeach Gerard,[46] a bitter fight ensued, which was finally settled in 1205 by the intermediary or legate of the pontiff, Cardinal Leo Brancaleoni, titular bishop of Santa Croce in Jerusalem.[47] The pope absolved Assisi and prescribed that they never again elect an excommunicate or an enemy of the Church to control the affairs of the city.[48] Assisi in her turn swore fidelity to the Church.

THE WAR WITH PERUGIA

Many of the vassals whose castles in Assisian territory had been destroyed in the uprising of 1198-99 had had recourse to Perugia, traditional enemy of Assisi, asking for citizenship there.[49] Any city which gave refuge to citizens from another hostile city was considered obliged to defend or restore their rights. Perugia had so decreed in its communal statutes. As a result, "it was required by its own charter to defend its (new) citizens and their property."[50] This was the proximate occasion of the war between

Perugia and Assisi. It was November of 1202, and Francis was twenty years old. The Assisians, convinced they were able to win, prepared with all the means at their disposal and with great enthusiasm. Francis, young, rather rich, and a great believer in the cause of the weak against the mighty, was among the most enthusiastic of all. The skirmish took place at Collestrada, where from dawn to dusk the battle raged, waned, and gained momentum. The Perugians, stronger in the long run, won. Francis, wounded, found himself among the prisoners.

7
THE CONVERSION OF FRANCIS

It is not easy to try to analyze the influences in the conversion of Francis of Assisi. His is a rich and profoundly intimate story which no one can adequately narrate. However, there are certain noteworthy elements which helped him arrive at that reflection and maturity which in turn brought him to a decision. Such elements represent successive steps in a journey towards a new horizon, a journey influenced by grace.

These steps are: his imprisonment in Perugia, which put an end to the dreams of a rosy future and opened to him the doors of reflection; his return to a city still divided by hatred among factions, ready to take up arms once again; his sudden recognition of the miserable plight of the poor which must have been a sword piercing his spirit, already touched from on high; his attempt to escape to southern Italy with a military expedition interrupted by the "mysterious" voice at Spoleto; the direct and voluntary experience of his pilgrimage to Rome and of what it meant to be truly poor and to have to beg alms; his upsetting yet revealing encounter with the leper; and, finally, the message of the Crucified at San Damiano.

PRISON IN PERUGIA

In those days a prison was really a prison—for the most part caves dug in the basement of the large municipal palaces. They were dark and damp; the prisoners had little more than bread and water.

For Francis this was his first encounter with a reality far different from his youthful dreams of pleasure and glory, and the beginning of a long and profound crisis. If it had not been for the defeat at Collestrada, perhaps we would never have had a Francis of Assisi.

Francis could keenly feel that something had betrayed him. Money, more and more money. Yet, what advantages had it given him? Beautiful clothes, the latest styles, friendship, affirmation in leading the youth of Assisi, organizing dinners and entertainment. Yet what had he gained? Where were his friends now?

In order to understand Francis' bitterness of soul, we must pause to look into his heart. From a few lines written by his first biographers we know that Francis possessed a certain nobility of spirit which kept him from being uncouth. He proved to be a thoughtless youth, but no one ever heard him pronounce trivial phrases or assume indecent attitudes. He held love and women in a chivalric spirit, that is, in a spirit of admiration and respect. It is that spirit which would develop into the "dolce stil nuovo" [a pleasing new way] as Dante Alighieri called it. His biographers agree that Francis, even in prison, preserved that joyful serenity which was a part of his nature. "Even if one's body is forced to live among these walls, his spirit is free."[1] Was it perhaps the spirit of chivalry which sustained him in prison? Most of all, there was the idealized figure of Walter III, Count of Brienne, (France) a noble knight, of whom his father had often spoken upon his return from his business trips to France. Walter was a knight who had carried out, and was still doing so, the most idealistic enterprises—a true promoter of chivalry.

In a bold expedition in 1199, he had freed the widow of Tancred, Queen Sibyl, and her three daughters, Albiria, Madonia, and Constance, from the prison of the Alsatian abbey and had brought them to Rome. The queen turned to Innocent III, asking him in the name of her eldest daughter, Albiria, to restore to them the ancient Norman kingdom of Apulia and Sicily, at that time in the hands of an evil German captain, Markwald. Innocent III, not daring to do it, sent her back to the King of France, Philip Augustus, who in turn invited his knights to take up the task. Sibyl promised her daughter in marriage to the "valiant knight" who would lead the expedition. Once again Walter of Brienne stepped forward, married Albiria in a solemn ceremony, and, having received from Innocent III the county of Lecce and the principality of Taranto, set about the task in 1200. Pietro di Bernardone, returning from France, explained all these events to Francis, who dreamed on. In the two legendary battles of June and October 1201, Walter defeated the imperialists and conquered the realm. Now, he was preparing to go to Sicily.[2]

Francis had hoped to be able to join his ranks for this task, but he was sick and in prison.

Francis' imprisonment lasted a year. We do not know the exact circumstances of his liberation; the *Legend of the Three Companions* states that Francis was freed the following year, "when peace was restored." However, this phrase cannot be accepted literally, because it is contradicted by documents from Assisi, which indicate that the war between Assisi and Perugia lasted intermittently until 1209. But during this time there were long intervals with only sporadic skirmishes; and one could, therefore, speak of "periods of peace." Francis' liberation could have taken place during one of those periods; or more probably, it was the result of a custom in force at that time in many Italian cities, including Perugia: prisoners of war who became ill were made part of a special group called *prigionieri malati*, whom it was possible to ransom. This would not have been difficult for Pietro di Bernardone.[3]

HOME TO ASSISI

Francis returned to Assisi in the very days that "the bailiffs of the commune were shouting through the streets in complaint against the new proclamations passed at Perugia against the exiles. New trumpets sounded; new cries echoed through the square. Old and young took up arms again. Once more war appeared in its role of 'eternal siren.' "[4]

Francis was not comfortable with the situation. His long period of maturation had begun, and he was looking at men and events in a different light. Although he had returned to his father's business, neither commerce nor profit interested him much. Why should he continue to live for money? Besides, after such a disastrous war, there was a period of great famine. There were poor people knocking on doors or sitting around the squares, too weak to do anything else. Every day new families were forced to sell their property in order to live. Even violence was all around: quarrels, fights, and feuds of honor. Francis saw all other kinds of disturbing things: the sick and the lame were maltreated; lepers were hunted down like mad dogs. There was enough, more than enough, to sadden the hearts of those who were able to see the cruel reality of things. Francis could not remain indifferent to such realities. Something within him had deeply changed.

SPOLETO: GETTING AWAY FROM IT ALL

The *Legend of the Three Companions* tells us that some "years passed."[5] It was spring of 1205 when Francis decided to escape from all this. Count Walter of Brienne once again came to public attention. His expedition to Sicily had been delayed because of the unexpected rebellion of the cities of Brindisi, Barletta, and Otranto in the wake of rumors of the death of Innocent III. In the meantime, Walter had established a splendid court in Lecce. "Sibyl, Albiria, Madonia, and Constance were installed there with a large following of the most beautiful and noble women, with French and Italian knights of renowned bravery."[6] The count was overcoming the last pockets of resistance in the rebel cities and recruiting soldiers for his next expedition to Sicily. Francis' dream slowly began to take shape: he could win glory on the battlefield and return to Assisi as a "knight"; thus he would be numbered among the nobility of the city. This must likewise have harmonized with the dream of Pietro di Bernardone, who was hoping that his son would soon find his path in life. The *Legend of the Three Companions* tells us that "an Assisian nobleman was planning to start for Apulia on a military expedition which he hoped would bring him money and honors. Hearing of this, Francis was fired with the wish to accompany him and to be knighted by a certain Count Gentile. He prepared magnificent equipment; and though his fellow citizen was a nobleman, Francis was by far the more extravagant of the two."[7]

Francis and Count Gentile first stopped at Spoleto,[8] the capital of the duchy, which was now in obedience to the Church. Perhaps they wanted to learn the particulars necessary for this adventure, for which Pope Innocent III had granted the same indulgence as the Crusades. But at Spoleto his previous illness returned and a dream or "vision," or perhaps his subconscious dissuaded him forever from the path of human adventure.

According to Francis' biographers—the *Legend of the Three Companions,* taken up by Celano in his *Vita Seconda* and by St. Bonaventure in his *Legenda Major*—the voice, having asked and learned where Francis intended to go, demanded: "Who do you think can best reward you, the Master or the servant?" Francis answered: "The Master." The voice questioned further, "Then why do you leave the Master for the servant, the rich Lord for the poor man?" Francis replied in the same words of St. Paul on the road to Damascus: "Lord, what do you want me to do?" He received the same answer that Saul did: "Return to your own place, and you will be told what to do" (Acts 9:6-7).[9]

Perhaps we need to clarify some ideas on "dreams and visions" which are often found in official and non-official biographies of Francis. The historian is not inclined—nor should he feel obliged—to accept them literally, especially when they present objective difficulties. Let us consider, for example, the difficulties presented by the "dream of Innocent III." In 1210, at his first meeting with Francis, Innocent III was perplexed at receiving the request to approve Francis' way of life. In his *Vita Seconda*, but not in the *Vita Prima*, Celano states that the following night the pope dreamed that the Lateran basilica was beginning to fall when a tiny, scraggly religious held it up with his shoulder so that it did not fall.[10] He recognized in that "religious" the man whom he had sent away the previous evening and, as a result of this dream, he immediately "granted the request."[11]

Here is the historical difficulty of the dream: the very same "vision" is applied to St. Dominic in the *Vita* written by Constantine of Orvieto in 1244, almost two years before the *Vita Seconda* of Celano, written in the years 1246-1247. We must remember that Celano, in his *Vita Seconda*, uses works and "reminiscences" sent to him by the companions of St. Francis in August 1246.

Of course, nothing forbids our accepting a vision in regard to both Dominic and Francis. However, the more probable solution is in recognizing that the hagiography of the thirteenth century uses the literary device of the "vision" to indicate that the will of God had been made manifest interiorly and with certainty to the servant of God. In our case that "vision" shows the certainty of the author that the pope, with the help of God, had understood that the sad state of the Church could be reformed through the work of men like Dominic and Francis.[12]

Returning once again to the "dream" at Spoleto, the historical facts give us another solution which is not only probable but almost certain. Walter of Brienne died in June 1205 as a result of wounds he received during a furious battle against the soldiers of the German leader Diepold of Vohburg at the castle of Sarno, to which Walter had laid siege. The news of his death probably reached Spoleto about a month later, at the very time that Francis and "Count Gentile" were getting ready to leave the city and continue their journey south. This was the "dream" of Spoleto, or better yet, the end of a youthful "dream." Francis must have asked himself what he would do in the south if the leader of the expedition were dead.

Another valid solution is suggested by Helen Moak, "that Francis was finally able to admit to himself that escaping from Assisi in search of exciting action in faraway places would not solve his intimate problems. If a solution was to be found for his internal doubts, he would have to look for it in his own country, in a familiar environment, among people he knew. And so it was."[13]

Francis returned to Assisi, deeply dejected, well aware that he would have to face a father who twice had spent a small fortune to prepare him for expeditions, as well as friends and acquaintances to whom he had bragged about the glory that would be his. He spent some months in a visible state of depression, aimlessly wandering around the streets and countryside of Assisi, having to bear the taunts of his fellow citizens. It seemed to be a time of idleness, a real waste of time.

On the contrary, however, this period was the most important one preceding his conversion; for it determined the course that his life would ultimately take. It was a period of interior struggle, of refining his capabilities. We could say it was one of periodic attempts to test and refine the resistance of his soul. This is the real perspective with which one should consider the two episodes noted by his biographers at this time: his trading places with the beggar in Rome, and his encounter with the leper.

Would he, who was on the verge of rejecting the society in which he lived, be able to appreciate and accept that which his society rejected?

THE EXPERIENCE OF POVERTY

In spring of 1206, Francis joined a group of pilgrims for a visit to the basilica of the apostles. In front of St. Peter's there was a multitude of poor people, clinging to the gates where the pilgrims passed. They implored, cried out, and held out their hands. The pilgrim from Assisi asked himself, "What is it like to be really poor?" He traded clothes with a beggar and joined the others in front of the basilica, begging in the Provençal language. When it was time for the meal which the deacons of St. Peter's served the beggars every day, Francis also joined in that *agape*. It left him with a vivid emotional impression and experience of fraternity; he took that impression with him back to Assisi.

MEETING THE LEPER

There was an even more painful aspect of life in society of those days—leprosy. It is most probable that Francis' concern for the poor had found support in the precepts of the gospel. We have no indication, however, that this concern also extended to the lepers; and in those days people hardly thought of them. Communal statutes put lepers outside the protection of the law. When they were discovered, their goods were confiscated and they were put into leprosaria forever. They were forbidden to enter the cities; and if they were found there, the citizens could legally attack them. Francis, like all the others, found them nauseating and repulsive. He had never even reflected on what it meant to be one of them, as he had done for the poor; nor did he ever imagine what would happen.

One day, as Francis rode along the plains of Assisi, caught up in his own thoughts, his horse suddenly reared. Francis looked up and was struck with terror. A leper stood before him, staring at him. Francis' first impulse was to throw him a coin and flee, but this was impossible—what he now was, or was becoming, stopped him from doing this. He slowly dismounted; went toward the leper; and let some coins fall into that disfigured, outstretched hand. He felt in some mysterious way that he himself was almost transformed into that suffering mortal; and in that transformation he understood the essence of Christianity: God is in every person. Alms could never be enough.

Francis reverently kissed that leper as one kisses a sacred object. Even on his deathbed he recalled the transforming effect of that encounter: "that which seemed bitter to me was changed into sweetness of soul and body."[14]

Now Francis was ready to hear the voice of the Crucified at San Damiano. He was ready for his final conversion.

8

FRANCIS BECOMES A PENITENT

Celano narrated Francis' conversion as follows: "One day, however, when he had begged for the mercy of God most earnestly, it was shown to him by God what he was to do . . . for it was extremely necessary that the gospel calling be fulfilled in him who was to be the minister of the gospel in faith and in truth. When the blessed servant of the Most High was thus disposed and strengthened by the Holy Spirit, now that the opportune time had come, he followed the blessed impulse of his soul, by which he would come to the highest things, trampling worldly things under foot."[1]

The decision was actually put into practice on the way home from a business trip to Foligno where "as usual he sold everything he had with him and, successful as a merchant, he left behind even the horse he was riding."[2] He stopped at San Damiano and told the "poor priest" of his decision. "He offered him money he had with him, telling him what he proposed to do. The priest was astonished and, wondering over a conversion so incredibly sudden, refused to believe what he heard. And because he thought he was being deceived, he refused to keep the money offered him. For he had seen him just the day before, so to say, living in a riotous way among his relatives and acquaintances and showing greater foolishness than the rest. But Francis persisted obstinately and tried to gain credence for what he said, asking earnestly and begging the priest to suffer him to remain with him for the sake of the Lord. In the end, the priest acquiesced to his remaining there. . . ."[3]

Thus Francis asked and obtained permission to be accepted at San Damiano as a *conversus,* thus becoming an *oblatus* or *donatus* or *conversus,* an official form of *penitent,* as we have clearly seen in our brief historical glimpse of the penitential movement.[4]

What happened next is further proof that this is the only valid interpretation of the narrative of Celano. Here we find perfect agreement between an incident related in the *Legend of the Three Companions*, which is the only Franciscan source that refers to this detail, and the Assisian statutes of the time. This proof is not to be underestimated because of the historical value of the legend itself. Pietro di Bernardone, exhausting all his efforts to convince his son to return home, turned to the civil authority; and making strong use of his position as *rei publicae benefactor et provisor*—as he will later be called by Marianus of Florence—that is, one who provided for the needs of and also helped in city affairs, requested its involvement in his case and accused his son of rebellion and dissipation. The statutes of the commune of Assisi punished anyone found guilty of such an offense with banishment from the city.[5]

According to the instructions of the same statutes, the judge issued a summons to appear in judgment. A nuncio would have either delivered it to the accused or he would have shouted before his house: "The guilty party is commanded and ordered to appear on the third day before the civil authorities to respond to the accusations presented by his father." Francis received the summons at San Damiano, as the *Legend of the Three Companions* attests, and "answered that, since by divine grace he had obtained freedom, he was the servant only of God and therefore no longer owed obedience to the civil authorities and was outside their jurisdiction."[6] The civil authorities did not want to press the issue and said to Pietro that "as Francis had entered the service of almighty God, he was no longer their subject."[7]

Their decision to give up the prosecution is quite significant when one recalls that Assisi was in the first years of civil autonomy. City authorities, quite jealous of their power, exercised it firmly, and if they had given up this power, it could only have been because they realized that Francis was no longer under their jurisdiction. It is precisely because he was a *conversus* (*oblatus* or *donatus*) and therefore a true *ecclesiasticus* or *clericus*, exempt from civil jurisdiction.[8]

Jordan of Giano also affirmed Francis' entrance into the "life of penance." He began his chronicle in this way: "In the year of the Lord 1207, Francis, who was by profession a merchant, with repentant heart touched by the breath of the Holy Spirit, began a life of penance in the habit of the hermit."[9] Ida Magli noted that "Jordan of Giano presents this penance of Francis, not as a common or transitory penance, but as a state, a *modum penetencie*": ("*Anno*

1207 Franciscus . . . in habitu heremitico modum penetencie est aggressus)."[10]

Celano repeatedly affirms that Francis wore the habit of penance. In the *Vita Prima* he said expressly: "It was the third year of his conversion when he began to repair the church (of the Porziuncola). At this time he wore a kind of hermit's dress, with a leather girdle about his wasit; he carried a staff in his hands and wore shoes on his feet."[11]

The same fact is repeated by Julian of Speyer[12] and in other *Legendae*.[13]

Francis resolutely bade farewell to all, publicly, before his father Pietro di Bernardone and Guido, the bishop of Assisi. It should be emphasized—something not considered very often—that the bishop, before asking Francis to give back the money to his father, advised him to think about the fact that this is the condition necessary for him to become a *conversus*: *"Si tu vis Deo servire, redde illi pecuniam quam habes."* "If you really want to consecrate yourself to the Lord, you must give back (to your father) the money that you have." *Deo servire* is the formula phrase that referred to the oblates. Francis replied: *"Quia Deo servire proposui, reddo illi pecuniam . . . et omnia vestimenta."* "Since I have decided to dedicate myself to the service of the Lord . . . I shall give him back not only the money . . . but also all the clothes."[14]

Francis left the scene of the renunciation, officially recognized as a penitent by the bishop of Assisi; as a penitent, he will permanently reside at San Damiano.[15]

FRANCIS, "BROTHER OF PENANCE"

The *Legend of the Three Companions* explicitly states that the eremitical penitential life of Francis lasted for two years: "Until the work of restoring the church of San Damiano was completed, blessed Francis still wore the garments of a hermit with a strap to serve as a belt, and he carried a staff and had sandals on his feet. . . . Two years after his conversion several men were drawn to follow his example of penitence, and they left everything in order to join him. . . ."[16]

This was the period of Francis' greatest maturation, a period which led him, little by little, to plan his future. Probably no one can tell us just how much his penitential experience affected his spirit and outlook; but one thing is certain—through the penitential movement Francis came to realize the lively desire spreading among Christians for a more evangelical life, and even more, for the urgent need of spiritual guides to show the people the way to remain faithful to God and the Church. He certainly saw how the Cathari heresy and other anti-ecclesiastical movements were spreading.[17] Perhaps he also realized that in that same "penitential movement" the real gospel meaning of *metànoia* had been forgotten or lost along the centuries. By Francis' time, *metànoia* retained only the external, physical aspect of corporal penance; and that was mostly a cultural or cultic phenomenon.[18]

Perhaps these two elements proved very weighty in the soul of Francis and brought him, after two years, to the decision to be not only a solitary-penitent, but also an apostle.

A factor of primary importance in this period of Francis' maturation and planning of future action was his closeness to Bishop Guido, who counseled him on the steps he should take. Another equally important element was his friendship with the Benedictine monks of Mount Subasio who, in their winter home in Assisi, next to the paternal home of Francis,[19] had seen him grow up and, together with Guido, were the only ones to foresee or understand something of the greatness in the singular behavior of the young man from Assisi.

FRANCIS' THEOLOGICAL AND BIBLICAL PREPARATION

Why should we rule out, in this same period of the life of Francis, some sort of preparation or theological and biblical study, both from the priest of San Damiano as well as from Bishop Guido himself, and probably under the guidance, if not the regular instruction, of the Benedictine monks?[20]

Today, in fact, the idea of Francis as "an ignorant man"[21] is rapidly dissolving. His writings, now minutely analyzed, demonstrate a certain literary education as well as a theological preparation and a biblical knowledge that cannot be overlooked.

Men of letters now admit that the composition of the *Canticle of the Creatures* reveals a notable literary preparation, among the best that could be obtained in a town of noblemen and rich merchants like Assisi.[22] Prof. Pasquale Tuscano recently wrote that "the *Canticle of Brother Sun* is anything but a song flowing from a naive, unformed soul, a text of religious poetry, a burst of romantic emotion. Its simplicity comes from a deep feeling and a cultural background that is difficult to evaluate, from a burning need to share his message of brotherhood, love, and humility with the heart of all of humanity, of his own and of all time." Still again, "the literary polish (of the *Canticle*) is doubtless. Even structurally the *Canticle* is carefully thought out and composed, and is accented by examples from the Bible and poetry."[23]

Branca affirmed that the religious message of Francis in the *Canticle* "is expressed in a poetic language of unsurpassed force, at least until Dante; with an immediate concreteness and a powerful use of allusion, with a miraculous freshness of impressions and sensations and an absolute precision of metaphysical and mystical concepts."[24] According to Baldelli, "the *Canticle* becomes almost a biblical and psalmistic reading in an artistic composition of rhyme, sound, and perhaps *cursus*—nothing playful or improvised."[25]

Concerning more directly the theological and biblical studies of Francis, no less a master of Franciscan criticism than Kajetan Esser has recently noted in his analysis of the text of the *Recensio prior* of the *Letter to all the Faithful* that this written instruction "would suggest the saint had a greater knowledge of Scripture than modern Franciscan research in general is willing to acknowledge."[26] Esser speaks as well of the "theological depth" that permeates the well-balanced division of the *Recensio prior*.[27]

If we admit, as the same critical analysis brings us to do, that the same *Recensio prior* (*1Lf*) should be included among the earliest writings of St. Francis,[28] we must find some human explanation for such "scriptural knowledge" and "theological depth" even in the very beginning of Francis' itinerant preaching.[29]

The most plausible explanation would seem to lie in the San Damiano period, that is in the period when Francis was the "Brother of Penance."

Sources are in agreement in relating that Francis spent much time in solitary meditation, wandering along the slopes of Mount Subasio and crossing the Valley of Spoleto. These places were dotted with monasteries, mostly of the Cluny tradition. Besides the huge Abbey of Mount Subasio, the Benedictine order had at least ten other monasteries of men in the territory of Assisi at the time of St. Francis.[30] In addition to these, the Abbey of S. Croce of Sassovivo (Foligno) was, in the first years of the thirteenth century, in such a state of prosperity that it was considered a separate congregation. A list, compiled in 1216, of the monasteries, churches, and hospitals dependent on S. Croce contains one hundred forty entries. These were situated along an uninterrupted line from Camerino to Rome, passing through Nocera Umbra, Perugia, Assisi, Foligno, Spoleto, and Orte.

As far as the more immediate neighborhood of Assisi is

concerned, the Congregation of Sassovivo possessed two abbeys and four priories in the diocese of Foligno, along with a further sixteen churches with a "monk with the title of prior" in residence,[31] many in the mountainous area, not far from Subasio. In the diocese of Spoleto the same congregation had three abbeys, twelve priories, and fourteen churches served by the monks. Among these we can note the Abbey of St. Peter of Bovara, whose structure is still visible along the highway between Trevi and Fonti di Clitunno. Between Assisi and Rome there were monasteries within a few hours' traveling time of one another, the maximum distance between any two of them, a single day's walk.

It must also be noted that the congregation of Sassovivo was founded with the specific purpose of giving hospitality to pilgrims. This can already be found explicitly stated in a document dated 1106.[32] Furthermore, one of the two institutions existing at Ponte S. Giovanni, near Perugia, was for the purpose of "restoring pilgrims."[33]

The Benedictine Abbeys of any importance were equipped with a library and scriptorium where the monks patiently copied the antique codices as well as the recent writings of their illustrious brothers. The only spiritual literature of the time came, in fact, from the monasteries.

From all of this historical information it would seem logical to suppose that Francis refined his theological, scriptural, and spiritual knowledge during his stays in these monasteries.

FRANCIS AND BISHOP GUIDO

We believe that the closeness, guidance, and advice of Guido were essential elements for the success of Francis' work with the penitential movement or "Third Order" which took its name from him, as well as for the Order of Friars Minor and that of the "Poor Ladies."

In the *Legend of the Three Companions*, immediately after Francis' public renunciation before his father, we read that Bishop Guido had "clearly understood that the servant of God had acted on a divine inspiration and realized that a great mystery lay behind what he had witnessed; therefore, from that hour, he became his protector. He helped and comforted Francis, loving him with tender charity."[34]

Guido's protection, therefore, dates back to the beginning of Francis' penitential life. When Francis began his itinerant preaching, and there were only six companions following him, the same *Legend* tells us that "only the bishop of Assisi, to whom the man of God often went for advice, received him with kindness."[35]

On the occasion of Francis' trip to Rome with his first companions to submit their way of life to Pope Innocent III, the *Legend of the Three Companions* tells us that "when they arrived in Rome, they found there the bishop of Assisi who welcomed them most gladly because he honored Francis and the brothers with a special love. He was happy to have men in his diocese whose life and behavior gave him great satisfaction. When he heard the reason for their coming . . . he . . . promised them his advice and help."[36]

Who was this Guido? Guido II (or di Secondo) was bishop of Assisi from 1204-1228, that is, he was Francis' bishop from the time of his conversion until his death. According to Fortini, "at this time the bishop of the Church of Assisi had reached the height of his power and wealth, so as to appear the strongest and richest feudal lord of the whole region. . . . He was avid for material goods and thirsty for power; he did not hesitate to fight without respite for his territory and wealth, with magistrates of the commune who did not want to submit to his will, with canons who wanted to escape the tribute owed him, and with the monasteries that rose against the bondage of submission." Yet, in spite of all of this, "it is he who, without hesitation, places his mantle over the man who stripped himself in his presence to make 'poverty' his way of life, the salvation of those who are spiritually tormented by their pride and cupidity."[37] "A secret presentiment made him realize that something solemn and mysterious was taking place at that moment in his court, touched by a contrast that went beyond the limits of time and place to reach the universal drama of a disturbed humanity."[38]

From that day forward, Bishop Guido remained close to Francis. He continued his battles with the commune, noblemen, middle classes, canons, and monks. Yet, in regard to Francis and his friars, he became both guide and protector.

The *Legend of the Three Companions* tells us that the "bishop of Assisi was a friend of the bishop of Sabina, Cardinal John of Saint Paul, a man full of divine grace who loved all the servants of God."[39] Salvatore Attal described the Cardinal as "a pious, prudent, and discreet man, who, because of his age and the dignity of his life, enjoyed great authority with the pontiff."[40]

This little piece of information given us by the *Three Companions* is of great importance because it helps us to deduce with certainty that Bishop Guido, with such an influential friend, must have been aware of the official attitude of Pope Innocent III concerning the new religious foundations, "poverty movements," and on the various measures taken in the last decade on all of them. Thus he could well counsel and aid Francis, as he had proposed, on what measures to take and the fundamental bases on which to found his fraternity if he wanted to be successful. Limiting our interest to the "poverty movements," we can summarize the attitude and relative measures of the Church concerning them in the period immediately preceding the time of Francis:

Pope Lucius III, in the Council of Verona (1184), held for the purpose of deciding political and religious questions, took radical measures against heresy and against its supporters and sympathizers. In the famous decree *Ad abolendum* he expressly condemned the Cathari, Patarines, Humiliati, the Poor of Lyons (Waldensians), Passagini,[41] the Josephines[42] and all those laymen who, under the guise of being religious, claim the right to preach in public without the authorization of the Apostolic See or of the local bishop. The reason for the condemnation was, therefore, the presumption of preaching without authorization.[43]

This condemnation was repeated by the statutes of the Synod of Toul in 1192.

Meanwhile, in 1186, Urban III, the successor of Lucius III, had promulgated the letter *Religiosam vitam eligentibus*, which is considered to be the first approval of the Humiliati, at least for those who had agreed to an explicitly religious-monastic type of community life at the church of St. Peter of Vico Bolbone, near Milan.[44]

Bishop Guido, a friend of a "prelate of highest authority," that is, Cardinal John of St. Paul, in addition to knowing what had happened from the time of Peter Waldo on, most certainly must have understood the programmatic lines of the new pontiff, Innocent III, which had begun to emerge from the very first years of his pontificate. It would, therefore, have been easy for him to direct Francis from 1206 onward to be successful in what he was planning.

THE POSITION OF INNOCENT III

Thomas of Celano described Innocent III as "burning with zeal for justice in the things that the cause of Christian faith demanded."[45] Pope Innocent's program can be summarized as a determined defense and expansion of Christianity through peaceful methods, such as preaching and persuasion, when possible and successful; and, when these were unsuccessful, by resolute and even violent methods.

A man of exceptional intelligence, he came to the throne of Peter in 1198, when he was only thirty-seven years old; it was the same year that Assisi won its independence, presumably with the participation of the sixteen-year-old son of Pietro di Bernardone. Innocent immediately realized that the decrees of condemnation such as those of the Council of Verona would not be enough to stop the heresies of the Cathari and Waldensians. First of all, it would be necessary to do something to recoup the losses wherever possible.

Dal Pino rightly affirms that: "As to the lay religious movements which had previously arisen, Innocent III assumed a totally new position; he attempted to bring back to the faith and to obedience to the Church as many as possible, uniting the various groups under one "propositum" and ceding on certain points proper to them, thus rendering the action more decisive. These points were: collective poverty and adhesion to other evangelical characteristics, the right to hold meetings, and the permission for preaching of a moral nature, in exchange for an explicit profession of orthodox faith and respect for the hierarchy. Such an effort of reconciliation certainly did not preclude the aim of recuperating some of the Church's lost strength by using prestige and power against the remaining more radical anti-hierarchical and heretical elements, which the pope had decided to fight against."[46]

Thus Innocent III was ready to re-admit into the fold of the Church those groups already included in the condemnation who wanted to return. From 1200 to 1202 he promulgated four letters by which he had accepted groups of Humiliati, allowing them diverse forms of life, even contrary to his first desire expressed in these letters, that of establishing a single rule for all of them— (*unum honestum et regular propositum*).[47]

In 1208 Innocent III accepted into reconciliation with the Church the Poor Catholics of Durandus di Uesca[48] and in 1210 the Poor Lombards, also known as *Pauperes Praedicatores*, of Bernardus Primus.[49] In regard to the various poverty and penitential movements, it was Innocent's intention to regain as far as possible the various spiritual forces of Christianity.

Besides this, we see delineated in the scope of his program an attitude that, beginning in the first years of his pontificate, seems to make his approval of the fraternity of itinerant preachers of Francis of Assisi in the spring of 1210 a foregone conclusion.

From the beginning of his papacy, Innocent showed that he

clearly understood that the spread of the Cathari and Waldensian heresies was essentially due to two factors: the lack of religious instruction on the part of the Christian people, especially those of the uneducated and illiterate lower classes, due in turn to the lack of preaching on the part of the clergy. Writing to Berengarius, bishop of Narbonne on May 30, 1203, the pope reproached him for his neglect of preaching and clearly attributed the spread of heresy in his territory to this fact: "You do not distribute the bread (of religious instruction) to your children who are asking for it, as it should be done according to your pastoral office. Meanwhile the heretics are taking advantage of this and dare to propose to them, publicly, their perverse doctrine."[50] At the same time it was quite evident that the crowds were drawn to the heretics more by the "poor way of life of the Cathari and Waldensian preachers than by their preaching."[51]

There was, therefore, a dire need to instruct the faithful and preach the word of God to all. Such preaching, however, would have to be conducted by people whose life corresponded to the word that was being preached. Since the signs of the times, both in the Catholic and the heterodox field, called for a return to the simple, poor, apostolic life, it was necessary that these preachers be truly poor, "powerful in their words and deeds," as can be found in more than one of the pope's letters. The importance that he attached to this two-fold element is well expressed in the terminology he used in *Etsi nostra navicula* of May 31, 1204, addressed to the Cistercian preachers in the south of France. "Your teaching should reflect your life in such a way that the people may see in your conduct what you are preaching in your sermons."[52] This plan of action became ever clearer in the mind and actions of Innocent III and remains basic to an understanding of his untiring activity regarding heresy. Only when peaceful means such as preaching and persuasion reveal themselves to be inadequate, that is, useless, did he resort to more resolute methods, such as the crusade against the Albigensians.

In the fall of 1203 he began to act, designating as apostolic preachers in the south of France the Cistercian Pierre de Castelnau and his confrere, "master" Raoul of the Abbey of Fontfroide; they were later joined by Arnaud, the Abbot of Citeaux. The mission began in the midst of great difficulties, some of which were even caused by the opposition of local bishops and clergy. So that the missionaries' work might be more effective, the pope gave them a wide range of powers, including the ability to substitute pastors and suspend bishops after an investigation. During the summer of 1206 the group was expanded by the arrival of Diego di Acebes, bishop of Osma (Spain) and Dominic of Caleruega, the future founder of the Dominicans.[53] After their first experience, all of them had to admit that their way of life was not yet as poor as that of the Cathari and Waldensians; and perhaps that was the main reason they had achieved such poor results. Diego, the leader of the group, took the initiative to send his entire retinue, servants and horses included, back to Spain, and began going around barefoot. The others imitated him, so that in the summer of 1206 the small group began evangelizing in real poverty. They practically renewed in themselves the ideal and the practice of the itinerant preachers of the previous centuries, a practice that Peter Waldo had tried to imitate some thirty years before. The experiment met with some success.[54] Innocent III followed this preaching experiment with great interest. On November 17, 1206, he sent his famous letter, *Excursus saeculi*, a letter fundamental for an understanding of Innocent's current and future attitude, to his legate, Raoul de Fontfroide. In it he invited Raoul and his companions to proceed with this new evangelical method. Furthermore, he asked him to look for more preachers, "wearing disdainful clothes, but with a burning spirit, . . . ready to imitate the poverty of the poor Christ, who would have no fear to approach those who are far from the Church, . . . so that, through the example of their life and the strength of their word, they may recall even the heretics from error."[55]

"Strengthened by this pontifical support," writes Thouzellier, "the mission, under the guidance of Diego, continued its fruitful apostolate during the winter of 1206-1207. In all humility, abstinence, and patience, the little group went around barefoot, without a rich entourage, through cities and towns where debates with the heretics could be anticipated.[56] It did not have further success. From the autumn of 1207 on, there was a strong resistance among the heretics, especially the Cathari or Albigensians. "Tenacious in their errors," wrote Robert D'Auxerre, well-versed in the chronology of the facts, "these unbelieving people do not accept the truth of any sort of document, although the value of the arguments are undeniable. For three months (May-August 1207) the apostolic preachers wandered with much zeal and fatigue through cities and villages, among dangers and difficulties, to gather small fruit: rare conversions and few confirmations in the faith."[57]

Innocent III was well aware of the situation. For that reason, in November 1207, he decided to have recourse to "worldly help." Writing on November 17 of that year to King Philip Augustus of France, he said that he was thinking of "the deplorable state of Toulouse where all the (spiritual) means tried up to now have been worn down by the inveterate heresy that nothing, neither reason nor threats, can shake."[58]

Therefore, he asked the king's help so that, "moved to repentance through warlike affliction, the heretics may return to the truth."[59]

Despite all of this, Innocent III still saw the value of "itinerant preaching, in strictest poverty," at least in those areas of Christendom where heresy, although a real danger, had not yet prevailed. As a matter of fact, while on the one hand starting the crusade against the Albigensians, a new letter, *Etsi nostra navicula* of March 28, 1208 (not to be confused with the letter of May 31, 1204, beginning with the same words) was sent to Abbot Arnaud of Citeaux. Whereas before he had delegated the Cistercians, he now directed his apostolic plan to "all the zealous orthodox defenders of the faith, powerful, as those of before, in *opere et sermone*, and of an irreproachable life." As he had done in *Excursus saeculi*, he once again invited the legates to procure the help of "such men, taken from any order or congregation, to exercise the office of preaching."[60]

Knowing all of this, Bishop Guido was easily able to guide Francis among the rocks which had destroyed many of his predecessors in the penitential movement. A good part of the success of the young man from Assisi can probably be attributed to the wise advice of the bishop of Assisi. "And this may well be the greatest glory in the varied and turbulent history of the bishops of Assisi," as Fortini has remarked.

When, only two years later, in the spring of 1210, Francis and his companions went to the Lateran, asking the pope for the approval of their "fraternity of itinerant preachers," based on poverty, but also on the two pillars of a "complete adherence to the Church" and "obedience to the hierarchy," Innocent III, assured of their "fidelity" either directly or through Cardinal John of St. Paul, had little or no hesitation to give them permission to "preach penance to all."

Francis of Assisi and his little group represented the realization of the "Lateran dream"—the Lateran would be upheld through the apostolic efforts and good example of this new band which, in just a few years' time would become an "army," fighting the heretics on their own ground, with the same weapons—in total poverty, but with an "ardent spirit," faithful to God and to the Church.

It seems appropriate to add a final word about the support Francis found among the Benedictines, and in particular from Cardinal John of St. Paul.[61] The *Legend of the Three Companions* affirms that "when he heard from the bishop (of Assisi) of Francis' life and sanctity, he desired to see him and some of the brothers." Having welcomed them into his home for some days, he was edified by their speech and behavior. "He saw that their works corresponded to what he had heard; and he commended himself to their prayers and, as a special favor, requested that they would consider him as one of themselves. Finally, he asked Francis the reason for their coming to Rome; and, on hearing what was on their minds, he offered to plead their cause at the papal court."[62]

From whom had the cardinal heard about Francis and his movement before inviting them into his home, and ultimately assuming the responsibility of representing them in the curia?

Cardinal John was a Benedictine. Therefore, after Bishop Guido's request for help in favor of Francis' proposed fraternity, it would seem natural for the cardinal to have asked for information from the most important representatives of local monasticism who would have been expected to have had some first-hand knowledge of events in Assisi and its surroundings, that is, the priors and abbots of the Benedictine houses in the region.[63] This information must have been of such a nature that it prompted him to act in their behalf.

9

FRANCIS AND THE PENITENTS

Without pretending to give a complete history of the relationship of Francis to the penitential movement of his time, something which will remain impossible to do for quite some time, it is our intention to point out certain easily-documented basic points.

THE RAPID INCREASE IN
THE NUMBER OF PENITENTS

In his *Vita Prima* Thomas of Celano tells us that Francis "went about the town and villages announcing the kingdom of God, preaching peace, teaching salvation and penance unto the remission of sins. . . . He acted boldly in all things because of the apostolic authority granted to him, using no words of flattery nor seductive blandishments. Men and women, clerics and religious hastened to see and to hear the holy man of God who seemed to all to be a man of another world."[1]

This passage is to be interpreted in the context of Francis' return from Rome where he had received official, although oral, recognition of his gospel fraternity from Innocent III and authorization for himself and his brothers to preach "penance to all."[2]

Meersseman notes: "The primitive theme of his preaching was penance and conversion. From the beginning his companions lived as simple *viri poenitentiales*."[3] It has been noted that the *Legend of the Three Companions* and the *Anonymus Perusinus* state that to whoever asked "where did you come from" the brothers simply replied that they were penitents coming from Assisi.[4]

The effects of the preaching of Francis and his brothers was described by Celano: "Thanksgiving and voices of praise resounded everywhere so that many put aside worldly cares and gained knowledge of themselves from the life and teaching of the most blessed Francis, and they longed to attain love and reverence for their Creator. Many of the people, both noble and ignoble, cleric and lay, impelled by divine inspiration, began to come to St. Francis, wanting to carry on the battle constantly under his discipline and under his leadership. All of these the holy man of God, like a plenteous river of heavenly grace, watered with streams of gifts."[5]

Because of Francis' preaching, in a very short time, in addition to the Christian reawakening that happened wherever he traveled, many faithful of every social class (*nobiles et ignobiles*), clergy and laity, were moved by divine grace to salutary repentance by the teaching of the saint. They turned to him with the express desire of serving the Lord forever under Francis' direction and teaching. This is the real meaning of Celano's *perpetuo militare*. Those of us who cursorily read the Latin expressions of that epoch, or read it in a poor translation, should keep in mind that "when we study the first biographies of St. Francis from the point of view of the ecclesiastical institutions of his time, we find a poetic expression of many juridical details, which show how meticulously Francis observed the prescriptions of canon law in force at that time, details more obvious to the reader of that era than to the modern historian."[6]

Analyzing the terminology of this passage from Celano, Schmucki notes that "the 'regular' terminology (*sub eius disciplina et magisterior militare* and *ad cuius formam, regulam et doctrinam . . . renovatur Ecclesia*) and the 'penitential' language (*saecularibus curis abiectis* and *compuncti*) presuppose that the clergy and laity who turned to St. Francis have made a commitment to a special form of religious life."[7]

This interpretation of Celano's text is supported by the passage which immediately follows it: "for he was an excellent craftsman; and, according to his plan, rule, and teaching, proclaimed before all, the Church is being renewed in both sexes, and the *threefold army* of those to be served is triumphing."[8]

Many editors, such as the Italian translators of Celano note that this "threefold army" can be interpreted in two ways: it may be an allusion to the three states of life which comprise the Church, i.e., clergy, religious, and laity, or to the three "orders" founded by Francis—the Friars Minor, Poor Ladies, and the Brothers and Sisters of Penance (Third Order who lived the Christian ideal in their homes)." They are merely repeating the interpretation of the editors of the Quaracchi edition in 1941.[9]

Schmucki, however, claims that such an alternative is "inadmissible": the word *militia*, when used in a religious context, usually meant the *servitium Deo* or clerical status; this is the meaning given it by Celano, Julian of Speyer, and St. Bonaventure.[10] Thus the *trina triumphat militia salvandorum* should be understood as "a triple religious institute flourishes for the elect."

These conclusions are confirmed by the analogous account of the *Legend of the Three Companions*: "Married men and women, being bound by the marriage vow were advised by the friars to dedicate themselves to a life of penance in their own houses." The *Legend* continues by adding: "Thus through blessed Francis' perfect devotion to the Blessed Trinity, the Church of Christ was renewed by three new orders as had been prefigured through his previous reparation of three churches. His three distinct orders were each in due time approved and confirmed by the sovereign pontiff."[11]

"It is an historical fact," says Meersseman, that "around 1215 in the urban centers of Italy we note a sudden increase in the number of penitents, even among married persons; and it is exactly this that the historians call the 'penitential movement of the thirteenth century.' Voluntarily embracing the penitential state with all that it implied, according to the centuries-old customs and laws of the Church, these pious laymen and women committed themselves to observe a rudimentary and archaic religious life, recognized by the Church. Before 1221 they were already grouped into local fraternities."[12]

These historical facts are interpreted by the same Meersseman whose interpretation carries more weight because of his reluctance to consider as "Franciscan" some pontifical documents of the thirteenth century. "The unexpected increase of the number of urban penitents is attributed, as we know, to St. Francis of Assisi who himself lived as a brother of penance before founding his religious order."[13]

Without forcing the issue at all, we can say that the best Franciscan sources clearly indicate that the penitential movement had a rapid increase in numbers from the very beginning of the itinerant preaching period of Francis and his brothers, and that the new penitents expressed the desire to be associated with him forever, under his guidance.

**FRANCIS IMMEDIATELY IS INTERESTED
IN THE PENITENTS**

Once he and his first companions had begun their itinerant

penitential preaching, Francis could certainly not forget or neglect the penitents. The unexpected growth of the movement and the increase of those who wanted to serve God directly under his guidance was primarily due to his and his brothers' preaching and therefore demanded his involvement.

Up until about 1960 there were very few who spoke about a specific intervention of St. Francis in regard to the lay group of his followers before 1221. Generally the writers quoted the sentences addressed by the saint to the inhabitants of Alviano, as quoted in the Fioretti. After his famous sermon to the birds, everyone desired to follow him and become his disciples. "Don't be in a hurry and don't leave, for I will arrange what you should do for the salvation of your souls."[14] Then, according to the suggestion of the author of the Fioretti, it was assumed that "the first germs of what would later be the Order of Penitents or the Third Order, sprang forth at that moment in the soul of the founder."[15] More progressive authors, "after accepting the traditional year of 1221 as the year of the precise organization of the Third Order" remarked, however, that "all else leads us to conclude that the tertiary movement had begun before this, perhaps many years before."[16]

Today, after recent numerous studies on the penitential movement of the twelfth and thirteenth centuries, modern historians more assertively admit the interest of Francis for the *poenitentes*. For the most part, they admit that the *Letter to all the Faithful*, unanimously recognized as an authentic work of St. Francis, does not directly refer to "all the faithful" but to those who had decided to follow him in the sense already indicated, that is as "Brothers and Sisters of Penance." Father Kajetan Esser, to whom all tertiaries, especially those of the Third Order Regular, should be grateful for his Commentary on the Rule (of Pius XI-1927)[17] and for *Love's Reply*, in which he shows that all of Franciscan spirituality comes from the idea of penance (*metànoia*),[18] presented a paper at the first meeting on Franciscan Studies, in which he affirmed that "It seems improbable to us that the *Letter* can be said to have been addressed *ad omnes fideles* [to all the faithful]. I believe that not even Francis, with his heroic idealism, could deviate so far from reality. . . . Those to whom the *Letter* was addressed would have to have been open, willing, and ready for a more intense Christian life."[19]

Ultimately, due in great part to the studies of Esser, new importance is being given to a document which has largely been forgotten up until the present time and which, in our opinion, is of primary importance for the penitential movement. We are speaking of the *Recensio prior* (*1 Lf*) of this same *Letter to All the Faithful*, generally considered as an earlier version of the more famous document.

The *Recensio prior* was discovered by Paul Sabatier in cod. 225 of the Guarnacci Library in Volterra (Italy) and was first published in 1900 under the title *"Haec sunt verba vitae et salutis quae si quis legerit et fecerit, invenient vitam et hauriet salutem a Domino"* (These are words of life and salvation: whoever reads them and puts them into practice will find life and salvation from the Lord). After a few brief interventions and observations about it by the same Sabatier, Boehmer, Goetz, and Lemmens in the following years, the document was ignored until the present day. However, when all the manuscripts of the *"Epistola ad fideles"* were collected by the scholars of the Collège of St. Bonaventure of Quaracchi-Grottaferrata in preparation for a new critical edition, it was clearly seen that the "Volterra text held a special place among all the material transmitted to us." It was then (1974) that Kajetan Esser made an extensive critical study which was published in *Collectanea Franciscana,* 1975 in German. In 1978 the *Analecta T.O.R.* published this study in English and Italian.[20]

From this meticulous critical study Esser formed some conclusions which are very interesting for the subject under consideration:

1) The Volterra text refers to the penitential movement. In his "Conclusions and Evaluations" Esser notes that "it is quite clear that we have before us a written instruction directed to people who have joined the penitential movement...a movement to which Francis and his fraternity were deeply attached. Verse 48, however, clearly shows that it is not to the Friars Minor themselves that Francis is writing. It therefore concerns *fratres et sorores de poenitentia in domibus propriis existentes,* [brothers and sisters of penance living in their own homes] that is, to those people who took on themselves a definite way of life in 1221, or at least to some parts of these, to whom Francis gave a *forma vivendi,* according to the testimony of the early biographies."[21]

2) Even if the date of the composition of the *Letter to All the Faithful*[22] is uncertain, this first draft must be dated many years earlier. "Undoubtedly we must suppose that between the (Volterra) document and the *Letter* (to all the Faithful) there is a space of time long enough to have enabled Francis and his friars to consider the negative experience of the penitents associated with them and modified the text; this period was sufficiently long to have allowed Francis to acquire the undisputed function

as a guide of the penitents, as we see unequivocally expressed in the conclusion of the *Epistola*."²³ In our opinion, this earlier time can also be supported regarding the date of 1221. "Today we are no longer obliged to fix 1221 as the year that the Franciscan penitential movement began, along with the foundation of the Third Order" because the testimony of the two *Legendae* excludes these later dates; it must be admitted that this document is anterior to that date, perhaps by many years."²⁴ We can also find support in the fact that in a critical analysis of the *Recensio prior* (1 *Lf*) we find technical similarities to the *Epistola ad clericos* which, "in its earlier form, belongs among the earliest writings of St. Francis."²⁵ Esser again asserts that "Both letters belong to that period in which Francis had not yet found his style of letter-writing."²⁶ Thus we may assume that Francis gave the penitents some directives for living from the very beginning of his itinerant preaching.

3) The *Letter to all the Faithful* could have undergone "a development similar to that of the *Regula non bullata*"²⁷ of 1221. As we know, the *Regula non bullata* is the result of that *Protoregula* of 1209 (1210), presented by the first brothers to Innocent III and orally approved by the pontiff; other precepts were added to it, little by little, as the development and growth of the *Fratres minores* required. The additions were made in chapters held twice yearly, at which all the friars, at least until 1217, participated.²⁸ In the same way, Francis could have added to and modified this Volterra text until he had the long or final edition, the *Letter to all the Faithful*. Esser notes that "Into this long edition, later experiences are sometimes incorporated; corrections are also inserted to preserve the orthodox purity of *facere poenitentiam*; likewise the first contours of a structured community take shape. All of this appears very different, however, from the simple core we find in the Volterra text."²⁹ "Most of all, the work of correcting and expanding the earlier document appears to have been directed toward curbing and repelling contemporary errors which from all sides threatened the movement of the brotherhoods of penance at that time."³⁰ For example, in the *Letter to all the Faithful* there is apparent a great deal of clarification or correction on the question of preaching, which the Waldensians and others claimed as their right, even though they were not clerics. In the *Recensio prior*, in verse 25, there is a paraphrase of Jn 17, which says "*Non pro eis rogo tantum, sed pro eis qui credituri sunt per verbum illorum in me....*" (I do not pray only for them, but also for those that will believe in me through their words). The longer edition omits the second

part and forcefully unites what follows to the preceding verb. There can be no doubt that the elimination of *pro eis qui credituri sunt per verbum illorum in me* is due to the fact that such a text probably created misunderstandings and false interpretations; the sentence could have supported the opinion of the Waldensians that whoever embraced the *vita evangelica* had the right to preach. In addition to this omission, the long version explicitly emphasizes that "the proclamation of the word of God is the exclusive duty of the clerics"—*et ipsi soli ministrare debent et non alii*.[31]

All of this leads us to agree with Esser's final observation: "Both documents, however, show in their own uniqueness that Francis was deeply concerned about the Brothers and Sisters of Penance and followed their development with greater sympathy than some historians are still willing to admit."[32]

FRANCIS GIVES A NORMA DI VITA TO HIS PENITENTS

Francis' concern for the penitents was concretized in practice even in the preparation or composition of a *norma di vita* or rule of life for them. This was explicitly stated by Celano, Julian of Speyer, St. Bonaventure, and Bernard of Bessa.

a) After having mentioned the *"triplice militia,"* that is, Francis' threefold institutions in the Church, Celano affirms: *"To all he gave a rule of life,* and he showed in truth the way of salvation in every walk of life."[33] As we have already mentioned, this was done shortly after his return from Rome where he had obtained the oral approval of his way of life (1209-1210) and permission "to preach penance to all." Thus a triple religious institute was formed at about the same time: Friars Minor, Poor Clares, and Penitents (Third Order). "Unfortunately the first biographer does not give us a clear idea of what this rule was. However, most probably Francis provided for the religious needs of the laity by means not much different from those followed in drawing up the *Protoregula* for the First Order or the *Forma vivendi* which he gave to the Poor Ladies of San Damiano."[34]

K. Esser, advancing the hypothesis that this *"norma vitae"* can be identified as the *Recensio prior* of the *Letter to all the Faithful* observes that "unfortunately, we have no further information on the contents of this way of life. The biographers, however, do repeat that it was a *salutis via* suitable for leading its followers *ad perfectionem status*. The letter under consideration could well be such a *documentum salutis.*"[35]

b) The same idea is confirmed by Julian of Speyer in his *Vita S. Francisci*, written between 1232-1235; he wrote that "In fact, he (Francis) presented suitable teachings of salvation to persons of every class, age, or sex; to all he gave a rule of life which, when followed, like an excellent guide, by one or the other sex, brought about the triumph of the Church through the triple militia of the elect. He organized three orders, in fact, as we mentioned previously . . . the third, certainly not a mediocre means of perfection, is called the Order of Penitents, which, common to clerics and laymen, virgins, continents, and married people, benefits one and the other sex."[36] We should also note in this text the word *continentes*, which certainly refers to those who, although united in matrimony, for ascetical motives abstain from marital contacts."[37] In fact, the Order of Penitents, because it motivated the renunciation of matrimony for celibates and a periodic continence during the legitimate times for married persons, was also called the Order of Continents."[38]

c) It would be impossible to forget the text of St. Bonaventure in his *Legenda Maior* where he tells of the "great numbers of people (who) adopted the new rule of penance according to the form instituted by St. Francis which he called the 'Order of the Brothers of Penance.' The way of penance is common to all those who are on the road to heaven and so this way of life includes members of both sexes, clerics and lay-folk, married or single. How meritorious it is in the eyes of God is clear from the numerous miracles worked by some of those who joined it."[39]

"Joining the Order of Penitents is defined by St. Bonaventure as 'letting oneself be bound by the laws of penance in the way received by the man of God.' The biographer presumed, therefore, a rule of Francis that determined a style of penitential life."[40]

d) Bernard of Bessa, former secretary of St. Bonaventure, in his *Liber de laudibus beati Francisci*, written after 1278, tells about the beginning of the three orders. He referred to the Third Order as the Order of the Brothers and Sisters of Penance, outlining in detail the spiritual program—"to live honestly in one's own home, participate in works of piety, and flee the pomp of the world," that is, to avoid the sumptuous appearance of a worldly life. He specified, finally, that in the outlining of the rules for these orders, St. Francis was assisted by Cardinal Ugolino, who furnished what "the holy man lacked in juridical knowledge."[41]

In regard to Bernard of Bessa's last statement, some historians tend to think that from it one cannot "deduce with certainty that the juridical collaboration and editing of the Cardinal was also extended to the rule of the penitents."⁴²

We note, however, that Bernard of Bessa made a general statement relative to the "rules of these orders." One cannot, therefore, limit the scope of his affirmation, claiming that it is true of one rule, but uncertain about another.

10

FRANCIS' DIRECTIVES FOR HIS PENITENTS

Unfortunately we do not possess the *forma vitae* which, according to the explicit affirmation of the biographers of St. Francis, the saint gave to those groups of penitents—old as well as new—who desired to follow him; or, at least, we do not have sufficient information to identify it positively from any of the documents that we do possess.

Nevertheless, we have irrefutable sources which enable us to know the directives, the new ideals and aspirations which Francis wanted to give to those groups of penitents. They are mainly two: the *Recensio prior* and the *Letter to all the Faithful*. In regard to the organization, even their externals, of these same groups of penitents, we have a third document: the *Memoriale propositi* or *Regula antiqua Fratrum et Sororum de Poenitentia* of 1221-1228.

In a complete study of the sources regarding the primitive Third Order and its spirituality, these three documents should be studied minutely, because without them and their historical progression, we can understand only very little of the Third Order as Francis wanted it.

THE "RECENSIO PRIOR" OR FIRST LETTER TO ALL THE FAITHFUL (1 LF)

We have already pointed out the importance of this first document which demonstrates, among other things, how Francis became interested in the penitents from the very beginning of his itinerant penitential preaching. This document was not included in the Quaracchi edition of the writings of St. Francis,[1] but has been included by Esser in his critical edition of the Opuscula.[2]

ITS CHARACTERISTICS AND DOCTRINE

According to the best modern critics, this document represents the nucleus of what would later be developed, perhaps, as we have already mentioned, progressively, into the long edition or the *Letter to all the Faithful* (2 *Lf*). It is more or less limited, containing only some essential ideas, which is what most of all convinces us that it was actually an earlier draft, and therefore contains the very first teachings that Francis set in writing. It is addressed, in letter form, to the penitents who, in ever greater numbers, turned to him for direction. The longer edition, on the other hand, contains a variety of themes, those which "had great importance in the religious movements (both orthodox and heretical) of the Church of those times."[3]

The *Recensio prior* (1 *Lf*) is clearly divided into two distinct but related parts. "It is impossible to determine whether or not the titles of the two chapters were in the original";[4] however, they do correspond to the contents, briefly describing "the lives of those *qui faciunt poenitentiam* (who do penance) (Ch. I) and of those *qui non agunt poenitentiam* (who do not do penance) (Ch. II)."[5]

First of all, Francis gives a clear indication of what *facere poenitentiam* means. Five elements are enunciated in the opening lines:

1. Love God;
2. Love one's neighbor;
3. Resist the sinful tendencies of our fallen nature;
4. Participate in the sacramental life, especially the Eucharist;
5. Act in conformity with the conversion that the person has accepted.

1-2. Francis, who knows the gospel well and bases his plan of life on the gospel, could not have put as the foundation for the life of the penitents anything but the commandment of love which, according to Christ's teaching, is the compendium of the message of salvation. He will elaborate on this point greatly in the long edition of the *Letter to All the Faithful* (2 *Lf*).

3. The realization of such a life of love of God and others requires, first of all, a constant effort to resist the tendencies of our corrupt nature, which is more inclined towards sin than virtue. The sentence "and hate their bodies with their vices and sins" should be understood according to the language and use of words of Francis who uses the word "body" in the sense of "flesh," that is, fallen nature, the cause of sin.[6] It does not mean, therefore, "body" in the modern sense, in which it is an integral

part of human nature. For Francis this body is also God's creature, to be loved, respected and taken care of. On the contrary, what the penitent must fight are the sinful tendencies of that fallen nature, the cause of "vices and sins." This is very evident in the expressions of the second part of the *Letter*, "Those who do not do penance," where we have in counterdistinction the behavior of those who have not accepted *conversio*. To those who "hate their own body with its vices and sins" as described in the first part, Francis contrasts those that "live in vices and sin and yield to evil concupiscence and to the wicked desires of the flesh... and are slaves to the world, in their bodies, by carnal desires, and the anxieties and cares of this life;... because all vices and sins come out and proceed from the heart of man as the Lord says in the gospel." It is, therefore, the internal, fallen human nature, the divided heart, that needs to be controlled.

4. This process, to be practiced continually, will not be possible through human effort alone; supernatural help is essential. Therefore a sacramental life, the source of grace, is necessary. In this first document directed to the penitents, Francis mentions only the Eucharist. However, it is his thinking (and this will be evident in the second version) that the penitent must also have recourse to the other sacrament, that is penance, more often.

5. Based on these solid foundations, the penitent is invited to "bring forth fruits worthy of penance," that is, to work constantly in correspondence and conformity with his decision to "go towards God" (*metànoia*). In this first version, Francis does not specify what these worthy "fruits of penance" are; he does so to a great extent in the second version (2 *Lf*).

"Though the phrases flow so simply from one to the next," Esser observed, "they reveal a deep consciousness of their vital connection for Christian living.... Only when a person overcomes pride and self-centeredness can the love of God and neighbor flourish (vv. 2-3), a love nourished by the Eucharist (v. 4)."[7]

The result of such conduct will be the attainment of that happiness which man desires so greatly. "Oh, how happy and blessed are these men and women when they do these things and persevere in doing them," because behaving in this way will effect the person's sharing in the trinitarian life of God: "the Spirit of the Lord will rest upon them and he will make his home and dwelling among them; and they are the sons of the heavenly Father, whose works they do; and they are the spouses, brothers, and mothers of our Lord Jesus Christ."

In no other work of St. Francis is such a highpoint of spirituality reached, nor will the person's insertion in trinitarian life be expressed in more precise terms.

This is the essence of the life of penance.

The rest of the first chapter is a sublime hymn praising the mystical-spiritual reality of the union in the Trinity. With obvious joy of spirit, Francis continues to describe "the happy fruits of such a life in the hearts of men, with a genuine touch of true mysticism apparent throughout."[8]

We should pay particular attention to the fact that, in paraphrasing Mt 12:50, "For whoever does the will of my Father in heaven, he is my brother and sister and mother," Francis adds the word "spouses"—"these men and women when they do these things and persevere in doing them . . . they are the spouses, brothers, and mothers of our Lord Jesus Christ." He explains, "We are spouses, when, by the Holy Spirit, the faithful soul is united with our Lord Jesus Christ."

This terminology is rare in the spirituality of Francis' day. In a study of texts pre-dating the *Recensio prior*, Pastor Oliver[9] showed that it was Richard of St. Victor (+1173), among others, who expressed a somewhat similar concept in his commentary on the *Canticle of Canticles*: "It is the Holy Spirit who gives the soul the love of God and the love of neighbor. From that moment on, the soul becomes a spouse."[10] If we admit a direct knowledge of this text by Francis, we must also once again ask the question of how and where he received his patristic education.

The second chapter of the *Recensio prior* enunciates, first of all, in concise phrases those things which are not compatible with the life of penance, and then describes at great length the unhappiness, abandonment by God, and slavery to the world experienced by those *"qui non agunt poenitentiam."*[11] In the midst of this description (vv. 11-14), Francis changes from the third person forms *illi et istae* and directly appeals to them: "Open your eyes, oh blind men . . . ; and you think you will possess the vain goods of the earth for a long time, but you are being deceived. . . ." He evidently does this to stress the importance and urgency of his warning.

Francis next exhorts them to treasure "these fragrant words of our Lord Jesus Christ," inviting those who do not know how to read (the saint knew that this included the great majority of commoners) to have these words read to them and entreats them to "conserve them close to your hearts, putting them faithfully into practice till the end because they are spirit and life."[12]

In concluding his study, Esser observed that "the importance of this (*Recensio prior*) is in the fact that it presents the core ideas by which Francis tried to shape the life of the Brothers and Sisters of Penance associated with him. We can therefore see Francis' concept of the interiority of religious life, something that is not so clearly seen in his other works. Every now and then the words of the saint touch the depths of theology and mystical life."[13]

THE LETTER TO ALL THE FAITHFUL

First of all, it must be pointed out that this *Lettera* is considered authentic by the scholars and experts, most of all because it is found in many ancient codices containing the writings of St. Francis and because the thought and spirit of this work are in complete harmony with the rest of his writings.[14]

Modern criticism, Franciscan and non-Franciscan alike, is also moving decidedly closer to two other conclusions concerning this work:

1) In spite of the title attributed to this work, it was not really addressed to all the faithful indiscriminately, but to those who followed Francis' spiritual direction. "The addressees of this work, as well as the relation between them, cannot refer to all Christians in general, but must be understood to have been individuals and communities united in a special way to Francis, who had given them a *forma vivendi* closely resembling the form of life of the Friars Minor."[15]

2) Although not absolutely certain, the most probable date for the composition of this work is around 1221.[16]

These conclusions of the scholars are of great importance to our current study. The first tells us that from the letter we can deduce with certainty the spiritual direction which Francis desired to impart to the followers of his movement, that is, to those *poenitentes* who were later to be known as the *Poenitentes beati Francisci*.

The second conclusion regarding the year of composition immediately reminds us that the year 1221 is the same as that of the *Memoriale propositi*, the first official rule of the followers of St. Francis, in what would eventually be known as the Third Order. Given the fact that the *Letter to All the Faithful* was certainly written by St. Francis, we see that even the *Memoriale propositi* is Franciscan, most of all in the sense that it juridically codifies the spirit of Francis contained in the letter. There is perfect correspondence of spirit between the *Memoriale propositi* and the letter; only the language is different. The *Memoriale propositi* is written in juridical language, the letter in exhortative. Thus, with regard to the *Memoriale*, Bernard of Bessa's statement referred to before, gains credence; there was cooperation between Cardinal Ugolino and Francis in drawing up the "forms of life" or rules for the three orders. Cardinal Ugolino, a noted jurist, gave Francis' thought juridical form. Thus, in the two documents dated in the same year we find the same thought of Francis, expressed in two different styles.

As a preliminary to our analysis of this work, we can say that it is an "earnest appeal to the readers to sanctify themselves by prayer, the use of the sacraments, mortification, and the practice of justice, charity, and humility; to spread peace by the forgiveness of enemies and by love for them; to observe the commandments and precepts of Christ; to show reverence and respect for the Eucharist; and to live the Catholic life in all its fullness. It is especially noteworthy for its dramatic descriptions of the last moments of the impenitent owner of ill-gotten goods."[17]

THE BASIC IDEAS OF THE "LETTERA AI FEDELI" (2 LF)

If, beginning with the idea that the *Recensio prior* (1 *Lf*) is a first draft of the *Letter to all the Faithful*, we try to find in the letter an organic and systematic development of the former, we would be in trouble. The later work is not the work of an academician who has been assigned the task of organically developing the five basic ideas so clearly stated in the earlier work. Rather, it is the work of a person in love with God, who freely reveals his inner soul, touching again and again those five themes, adding new ones, developing them, and passing from one to the other with no other concern than that of being able to give abundant spiritual nourishment to his followers. Thus we find in it the original ideas of the spirituality of Francis.

1) The letter opens and closes with the greeting, "I, Brother Francis, your servant and subject" (*Francis and Clare*, pp. 67, 73). Francis first of all introduces himself as a brother. From his constant reading of the gospel he has learned the universal brotherhood of all creatures, beginning with that most eminent creature, the human being. This is why Francis could not live alone as a penitent hermit; he had to live as well for those for whom Christ had died. This leads us to understand his continuous travels and preaching, his apostolate and desire to communicate and bring his discovery of God's love to all, either personally or

through his companions. He even desired to reach the infidels, from whose land he had recently returned. When his strength had already begun to fail him (1220 and 1221 are the very years that, according to his biographers, Francis' serious illnesses began), Francis tries to reach everyone by means of his writings. He wrote to the rulers of the people (magistrates, consuls, judges, and governor); to the clerics; to the brothers gathered in chapter; to all superiors; to the guardians; and even to "all the faithful" who have followed him.

2) The letter is a "summary of the gospel," a *vade mecum* to committed Christians wherein the essential themes of Francis are expressed, those same essential themes which he learned from a constant, loving reading of the gospel. From this aspect we may consider the letter as a development of the fundamental ideas which Francis had already given to his penitents in the *Recensio prior* with the words, "How happy are these men and women"; that is, a person's happiness can only come through the love of God. "How happy and blessed are they who love God, that is, those that respond to the love that God had first for us."

3) Now, filling his hands with the "fragrant words of my Lord" (v. 2) Francis will demonstrate at length the love of God, one and three (vv. 4-14).

The love of the Father, the beginning and end of mankind, has affected the history of salvation by his saving interventions (vv. 4, 11) directly and through the prophets in the Old Testament, and by means of Jesus Christ in the New. He willed that his Word, so worthy, so holy, and glorious (v. 4) would take on "our humanity and frailty" (v. 4) "and the will of the Father was such that his blessed and glorious Son, whom he gave to us and who was born for us, should, through his own blood, offer himself as a sacrifice and oblation on the altar of the cross (v. 11) . . . and wills that all of us might be saved by him" (v. 14).

The love of the Son who, "being rich beyond measure" (v. 5), desired to descend to our level in humanity and frailty, "took on our weak human nature" (v. 4), and "with the most blessed Virgin, his mother, willed to choose poverty" (v. 5). "And as the passion drew near, he celebrated the Passover with his disciples" (v. 6), leaving for us in this way the Eucharist. He is the saving mediator (vv. 11-12) through whom one enters the kingdom of God (v. 23). Jesus is the Word of God (v. 4) and our brother (v. 56). He is the true light (v. 66) and wisdom of the Father (v. 67).

The love of the Holy Spirit makes us children of God and

spouses, brothers, and mothers of Our Lord (v. 50). "And upon all men and women, if they have done these things and have persevered to the end, the Spirit of the Lord will rest and he will make his home and dwelling among them. They will be children of the heavenly Father whose works they do. And they are spouses, brothers, and mothers of our Lord Jesus Christ" (vv. 48-50).

The continual contemplation of the love of God, one and three, brings forth from Francis the three stupendous exclamations never to be repeated or surpassed in his writings: "Oh, how glorious it is, how holy and great, to have a Father in heaven! (v. 54) Oh, how holy, consoling, beautiful, and wondrous it is to have a spouse! (v. 55) Oh, how holy and how loving, pleasing, humble, peaceful, sweet, lovable, and desirable above all things to have such a Brother and Son, who laid down his life for his sheep . . ." (v. 56).

It is obvious that the trinitarian concept is at the basis of Francis' teaching. It is well to remember that the trinitarian humus was abundantly fostered in monastic theology, which was about the only one to produce important spiritual works.

In speaking of the Provençal trinitarian humus, Zorzi proved that "interest in the Trinity was not limited to the speculative sphere of the professors, or of students of higher education, but had become a theme of the common people . . . a result brought about even by the Gallican liturgy, so trinitarian by tradition."[18] Even the Provençal troubadours used the trinitarian doctrine as material or for underlying motif of their songs, which leads us to conclude that the common people for whom these songs were written lived in that atmosphere and understood the subject. It would be interesting if we could pinpoint the effect that the popular Provençal culture had on the development of Francis who, as is well known, loved to sing in that language in moments of joy and enthusiasm.[19]

4) When faced with this love of God—of the Father, Son, and Holy Spirit—the penitent will respond with his love in a radical, total, and practical way. This response will involve the universal praise of God (vv. 18-21, 61-62); the metànoia-conversion that means opposition to the sinful tendencies of our corrupt nature (vv. 37, 40, 46); the sacramental life which it entails (vv. 22-24, 34); and the other virtues that we will discuss in greater detail in another chapter.

5) The result of all this is our insertion into the life of the one and triune God. Even though the *Letter to all the Faithful* is three times as long as the *Recensio prior*, Francis retains almost word

for word the phraseology he used in this sublime point of the earlier document, without any additional thoughts or emphases.

This insertion into the trinitarian life of God represents, from the spiritual aspect, man's supreme happiness. This is Francis' goal, and the one he wanted for his followers as well. After this insertion of the "new" man into the life of God, his life will be a hymn of praise to the goodness of the Lord (vv. 61-62).

6) The opposite of this insertion is that already described in the second part of the *Recensio prior*—of those who do not do penance; this is explained and elaborated in verses 63-85. These people are blind because they are deprived of the "true light" of the "wisdom of the spirit"; they are "sons" of the devil, and "knowingly lose their souls" (vv. 66-68).

The *Letter* continues with the description of the "impenitent dying man" (vv. 72-73), which has been called a splendid passage of dramatic composition. It closes with the exhortation and plea "in that love which is God" (Francis' ending phrase in the *Recensio prior* as well) to "receive these words . . . of our Lord Jesus Christ with humility and love, and observe (them) and put (them) into practice (vv. 86-87).

"And to all men and women who will receive them kindly (and) understand their meaning and pass them on to others by their example: If they have persevered in them to the end, may the Father and the Son and the Holy Spirit bless them. Amen" (v. 89).

11
THE SPIRITUALITY OF FRANCISCAN PENITENTS

CHARACTERISTICS OF THE FRANCISCAN PENITENTS:

**ADHERENCE TO CATHOLICISM AND
FIDELITY TO THE CHURCH**

When we examine more closely the characteristics which, according to the *Letter to All the Faithful*, should dinstinguish the followers of St. Francis in the penitential movement, we must arrive at the following conclusions:

First of all, their beliefs and their life style or *forma vitae* will be strongly anti-Cathari and anti-Waldensian, that is, they will correspond to Francis' basic principle of complete adherence to Catholicism and an absolute fidelity to the Church. Francis mentioned neither the Cathari nor the Waldensians in his letter, but it is evident that he had in mind heterodox and anti-ecclesiastical preaching, which he tried to counteract by insisting, almost imperceptibly, on the points of Catholic doctrine. Thus, he emphasized the physical reality of the person of Christ against the docetist ideas of the Cathari regarding the Incarnation of the Word: "Through his angel, St. Gabriel, the most high Father in heaven announced this Word of the Father—so worthy, so holy and glorious—in the womb of the holy and glorious Virgin Mary, from which he received the flesh of humanity and our frailty" (v. 4). These words, read against the doctrinal milieu of their time, carry a theological value which is quite important. Along the same lines, Francis rejected the docetism of the Cathari regarding the passion of Christ, using the realistic sentence of Lk 22:24—"offered himself, through his own blood, as a sacrifice and oblation on the altar of the cross."[1]

EUCHARIST AND PRIESTHOOD

Francis' adherence to Catholicism was particularly emphasized in whatever concerned the doctrine of the Eucharist and the priesthood, two areas openly denounced by the Cathari and Waldensians.

Francis understood that, according to the teaching of Christ, no spiritual life was possible without the Eucharist. He especially loved the Gospel of John because it gives such pre-eminence to the Eucharistic discourse of Christ (6:32-72). Francis also realized that ordinarily without the sacrament of penance there would be no remission of sin. These two sacraments, Eucharist and penance, in their turn, cannot exist without the ministry of the priesthood, which is conferred through the sacrament of holy orders. It is this sacrament which gives the power to consecrate the Body and Blood of Christ and to forgive sins. The Cathari and Waldensians contested the ministerial power of unworthy (or those they considered unworthy) priests as if the power to consecrate and absolve came directly from the *vita evangelica*. Francis took up a position against this teaching and remained faithful to the Catholic stance. For him, the call and return to evangelical simplicity neither implied nor demanded rebellion against the hierarchy. Peter Waldo had also called for a return to evangelical simplicity; but, at the same time, he had felt the need to shout against Rome. Francis did not do likewise because his foundation was the gospel, in which he found, in addition to absolute poverty, the Church with her guides and pastors. He therefore exhorted his penitents to respect priests, even unworthy ones, because they alone have the power to consecrate and to forgive sins. In this context, the following salient points can be noted in the *Letter to All the Faithful*:

v. 33: "We should show respect for the clergy, *not so much for them personally, if they are sinners,* but by reason of *their office,* and their administration of the most holy Body and Blood of Christ which *they sacrifice* on the altar and who receive and administer to others."

v. 22: "... We must also confess all our sins *to a priest* and receive *from him* the Body and Blood of our Lord Jesus Christ."

v. 34: "and let all of us firmly realize that no one can be saved except through the Blood of our Lord Jesus Christ which the *priests pronounce, proclaim, and administer.* And *they alone must administer them.*"

The *Letter to All the Faithful* seeks to remove the dangers of heresy in a constructive way, while the *Memoriale propositi* seeks to avoid the same danger by a marked juridical regulation.

In the *Letter* Francis stated: "We must be Catholics . . ." (v. 32).

The *Memoriale propositi* declared that "no heretic or person in bad repute because of heresy may be admitted (to the fraternity)" (Nullus haereticus vel de haeresi diffamatus recipatur.) (n. 32).

Francis exhorted his followers to "receive . . . the Body of our Lord Jesus Christ," without determining how often; he only provided the theological reason: "He who does not eat his flesh and does not drink his blood cannot enter the kingdom of God." (v. 23), and "no one can be saved except through the Blood of our Lord Jesus Christ" (v. 34).

The *Memoriale propositi*, on the other hand, gave a specific command, in accord with the ecclesiastical discipline of that day: "They are to receive Communion at Christmas, Easter, and Pentecost" (n. 15).²

Esser observed that in "his letter, Francis not only warned of dangers, but seeks to construct. His writings do not merely contain an invitation to orthodoxy, but are an admonition and exhortation to a truly Christian life. With this, Francis presented the 'new man' that the penitent should become."³

THE NEW MAN: A) THE STATE OF PENANCE IS A JOURNEY TO GOD: B) THE SPIRIT OF LOVE

As we have already observed, once Francis entered into the Order of Penance in 1206, he must have realized very quickly that the evangelical sense of *metànoia*, as described in the first chapter, had been distorted and maintained only the external aspect, at times ostentatious and showy; the interior element of "*conversio*," a turning to God, was often lacking.

In speaking of the new ideals, aspirations, and meaning which Francis wanted to give his penitents, we can immediately mention two elements which, even singly, indicate the radical change he gave to the nature and meaning of the penitential movement:

1. Penance is not a state, but a journey that leads to God. The life of penance can no longer be regarded as something unavoidable and unnatural for man, a logical consequence of the human condition, to be accepted with a stoic spirit. On the contrary, it is spontaneous, the result of our response to the love of God, and is enlivened by his spirit. It is not something static, but dynamic in the fullest sense of the word. Before God, man must

certainly acknowledge being a creature, totally dependent on him and, at the same time, confess the infinite greatness of divinity and, by comparison, the depths of his own nothingness. At the same time, however, man also understands that his vocation is a call to greatness which can be reached by means of a continuous journey or passage towards God-likeness: "Be perfect, as your Father in heaven is perfect." This greater similarity is reached through a continuous *metànoia*, or conversion, a continual aspiration and ascent towards God.

In synthesis, the "life of penance" is a road of ascent and a means for this ascent. This is a fundamental point of spirituality for Franciscan penitents, those of yesterday as well as of today.

2. The spirit of love, which continuously grows in the heart of the penitent is a part of the new concept of the "life of penance" discovered by Francis. For him there is only one reality: God who loves on the one hand, and the whole world, including mankind, in a penitent stance in the face of this love—an attitude of absolute humility, of total recognition of the relationship between God the Creator and the world his creature. It is this relationship of love between God and man, between God and creation, which is for Francis the only light, the only reality,[4] a relationship of love which only the gospel, that is, the call to *metànoia*, makes possible. This love is augmented and deepened to the measure in which we accept and respond to it, in the measure in which we put that call to conversion into practice. Francis is the man of penance in the sense that he accepted the gospel as a message to live in the world. For him, the gospel was first of all an interior state; it gave meaning to his life and it showed him the proper attitude towards life.[5]

The consequence of these two elements is the "new man," the penitent, the follower of Francis, who lives in love because he has tasted and seen "how good is the Lord."

In this light we can also state that for Francis *facere poenitentiam* meant and implied, most of all, loving God. The *Recensio prior* gave us, right from the beginning, a basic rule in the concept of Francis: a person will only be able to find the happiness he longs for through love—"All those who love the Lord with all their heart, with all their soul, with all their mind, and with all their strength . . . how happy they are, who do these things and persevere in them." He retained the same concept in the *Letter to All the Faithful*: "How happy and blessed are those who love God and do as the Lord himself says in the gospel, 'You shall love the Lord God with all your heart and all your mind, and your neighbor as yourself" (v. 18).

This person will respond to God's call by his love, which will be manifested first of all in prayer, that is, in adoration, praise, and petition.

v. 19: "Let us love God, therefore, and *adore him* with a pure heart and a pure mind because he who seeks this above all else has said: The true worshipers *will adore* the Father in spirit and in truth."

vv. 61-62: "Let every creature in heaven, on earth, in the sea, and in the depths, *give praise*, glory, honor, and blessing to him who suffered so much for us, who has given so many good things, and (who) will (continue to) do so for the future. For he is our power and strength, he who alone is good, (who) is most high, (who is) all-powerful, admirable, (and) glorious; (who) alone is holy, *praiseworthy*, and blessed throughout endless ages. Amen."

v. 21: "And let us praise him and *pray to him* day and night saying: Our Father who art in heaven, since we should pray always and never lose heart."

The service of God will be the first and most decisive factor in the life of this person, the Franciscan penitent, who feels his whole being pervaded and moved by the love of God.

This person will also love his neighbor. Perhaps in few other ages was the love of neighbor as difficult as in the time of Francis, when society was divided by religious and social animosity.

Esser states that "love in the life of penance is fulfilled in the love of one's neighbor."[6] Francis said "and let us love our neighbors as ourselves. And if there is anyone who does not wish to love them as himself, at least let him do no harm to them, but rather do good" (vv. 26-27).

OTHER VIRTUES FOR THE PENITENT

Always based on those valid truths, that is, that life is a journey to God under the impulse of love of God and neighbor, the follower of Francis will be a penitent in spirit and practice and, as a logical consequence, will follow the final exhortation of Francis: "Let us perform worthy fruits of penance," that is, fruits corresponding to the ongoing *metànoia*. Francis did not insist predominantly on external mortification, although he did make clear reference to it in vv. 37 and 46 as well as implied it in the subjection of the material to the spiritual. He emphasized, however, those virtues which demonstrate and support the continuing interior change which can best be described as "tending towards

God" and which, in the final analysis, are identified with the two main ideas we have been treating.

Here, then, are the principal virtues suggested by Francis:

a) *Mercy*—we are reminded of "the golden rule"; judge not is a valid criterion, even for those who have the power and the duty to do so. "But those who have received the power to judge others should exercise judgment with mercy as they themselves desire to receive mercy from the Lord. For judgment will be without mercy for those who have not shown mercy" (vv. 23-29).

The person in authority should also be merciful: "The one to whom obedience has been entrusted and who is esteemed as greater should be as the lesser and the servant of the other brothers. And he should use and show mercy to each of his brothers as he would wish them to do to him were he in a similar position" (vv. 42-43).

b) *Charity and humility*—"Let us then have charity and humility" (v. 30).

c) *simplicity, humility, and purity*—"We must not be wise and prudent according to the flesh; rather, we must be simple, humble, and pure" (v. 45).

d) *servants and subject to all*—"We must never desire to be over others; rather we must be servants and subject to every human creature for God's sake" (v. 47).

3) *self-contempt*—"And let us hold ourselves in contempt and scorn, since through our own fault all of us are miserable and contemptible, vermin and worms, as the Lord says through the prophet" (v. 46).

Even when Francis exhorts his followers to external mortification, he points out the proper significance and the spiritual values which must be united to it.

f) *Almsgiving*—is recommended for its value for remission of sins and its intrinsic value of love for others. This leads to deeds which remain for eternal life: "Let us then have charity and humility; let us give alms since this washes our souls from the stains of (our) sins. For people lose everything they leave behind in this world; but they carry with them the rewards of charity and the alms which they have given, for which they will receive a reward and a suitable remuneration from the Lord" (vv. 30-31).

g) *Fasting*—"We must also fast and abstain from vices and sins and from any excess of food and drink" (v. 32).

"We must hate our bodies with (their) vices and sins, because the Lord says in the gospel: All evils, vices, and sins proceed from the heart" (v. 37).

"We must also deny ourselves and place our bodies under the yoke of service and holy obedience, as each one has promised to the Lord" (v. 40).

THE SUBLIME SPIRITUALITY OF THIS "FORMA VITAE"

The core part of the letter shows clearly that "the revolutionary demands of the *vita evangelica*—the spirit of selfishness must be killed so that the Spirit of the Lord may rest in the 'new man' and live in him forever. . . .

"What Francis says in verses 49-53 help us to penetrate into the depths of Christian mysticism which we seek in vain elsewhere. Can the Christian be given any higher ideal than this?"[7]

Esser continues: "This is the new man, the Franciscan man, who forgets himself and completely renounces himself in order to serve all people and all creatures in the Spirit of the Lord, and to do the will of God. It is this very part of the *Letter* in which the need for a radically 'christian' life becomes evident. Francis insistently asks as a normal consequence much more of his followers, the Christians *qui habitant in universo mundo* and follow him; he demands much more than the mediocre Christianity lived in the society of the times. Anyone who carefully meditates on this document and takes to heart what we have been saying, will have a clear impression of how Francis fought to bring to reality a radical form of Christianity among the laity who wanted to follow him, and how he did everything possible to bring those Christians who did live their faith to a renewal of life *secundum formam sancti Evangelii*. He pursued this plan with such dedication that the Franciscan form of life which unites the Friars Minor, the Poor Ladies, and the *Fratres et Sorores de Poenitentia* has rarely been more clearly presented than in this letter. Through the operation of the Spirit of the Lord, there results a radical change in the values of a purely natural human life which, after all, is the earthly life lived by almost all Christians in spite of the 'Sermon on the Mount' and the entire gospel.

"Of all those who would follow him, Francis demands a radical Christianity that goes against our human nature; there could be no compromise. With a surprising matter-of-factness, he takes the *spiritus carnis*, i.e., the egoistic and authoritarian 'I,' which always tries to be the center of attention, and replaces it with the 'Spiritus Domini,' living, desiring, thinking, and working according to the Spirit of the gospel. This is *metànoia*, the way that

Francis saw to *agere poenitentiam*. This is the source of penance as understood in the Franciscan sense. For this reason this work, to whomever it was addressed, can be accepted as an authentic basis for every life and aspiration within the Third Order and, most of all, as the foundation for the renewal of the order in our times."[8]

COROLLARY

"PENANCE" AS THE FUNDAMENTAL CHARACTERISTIC OF THE THIRD ORDER

Modern scholars of "penitential spirituality," still very few in numbers, point out how penance-metanoia-conversion, together with the "works of mercy" have always been and must remain the characteristic element of the spirituality of the Brothers and Sisters of Penance, that is, of the whole Franciscan Third Order.

First of all, it should be pointed out how "within the sphere of Franciscan spirituality one can identify three principal streams flowing from St. Francis, but they are distinguished from one another by their orientation," that, is, their emphasis,[9] which has become identified as the characteristic of one or the other of them. These three "streams" are identified with the three orders of St. Francis.[10]

Starting from a different perspective, one could point out that besides accepting the "dominant ideas of Franciscan spirituality" that are elements of a common patrimony, there is a store of spiritual elements that characterize each group within the sphere of the Franciscan family. For example, minority characterizes the three branches of the First Order, and penance the many congregations of the Third Order.[11]

We would be justified in trying to show how such characterization became a reality in the very beginnings of the Franciscan movement.

Shortly after the beginning of Francis' itinerant preaching, on their return from receiving the oral approval of the new fraternity from Innocent III, the rapidly growing group had to have a change in the emphasis of the characteristics by which it presented itself to the people. In their primitive preaching, before going to Rome, to those who asked them "where do you come from?" they "confessed with simplicity to be penitents from Assisi";[12] soon (we don't know exactly when) they began to call themselves "Friars Minor."

Burchard of Ursberg, as early as 1210, referred to the "Poenitentes de civitate Assisio" as *"Pauperes Minores."*[13] Jacques de Vitry, in his letter from Genoa in October 1216 clearly stated that the *"Pauperes de Assisio"* were commonly called *"Frati minori"* and the followers of St. Clare the *"Sorelle minori."*[14]

The Rule of 1221 says: "and whoever is the greater among them should become like the lesser."[15] Schmucki notes that "this passage bears all the signs of relative antiquity. Most probably it was added very early to enrich the biblical and disciplinary elements of the Proto-rule.[16] From Celano's remark in the *Vita prima* it seems that Francis was struck by the expression "they are to be minors" as soon as it was suggested and wanted it to become the actual name of his fraternity.[17]

Although Francis' understanding of "minors" is doubtlessly the evangelical one,[18] it cannot be denied that the social-political situation in Assisi, the home of the first friars, where the *maggiori* and *minori* competed for control, had some influence on Francis, causing him to decide that his followers should be called and really be "minors" by choice, without any association with the *minori* of the city in constant conflict with the *maggiori*. The novelty was quite evident: even those who were *maggiori* "in the world" voluntarily became "minori" like Francis, wanting to compete with no one.

Minority will also be the characteristic of the friar's spirituality.

Another element characteristic of the new fraternity soon developed—poverty, chosen for the love of God and "to follow in the footsteps of his Son."[19] From the moment he heard the gospel passage on the "mission of the apostles" Francis understood that the *vita evangelica* included life in poverty. Francis had practiced poverty since the first days of his conversion; now he began to understand it as an essential element of the *vocatio evangelica*.[20] The gospel passage showed Francis why and how he would have to practice poverty from then on. This very same desire to accept and put into practice the message of the gospel text is equally evident in the story of the conversion of Bernard of Quintavalle, his first companion. Heeding the advice of Francis, he "hastened therefore to sell all his goods and gave the money to the poor, though not to his parents; and laying hold to the title to the way of perfection, he carried out the counsel of the holy Gospel: If thou wilt be perfect, go, sell what thou hast, and give to the poor, and thou shalt have treasure in heaven; and come, follow me."[21]

Then follows the important remark that "his conversion to

God was a model to others in the manner of selling one's possessions and giving them to the poor."[22]

Even the short allegorical work, the *Sacrum Commercium*,[23] considered as "the testimony of the spirituality that the Franciscan community was developing right after the death of St. Francis . . . ,"[24] tells us that poverty was, from that time on, considered as a fundamental characteristic of the spirituality of the Order of Friars Minor. From the prologue on, in fact, "it affirms categorically that poverty is the most important among the various virtues that prepare the heart of man to receive God."[25]

These two elements—minority and sublime poverty—also became the two basic points for the spirituality of the Second Order, the Poor Clares; to these was added, mostly because of the ecclesiastical disciplines in force at that time, the total exclusion from the world, within a strict cloister and without any external apostolic activity; in this way the order was also characterized by the contemplative life.

Finally, it was "penance" that remained the primary characteristic of only the Order of the Brothers and Sisters of Penance. Such a characteristic has once again been found in the numerous studies on the Franciscan penitential movement.

12

THE "MEMORIALE PROPOSITI" OF 1221-1228

THE NUMERICAL GROWTH OF THE PENITENTS
AND NECESSITY OF LEGISLATION

The increase in the number of penitents following the preaching of Francis and his early companions in the period between 1210 and 1220 must have been enormous. Even if we cannot recreate the atmosphere of the times and pinpoint the impalpable elements that motivated the more committed Christians in the footsteps of the Franciscans, from what we have already observed and from the historical and social characteristics of that period, it is possible to reconstruct some of the data that helped create that phenomenon.

First of all, on the spiritual side, there was always a need for spiritual guidance that had motivated people to follow the itinerant preachers during the preceding centuries. The innate sensitivity of the Christian masses was convinced that there was something out of kilter with the gospel in the teaching of the Cathari and Waldensians who continually spoke out against the bishops and priests, preaching rebellion and de-emphasizing the sacraments. Even if these preachers actually lived the poverty that they preached, their teaching and even their lives were in contrast with the authority and teaching of the Church.

When the simple poor man of Assisi and his companions began to preach peace, harmony, love of God, and respect for priests because they have the ability to confect the Eucharist, without which, as the Gospel says, "you do not have life within you," these dedicated Christians immediately understood that his was a new message, different and true, and one that they should listen to. The life of the *Poenitentes de Assisi* was also convincing in its humility, industriousness, patience, and true poverty.

Following them in the Order of Penance meant to have secure guides and yet to remain faithful to God and to the Church.

Esser notes that "Burchard of Usberg attributes this rapid expansion (of the Friars Minor) to (their) activities against the heretics of the time, whose orthodox corrective they are."[1] The growth of the Order of Penitents can be explained in the same way. Penitents old and new entered this order because it bore Francis' stamp of catholicity. "Thus could the forces, aroused and enkindled by the religious movements of the High Middle Ages, flow freely into the Franciscan movement, just as the Lord guided them, without any 'worldly' barrier to hold them back."[2]

From the social point of view, there had been for some time certain elements that prompted a strong tendency to the "common life." From the end of the twelfth century groups of faithful had tried to form confraternities and associations based on mutual help, common life, and collective work. Their purpose was sometimes religious and sometimes economic; thus one could dedicate oneself more completely to God and/or make better provision for one's life support.[3]

We should also keep in mind the number of widows of the Crusaders who had died during the expeditions to the Orient. Common misfortune brought these women to seek one another's company and friendship, creating in this way a noticeable growth of beguinages and other groups. The common life was also a means for many to defend their rights.[4] Thus we see that following Francis in the Order of Penance also brought advantages, when viewed from a purely sociological aspect.

These elements alone would have been enough to explain the rapid growth and spread of the Order of Penance. However, since the penitents lacked any central government or administration, there were probably many variations in behavior, internal life, and external relationship, particularly their relationship to civil authority. This was reason for great concern. On the spiritual side there was a necessary concern against heresy. The preaching and propaganda of the Cathari and Waldensians was always active, especially in southern France and the large cities of northern Italy. In Lombardy and northern Italy the Poor Lombards, the Arnoldists, and the remainder of the Pataria were equally vociferous.[5] Without some kind of structure it would be very difficult for the penitents to remain in orthodoxy. They grew in number but were always "simple," uneducated people. They knew Francis' exhortations, but there was no legal apparatus that gave the movement power of control over its own members.

From our careful examination of the two versions of the *Letter to All the Faithful* we have already noticed that the *Recensio posterior* (2 *Lf*), whatever its date of composition, is a striking witness of the corrections and specifications needed in the interim to keep the *facere poenitentiam* in orthodoxy.[6]

We must also bear in mind that the first decade of the thirteenth century saw a very rapid change in the civil order and in the relationship between the *societates religiosae* and the communes where they arose. The main cause of concern for the civil authorities, along with the growing number of citizens who were tending toward these "societies" for the reasons already indicated, is that the *fraternitates* were asserting their own privileges to the civil authorities. Most important was their exemption from the obligation of pledging loyalty, bearing arms, and assuming civil positions. The first pontifical bulls, written between 1221 and 1228 in favor of the penitents, are indisputable proof; we shall treat them shortly.

It was therefore necessary to provide a legislative document for the large movement of penitents, a document that could establish some kind of compact organizational structure. This task was undertaken by Cardinal Ugolino of Segni, who had often served as papal legate in central and northern Italy and who, since 1217, had acted as Francis' advisor.

CARDINAL UGOLINO

Born in Anagni of the family of the Counts of Segni, probably in 1170, he received his early education at the bishop's school in the same city; he continued his studies in Paris and then studied law at the University of Bologna. He was a great-nephew of Innocent III, who made him a cardinal deacon in 1198 and sent him as papal legate to southern Italy. He immediately showed himself very capable in resolving diplomatic negotiations. He was made cardinal bishop of Ostia in 1206.

The following year he was sent to Germany as papal legate in the dispute between Philip, Duke of Swabia, and Otto IV of Brunswick,[7] both of whom had been elected king of Germany by opposing factions.[8] Ugolino was again in Italy in 1209.

To understand fully the cardinal's personality we must keep in mind Innocent III and the development of his line of action in regard to the religious-penitential movements and the new religious orders that were forming in those years, as we have already examined them.[9] Cardinal Ugolino would have been an integral part of that line of conduct because he lived in Rome near his uncle during those critical years. Celano informs us that the usual attitude of the cardinal was to lovingly welcome all the religious and those "particularly who loved the noble insignia of blessed poverty and holy simplicity."[10] That would seem to indicate that, along the same line as Innocent III, he had understood that the most effective weapon to defeat the supporters of the Cathari and Waldensian heresies was a support of the movement started by Francis, including the laity, who followed in the renewed Order of Penance.

Ugolino was directly involved in the preparation and direction of the Fourth Lateran Council (Nov. 11-30, 1215). Two days after the death of Innocent III, which took place in Perugia on July 16, 1216, Honorius III, Cencio Savelli, was elected there. The new pontiff, knowing and appreciating the stability and diplomatic talent of Cardinal Ugolino, made him his legate to the cities of northern Italy (1216-1219), cities which were free communes, deciding individually their relationship with the Church. Because of the independent spirit that had created their autonomy, the more important cities were also threatening the ecclesiastical privileges included in the formula *ecclesiastica libertas* and did little to prevent the spread of heresy. It was clear that some organization also had to be given to the exuberant Franciscan movement that was rapidly growing into the three principal configurations—Friars Minor, Poor Ladies, and lay penitents. Whether or not it was their first meeting, we do not know; but Francis and Ugolino definitely met in Florence in 1217. The *Legend of the Three Companions* tells us that "after the death of Cardinal John of St. Paul (1215),[11] another cardinal, Ugolino by name, then bishop of Ostia, was divinely inspired with a particular love of blessed Francis, and he took to his heart also all the friars and protected them and cared for them together with blessed Francis."[12]

Sabatier seems to have fully accepted the claim of the *Three Companions* when he wrote: "Under his successor, Honorius III, the most important personage of the curia was precisely Cardinal Ugolino. . . . He defended the Franciscan movement which was violently attacked on many sides, ending up by exercising with unfailing zeal the job of protector of the order, a long time before he was officially given the appointment."[13] Even though we know that Cardinal Ugolino became the official protector of Franciscanism only in 1220, we can believe the claim of the *Three Companions* if we see that at the meeting in Florence Ugolino's authority over Francis was such as to dissuade the saint from going to France when he had been determined to do so. There is no doubt that in this meeting in Florence they spoke about the necessity of giving a legislative organization to the three branches of the Franciscan movement. This is the only way to explain what took place in the legislative area in three short years—the Rule for the Poor Ladies of 1219, the *Regola non bollata* for the Friars Minor in 1221, and the *Memoriale propositi* for the lay penitents in the same year.

Francis' absence from Italy (June 1219, spring-summer 1220) brought about much confusion within the movement itself.[14] For this Francis was authoritatively "invited" to present himself to Cardinal Ugolino as soon as he returned from the Orient, which explains why he landed at Venice instead of Brindisi, since Ugolino was waiting for him in Bologna. In this meeting in Bologna there may have been a clash. Francis was strongly urged to prepare legislative texts immediately; thus the "earlier rule" came into being. It may have been at this time that Francis prepared the later version of the *Letter to All the Faithful* for the lay penitents. Cardinal Ugolino himself would have been the one to convert the main lines into legislative style, basing them on the ancient legislative norms for the penitents and the more recent ones regarding the Umiliati (1201), the Poor Catholics (1208), and the Poor Lombards (1212).

CARDINAL UGOLINO AND THE "MEMORIALE PROPOSITI"

Ugolino's juridical-editorial collaboration in the preparation of these rules is affirmed by Bernard of Bessa[15] and has been historically accepted. His collaboration is also claimed by the anonymous author of the *Vita di Papa Gregori IX*,[16] an important fact that has often been overlooked. For this author, Ugolino's organizational share in the work of the provision of the rule for the Poor Clares and the penitents was so great as to make him claim that the cardinal was the founder of these two orders: "In the period in which he was bishop of Ostia, Ugolino founded and brought to completion the new orders of the Brothers of Penance and of the Sisters Recluse."[17] If, by the expression "Sisters Recluse" we understand the Poor Clares,[18] the author must have been prompted to make this exaggerated claim by the accepted fact that in 1219 Cardinal Ugolino gave the community of Poor Clares the rule that later became known under his name.

When, around 1240 the author of the *Vita* wrote this, the only rule in effect for the Poor Clares,[19] other than the *ordinationes propriae* in force only in San Damiano, was the rule of Cardinal Ugolino.[20] Thus, the claim that Cardinal Ugolino "founded and completed" the Order of the Brothers of Penance as well, probably rests on the claim that he prepared a rule for them too.

In 1221 Cardinal Ugolino was at his peak. Guido Levi writes in his Preface of the *Registri of Cardinal Ugolino* that "in 1221 he left on the new mission assigned him by Honorius III, strong in the trust of the pope and of the emperor, and already efficient in negotiating because of the experience he had had in the previous missions entrusted to him in Germany (1207-1209) and in Lombardy (1216-1219). His guide was the legislation of the Lateran Council which was taking on new vigor because Frederick II, by receiving the Cross of the Crusade together with the imperial crown from the hands of the bishop of Ostia, had also strengthened by his sanctions the laws against heresy and against the attacks on ecclesiastical liberty."[21] "The main points of the mission assigned to the cardinal" were "the preaching and preparations for the Crusade, the pacification of every disagreement that would impede the unanimous progress of the undertaking, the protection of the privileges of the Church and of the clergy, and the uprooting of heresy."[22]

This reconstruction of the aims of the work of Cardinal Ugolino in the year 1221 sheds great light, we believe, on the nature and purpose of the same *Memoriale propositi*. In preparing it, probably with the help of his collaborators, Cardinal Ugolino had to keep in mind the traditional legislation of public penitence which was also included in the *Decretum Gratiani*[23] he would surely have studied at Bologna, and the *Propositum* from the beginnings of the century;[24] he probably had even had a personal hand in the composition and editing of these latter documents, since he was so close to Innocent III who had approved them.

THE MEMORIALE PROPOSITI

The *Memoriale propositi* of 1221 is no longer extant as it must have come from the hands of Francis, Ugolino, and, perhaps, some of his jurists. The earliest extant copy is that of the final edition of 1228, practically identical in the various codices discovered between 1901 and now. The best-known version is the first one to be discovered, the text found by Paul Sabatier in 1901 in the Franciscan monastery of Capistrano (L'Aquila),[25] in one of the codices of St. John Capistrano, and published by Sabatier in his *Opuscules de critique historique*.²⁶ Its title is "Memoriale propositi fratrum et sororum de Poenitentia in Domibus propriis existentium inceptum anno Domini MCCXXI tempore domini Gregorii noni papae III Cal. Iunii indictione prima tale est."²⁷ (The document of the way of life of the Brothers and Sisters of Penance who live in their own homes, begun in the year 1221 at the time of Pope Gregory IX, May 20, 1228, according to which those who promise to live do so, contains the following content.)²⁸

This text of 1228 probably represents an evolution, although we do not know how great a one, from the text of 1221.²⁹ One of the substantial modifications was certainly regarding "the oath." Number 17 of the *Memoriale* reads:

"All are to refrain from formal oaths unless where necessity compels, in the cases excepted by the sovereign pontiff in his indult, that is, for peace, for the faith, under calumny, and in bearing witness."³⁰ The phraseology clearly refers to and is taken directly from the bull *Detestanda* of Gregory IX (May 21, 1227), in which we read: "Nobis humiliter supplicastis, ut vobis indulgere misericorditer dignaremur ne aliquod iuramentum, nisi forsan paci et fidei, calumnie vel testimonii, facere teneamini."³¹ According to the statement of the pontiff, the penitents themselves had asked him, contrary to the usual total prohibition of oath taking, to be subject to the obligation of oath in those four cases. It seems that there is a spirit of accommodation on the part of the penitents, who wish to avoid a total frontal clash with the civil authorities.

A quick overview of the contents of the *Memoriale propositi* shows us that;

The organization of the Order of Penance and its insertion into society are based on an austere principle of personal sanctification.

The rule is strict and demands vocation and dedication. The law of poverty, as we have seen, the foundation of the whole penitential movement of the eleventh-through thirteenth centuries, contradicts the "worldly" life because *conversio* demands a renunciation "of the world." Humility in dress and abstention from entertainment and dancing, abstinence and fasting, prayer and frequent reception of the sacraments, examination of conscience and religious instruction of the Brothers and Sisters of Penance are fundamental characteristics of their identity.

Like the other two Franciscan orders, the Third Order is "the school of the gospel" and demands adherence to it of thought and action.

Most of all, it demands a life of prayer and more intense sacramental life than is asked of "plain Christians." Those who know how to read will say the canonical hours, as clerics do, and the others will say the office of the *Paters* and *Aves*. All will nourish spiritual growth through daily examination of conscience and monthly instruction.

On these spiritual foundations the Brothers and Sisters of Penance will carry out in a very special way the main Christian virtues, beginning with justice and charity.

They will give back what the law requires, make a will immediately to avoid quarrels among their heirs, make peace with their neighbors, cultivate good relations with others, be peaceful and bear peace rather than arms.

Charity shall be carried out beginning with the members of the fraternity, brethren infirm in body or soul, in need of prayer and tactful advice, and special suffrages for the dead. From the offering that each penitent would bring to the monthly meetings and instruction, a form of charity fund will be formed that would eventually lead to a series of uninterrupted charitable activities such as those in hospitals, hospices, and all kinds of institutions; from these grew the charitable work of the Franciscan tertiaries on behalf of the lowly, needy, and suffering in every nation throughout history.[32]

"From the roots of a profound and vigorous personal sanctity the Order of Penitents who neither left their homes nor went far from them, spread across the known world; this school of the gospel was beneficial and fruitful in the life of the times."[33]

THE APPROVAL OF THE MEMORIALE PROPOSITI

Was there an approval, implicit or explicit, of this rule? By which pontiff?

Both the *Legend of the Three Companions* and the *Anonymus Perusinus* affirm that there was an approval of the organization of the Order of Penance and its legislation. After recounting the foundation of the three orders by St. Francis, the *Three Companions* states: "His three distinct orders were each in due time approved by the sovereign pontiff."[34] The *Anonymus Perusinus* ends the story by claiming that "the brothers instituted an order for them.... It is called the Order of Penitents. They had it confirmed by the supreme pontiff."[35]

Unfortunately Franciscan history has not yet been able to single out the document or series of documents that the biographers of the thirteenth century considered as "official approval" of the Order of the Penitents of blessed Francis, although it is exclusively to this order that the *Legend of the Three Companions* and the *Anonymus Perusinus* are referring.

Many authors admit of an "oral approval" of the primitive *forma vitae* of the penitents by Honorius III; this oral approval usually refers to the *forma* of St. Francis, not to the *Memoriale propositi* in any form known to us.[36] Such a premise is based mostly on some expressions used by Gregory IX, successor to Honorius III, in 1227. The expressions concerned are contained in the bull *Detestanda* (May 21, 1227) addressed to the "universis fratribus dictis de Poenitentia per Italiam constitutis." In it we read that "Our predecessor, Pope Honorius of happy memory, noting how you who do fruitful penance were opposed with indescribable difficulties by the sons of this world, and were therefore deserving to be helped in your praiseworthy conduct, defending your order in the charity of Jesus Christ, treated it with particular favors (*gratia speciali*), commanding all the bishops and archbishops of Italy to defend your immunity from taking oath, etc."[37] For the aforementioned authors, these words imply at least an oral approval.

There is also a dispute concerning the approval by Gregory IX. Some historians continue to insist that the *Memoriale* did not receive official approval in 1228. At the same time, however, we cannot overlook the fact that the words *tale est* which precede the legislative text were the usual formula the popes used to introduce a *Propositum* that they approved with a papal bull.[38]

It is also generally accepted that the extant *Memoriale propositi* is not identical to the original one of 1221. As we have seen, it obviously underwent modifications and additions from 1221-1228. It is, however, equally well-known that, from 1228 on the *Memoriale propositi* "was considered an unchangeable rule, one that should not be touched, in the same way as the rules of St. Augustine and St. Benedict. . . . After 1228 the penitents were content, as were the Minors after 1223, to accompany their rule with a commentary on the less clear passages."[39] In fact, all the examples of the *Memoriale* found until the present time are substantially identical.

What happened, therefore, in 1228 that was so important that it made the "rule" stable and unchangeable?

Meersseman observed that "the voluntary penitential state had always been acknowledged. The *Memoriale* that expressed the obligations (of this state) did not, therefore, have to be solemnly approved. By this date the Holy See had already confirmed the essential privileges inherent to that state (with bulls 1-5)."[40]

There still remains the question of why, only after 1228, the *Memoriale* was considered unchangeable. The question is not yet resolved.[41]

13

THE PENITENTS FROM 1221 TO 1289

THE "FRANCISCAN" SENSE OF SOME
PAPAL DOCUMENTS, 1220-1230

Between 1221 and 1227 we have five important papal documents, usually directed to the bishops and prelates of Italy and dealing with problems concerning the "Brothers of Penance." One of these is addressed to "All the Brothers called of Penance."[1]

The first of these documents is the bull *Significatum est nobis* (Dec. 16, 1221) of Honorius III, in which he orders the bishop of Rimini to protect the penitents of Faenza and the surrounding area against the oppression of the magistrates who were obliging them to take the oath, bear arms, and "to follow them (in war) when asked."[2]

The bull *Cum illorum* of the same pontiff, dated December 1, 1225, notifies the bishops and prelates of Italy of the exemption from interdict which the Brothers of Penance enjoy.[3]

In 1226 (or 1227—"the twelfth year of our pontificate") the bull *Ad audientiam nostram* of Honorius III orders the bishops of Italy to protect the penitents against the authorities who obliged them to fulfil military service or to exercise public office and imposed many taxes on them.[4]

The fourth bull is *Detestanda* of Pope Gregory IX (May 21, 1227) sent to "all the aforementioned Brothers of Penance." It specifies that the penitents are not required to take oaths except in the four specific cases; that they cannot be taxed more than other citizens because of the fact that they are exempt from military service; that they may use the fruit of their goods for pious works; and that they cannot be punished because of the debts or crimes of their fellow citizens.[5]

The fifth bull is *Nimis patenter* of the same pontiff, May 26, 1227, in which the whole Italian episcopate is ordered to protect the penitents against the authorities who were demanding service, oathtaking, holding public office, and even daring to recall to their homes, through taxes or multiple obligations, "those who do penance and have retired to live in seclusion."[6]

A large interpretative tradition, Franciscan and non-Franciscan alike, has for centuries considered these documents as directed or related to the "Franciscan Order of Penance."[7] Meersseman has recently contested that attribution, not only negating the "Franciscan exclusivity" with which they have been interpreted, but even excluding all reference to the Franciscan Order of Penance, and in turn attributing them almost exclusively to the ancient "Order of Penance."[8]

We are of the opinion that the question of the documents cannot be solved by internal criticism, but through their study within the historical milieu in which they were written. That is, only a careful reconstruction of the "atmosphere" of that time and the characteristics of the penitential movement in that period can give us sufficient indications to solve the dispute.

We must first of all keep in mind the renewed spiritual fervor caused by the person of Francis of Assisi, and by his preaching and that of his friars. In this we must pay particular attention to the non-Franciscan sources, those that are exempt from the temptation to glorify Francis for their own interest; we must follow the example of Sabatier and Esser in this regard.[9] These witnesses, such as Burchard of Ursberg,[10] and Jacques de Vitry,[11] are the most reliable and authoritative. From them we see that "the religious ideals to which the authentic Christians of the age aspired, too often betrayed by the heretical interpretations, took form in Francis and his order. In them the authentic faith was revived. Their style of life represented the pure ideal of perfect Christian life."[12] "In Francis appeared . . . the sign . . . of an authentic apostolic life, like that the heretics also wanted, but, unlike them, integrally Catholic."[13] The penitents entered into this atmosphere. Who were the *poenitentes* of the papal bulls? Only a false historical criticism could claim that they were not predominantly *Poenitentes b. Francisci*. In fact:

a) "The sudden numerical growth" of the penitents in the Italian urban centers around the year 1215 that the documents certify "is attributed to St. Francis of Assisi."[14]

b) The origin of the first rules of the penitents, after the various *proposita* of the first decade of the thirteenth century, always refers to the time and circumstances of the earliest Franciscan preaching. The very same Meersseman posits the composition of the first rule or *propositum* for the penitents,[15] which he tries to reconstruct, as around 1215, in conjunction with the religious rebirth which historians refer to as the "penitential movement of the thirteenth century," or "the penitential movement caused by St. Francis."[16] "By this time the penitential preaching of St. Francis and his companions . . . had produced the well-known result: many married people had embraced the canonical state of voluntary penance *in domibus suis* and in every city or village where these penitents were sufficiently large in number, they founded a local fraternity, in the style of the ancient confraternities."[17] If by the term "Franciscan penitents" we mean Christians who entered the "Order of Penance" under the exhortation, guidance, teaching, and ideals of St. Francis and his companions, we do not see how these penitents can be classified as other than "Franciscan."

c) Likewise, the same scholar relates the *Memoriale propositi* of 1221-1228 to the Franciscan penitential movement: "In 1221 the fraternities of the Romagna, scene of the first apostolic journeys of the companions of Francis, adopted a common statute entitled *Memoriale propositi*."[18]

d) The various groups of penitential fraternities, known toward the end of the twelfth century, with the advent of Franciscanism and its consequent penitential movement either retained their own characteristics and specific name or they disappeared entirely, most certainly absorbed by the renewed penitential movement, that is, the "Franciscan" one.

In conclusion, speaking of the development of the penitents within the period of 1221-1289 and the relative questions, we should avoid two extreme positions:

1) On the one hand, those who would like to believe that by this time all penitents were Franciscan. It is they, in fact, who have generally held that these papal documents were "exclusively Franciscan."[19]

2) Those who, on the other hand, do not admit to any institution of an Order of Penance by St. Francis[20] or who claim that the Third Order "became Franciscan with the rule of Nicholas IV."[21]

Concerning the first position we must admit that the *Ordo Poenitentiae* was not the only organism of penitential orientation in the thirteenth century. Among the other groups we must include the Umiliati who for the whole century, especially in Lombardy and the surrounding area, share the preference of the Christian people with the penitents.[22] From 1248 on, there are the *Fratres de Poenitentia Iesu Christi* of Hugh of Digne;[23] in the area around Siena there are the "Friars Servants of Mary," begun around the year 1233, who "can be considered the projection" of the "lay penitential movement developed in Italy with the Brothers and Sisters of Penance."[24] In addition to these, there were large groups, each having its own characteristics; there were various spontaneous local religious associations of lay origins, mostly called "Confraternities."[25] There are also isolated penitents who continued to profess and follow some form of penitential life as it was already well defined since the tenth century. In all the areas of Italy and Europe studied in recent years[26] we can find *conversi*, oblates, and recluses living near monasteries and convents throughout the entire thirteenth century.[27]

However, in looking at the events towards the end of the century, mainly at the codification of a "Franciscan" rule for a "Third Order" that claimed to be founded by Francis, we must admit that the pole of attraction for the penitents throughout the thirteenth century was prevalently, and increasingly so, the ideal of St. Francis. In 1289 Pope Nicholas IV did nothing more than codify a pre-existing reality, so much so that the resistance to his changes were few and quickly overcome.

Concerning the second position, we must once again consider the claims of Julian of Speyer and St. Bonaventure.[28] Any judgment on St. Francis' "creation" of an order of penance cannot avoid dealing with these clear "narrative documents."

THE INTERNAL LIFE OF THE FRATERNITIES AND THE "FRANCISCAN EVOLUTION"[29]

The internal life of the fraternities of penitents that were becoming ever more numerous in the cities of Italy from 1215 on was soon to be regulated by the *Memoriale propositi*, whose norms, after all, followed for the most part the same lines as the preceding legislation.

For each fraternity the *Memoriale* prescribed, in addition to personal attitudes and acts (laws on dress, fasting, sacraments, etc.), certain collective actions such as the monthly meetings, and regulated a communal life that involved the presence of certain persons such as the minister, the visitator, and the "suitable person" for instruction.

Since the fraternity was, for the most part, constituted of persons living *in domibus propriis* and therefore in various parts of the city, it met for its monthly meeting in a church "chosen by its ministers . . . , and they had the hour and place of the meeting announced by the nuntius of the fraternity, who notified all the members by visiting each one in his own home."[30] When there was more than one fraternity of penitents in a larger city, it became normal for each one to meet in a neighborhood church or an area most convenient for the members of each fraternity. When the fraternities were in a parochial territory, they would meet in the parish church. We must bear in mind that the fraternities grew most of all because of the preaching of the Franciscans, and this element had influenced the development of the characteristics of the penitents. When, towards the middle of the century, owing to the increasing clericalization of the Friars Minor, the Franciscans began to have their own churches, it became natural for the meetings of the fraternities to be held mainly in them.

As early as 1227 the Friars had received the church of St. Donatus in Bassano, in 1228 the church of Santa Croce in Florence. The *Bullarium Franciscanum* reports the concession of eight churches to the Friars Minor during the papacy of Gregory IX.[31] It is generally accepted, however, that only a very small part of these concessions are included in the famous Franciscan collection. Moreover, in 1240, with the bull *Quoniam ut ait,* Gregory IX granted indulgences to the faithful who gave offerings for the building of churches and houses of the Friars Minor. This bull was repeated at least thirty-eight times, for similar reasons, during the pontificate of Innocent IV.[32]

These facts must be considered together with many other factors that illustrate the favor and sympathy of the papacy for the Order of Friars Minor—elements which must have been overlooked by those who deny or are surprised by the attraction that the friars had for the penitents.

As early as 1230 Pope Gregory IX, writing to the patriarchs of Antioch and Jerusalem and to "all the prelates who would have read . . ." the bull to receive the Friars Minor into their territory, to permit them to have their own oratory and to preach in the parish churches (if the preachers had been approved as *viros idoneos* [suitable men] by their ministers).[33] The papacy had begun to see in the friars those *viros idoneos* to whom Innocent III had already appealed in the struggle against heresy[34] and who were sent forth in 1215 by the Lateran Council as "necessary to preach the word of God."[35]

In the bulls *Nimis iniqua* and *Nimis prava* of 1231 the pope chided the prelates to whom the letters were addressed because they had put restrictions on the preaching of the friars, and on their possession of oratories where they could recite the "divine office."[36]

In 1234 Gregory IX recommended the Friars Minor to the prelates as "apostles who preach the word of God" and reminded them that, receiving them as prophets even they, the prelates, would receive the reward of the prophet.[37] Even higher praise and recommendations were expressed in the bull *Quoniam abundavit* (1237) in which the pope recommended the friars to the prelates of the entire Church "by the reverence one must have for God and the Holy See."[38] Therefore they should not "impede the faithful from attending the sermons of the friars or from confessing to the priests among them."[39] The pope came to the point of asking the prelates to cooperate with the friars so that the fruit of their ministry could be more easily obtained. Landini concluded that "this bull clearly assigns the Friars Minor the task of being co-workers of the bishops by preaching against heretics and hearing the confessions of the faithful."[40]

"Gregory IX not only found the Friars Minor to be a salutary answer to the spiritual problems of the Church, but he also employed the order's priests and learned men as apostolic visitators, mediators in disputes, preachers of crusades, legates, and inquisitors."[41]

Pope Innocent IV (1243-1254) continued along the same lines as his predecessor, favoring in every way the Friars Minor, at least until the bull *Etsi animarum*, dated only one month before his death. He defended the privileges already conceded to them and granted others. Thus, the bull *Nimis iniqua* of Gregory IX[42] was re-promulgated at least five times in a brief span of time against bishops of as many regions. Among the new privileges granted the friars was a very important one—to be allowed to bury in their churches the faithful who had requested so, either due to devotion or a will. This was granted with the bull *Cum a nobis*, February 25, 1250.[43] Two months later "the churches of the friars to which a convent was attached received the title of 'conventual church' (*ecclesia conventualis*). To such conventual churches went many privileges, one of them being burial rights together with cemeteries."[44]

In order to understand the practical importance of such privileges, it is sufficient to remember the special "popular spirituality" of the time: to be buried in the churches of the friars meant to participate—for as long as the soul required—in the merits of their Masses and prayers. It is obvious that one practical way to be buried in such churches was to be a part of the fraternity of penitents connected with them.

It was more than natural, therefore, that the penitents followed the friars ever more closely. Affiliation with them was also a guarantee for a privileged place in the Church. This explains how, towards the end of the century, Nicholas IV found before him an *Ordo Poenitentiae* that he not only defined as "Franciscan," but which he could say was "founded by St. Francis."

THE "VIR RELIGIOSUS" AND THE VISITATOR

According to the norms of the *Memoriale propositi*, at their monthly meetings, the fraternities of the penitents, "if it be convenient at the time, . . . are to have some religious who is informed in the words of God to exhort them and strengthen them to persevere in their penance and in performing the works of mercy."[45]

This was a basic requirement of the Order of Penance that merits our closer attention. We have already noted the consistency of the teaching of Ratherius of Verona.[46] This disposition will be repeated almost literally in the Rule of Nicholas IV (1289) and in the rules that have followed it, for both the Secular and Regular branches of the Third Order.[47] It must therefore be regarded as a norm that even today touches the essence of the spirituality of the Franciscan family. "These two subjects, persevering in penance and mercy, or active charity, represent and summarize" in the opinion of Matanić, "the specific aims of the *Ordo Poenitentium*, constituting its *raison d'etre* in the ecclesiastical community."[48]

The *Memoriale* did not specify who should be the *"vir religiosus"* to exercise the task of exhorting and strengthening the penitents, nor how he should be chosen or elected. It is understandable, however, that since the fraternity, as well as the whole Christian population, ultimately rely on the pastoral direction of the ordinary of the diocese for all their spiritual needs,[49] it was his duty to assign the task. The ordinary could have chosen him from among the diocesan clergy as well as from any one of the religious orders in his diocese. Even on this point there could well have been some natural evolution, according to the situation we have already described. In the beginning diocesan priests were more frequently chosen; as the Order of Friars Minor grew in numbers and importance, the bishop often found it more suitable, convenient, and efficient to name one of them. It almost became natural when the fraternity was in the area of a Franciscan church.

The *Memoriale* also provided for the presence of a visitator for the fraternity.[50] A careful study of the various articles concerning the topic shows us that the visitator is the supreme and final authority in all that concerns the spiritual and juridical development of the fraternity. On this matter the *Memoriale* once again does not specify how or by whom the visitator is appointed, nor whether he is a cleric or layman, or how long he should fulfil this function. Always keeping in mind that the juridical and moral life of the fraternity was under the jurisdiction and responsibility of the bishop, we must suppose that the choice of the visitator must have been at the discretion of the bishop. This supposition, however, was not always followed by the penitents; there are cases where they elected their own visitators. This probably caused disagreement with the bishop and the Friars Minor. The problem was finally resolved in the Rule of Nicholas IV; an earlier rule, the *Regola di Fra Caro* (Rule of Friar Caro) specified that the visitator was to be a priest of an order approved by the Church (*sacerdos alicuis approbatae religionis*). To this Nicholas added the precept that the visitator should be taken from the Order of Friars Minor because the "present form of life (of the penitents) was instituted by blessed Francis."[51]

THE PENITENTS AND THE CIVIL AUTHORITIES

The privileges and exemptions of the penitents had been gradually defined and specified throughout the centuries. By the thirteenth century they were recognized by common law throughout Europe because the "penitents were considered ecclesiastical persons.... The right to bear arms was not only prohibited to the reconciled penitents, but also for the voluntary penitents. They were therefore exempt from military service; and when the civil authorities tried to oblige them to take up arms, it was the job of the bishop to protect them against such oppression. The penitents were exempt from any public office or function as well; therefore the bishop had to prevent the municipalities from bothering them and trying to enforce their acceptance of such jobs."[52]

Generally, the civil authorities aware of the power, not exclusively spiritual, of the Church, recognized these privileges and exemptions. "Bishops, abbots, lord, and magistrates, in order to have the collaboration of the voluntary penitents, guaranteed the recognition of their '*status religiosus et ecclesiasticus,*' in effect granting them the '*immunitates*' given to '*piis locis et ecclesiasticis personis*' from duties of a political, organizational, administrative, or military nature, provided that they wear the habit of penance. This immunity, linked to the habit of penance, was also confirmed by Frederick II in 1220."[53]

There were also, however, frequent cases where the civil authorities seemed to forget the privileges and exemptions of the penitents and dealt harshly with them. One must keep in mind, on the other hand, that the civil authorities understood this opposition to bearing arms as a claim of some kind of ecclesiastical privilege; for those who wanted to avoid military service, it even provided a sufficient motive for embracing the penitential state. The exemption from service in the *militia* and from public office . . . was often a source of irritation within the cities."[54]

Another point of controversy was the "oath of loyalty." We must remember that the promise of fealty, by which the subject swore to follow the "lord" "in peace and war" was considered the foundation of the social order. It was the counterpart asked of the subjects for the lord's pledge of protection. Beginning in the second half of the twelfth century, when the feudal system was gradually replaced by the "independent communes," the cities also felt that they needed a promise of unity and loyalty from their subjects if they were to last. This was even more important than before, because the communes were not supported by the defenses and assistance of the empire. On the contrary, they were often required to defend themselves against it.

The penitents, however, refused to take the oath. Even though there was no prohibition against the oath in the penitential legislation, the penitents understood that they could not swear to "follow the civil authority in peace and war" when they could not take up arms. Some penitential movements developed such as aversion to oaths, that they believed that the taking of any oath, in any circumstance, was illicit and sinful. Such was the case of the Poor Lombards whose position, which was recited in their profession of faith, is explicitly mentioned in the bull *Cum inaestimabile* (June 14, 1210), by which they were readmitted to communion with the Church.[54a]

The bulls mentioned at the beginning of this chapter are examples of the disagreements between fraternities or groups of penitents and the civil authorities. These same bulls were restated many times throughout the thirteenth century, which indicates that the difficulties continues for quite some time.

RELATIONS BETWEEN PENITENTS AND THE FRIARS MINOR

Considering what has been said about the Franciscan ideals as a pole of attraction for the penitents and about the prestige and advantages one could have by being affiliated with the Friars Minor, it would seem logical that the relationship would run smoothly. Documents, however, tell us otherwise.

The most significant bull is *Vota devotorum* of Pope Innocent IV. In this letter of June 13, 1247, the pope ordered the provincial ministers of the Friars Minor in Italy to take an interest in the penitents. Assuming that this order meant that the ministers were not doing so, we must ask ourselves why. It is not difficult to find a probable cause in the behavior of the laity as we know from other sources about the penitents. The first reason is that a certain independent spirit had been growing in the laity for some time.

We can establish that, beginning with the time of the Gregorian reform, there are signs of a "reaction against a certain inferiority complex" on the part of the laity regarding the clergy. This probably increased as the number and quality of penitents did, as well as a spirit of independence or self-direction in the spiritual life. This spirit became even more noticeable in the thirteenth century. Meersseman wrote that "at first they had been hampered by their ignorance of Latin. As greater numbers of them learned to read and write, to manage their affairs better, and to participate more actively in the government of the commune, they wanted to become like "clerics" while remaining "laymen." Many of them also desired to live a more intense religious life, following the example of the mendicants, but as married laity, remaining in their own homes. . . . A saint as their founder (St. Francis) was convenient for them, because it enhanced their prestige; but submission to a clerical order, even one founded by the same saint, was not at all to their liking."[55]

The two contrasting elements (attraction to the Friars Minor, held in highest esteem by the Apostolic See and natural possessors of the Franciscan ideals, contrasted with their desire for independence) help to explain the less than ideal relationship between the penitents and the friars.

This independent spirit sometimes caused the penitents to elect their own visitator rather than ask the bishop for one, which seemed rather unorthodox and eventually put them in conflict with the bishops.

The other important element involved was the conflict between the penitents and the civil authorities. Taking the side of the penitents or defending them would have involved the friars in the disputes as well.

For these reasons (and perhaps some others we cannot identify), after the generalate of Brother Elias (1227-1239) the Friars Minor began to be less involved in the fraternities of the penitents.[56] Pope Innocent IV tried to remedy this with the bull *Vota devotorum* in which, as we have seen, he commanded the provincial ministers of Italy and Sicily to exercise the office of visitator of the penitents, either personally or through friars who were suited for the task; the purposes and powers listed are practically identical to those established in the *Memoriale propositi*. The pontiff also said that he had come to such a decision because of a direct request of the same penitents (*eorum precibus annuentes*).[57]

In August of the same year he repeated the same letter, addressing it to the provincial ministers of Lombardy, presently in Northern Italy.[58] A month later the pontiff increased the power of the provincial ministers of "Italy and the kingdom of Sicily," granting them the power of absolving from excommunication those penitents who incurred such a penalty for siding with the "deposed" emperor, Frederick II. However, not all penitents were happy with these pontifical arrangements. The most vociferous against them were the penitents of Lombardy. In fact, a year later, on November 10, 1248, in the bull *Licet vos*, addressed to the "Brothers of Penance of the Province of Lombardy," he revoked in effect all the concessions he had granted the year before, commanding them to remain humbly subject to their bishops in everything, especially in that which pertained to the office of visitator.[59] From the bull we learn that not only were the penitents of northern Italy in disagreement with those of southern Italy and Sicily in presenting the request that had elicited the *Vota devotorum*, but they knew nothing about it (*vobis, ut asseritis, insciis*).

In 1251 the bishop of Florence was notified of a similar repeal and, due to a request of the penitents of the city, he was granted the power to exercise the office of visitator "by apostolic authority."[60]

Towards the middle of the century, therefore, the office of visitator was once again exercised by the bishops or their delegates.

Concerning the disinterest of the Friars Minor during this

period, and the reasons for it, we turn to the famous passage of the work *Determinationes quaestionum*. This work, written around 1266, has been traditionally attributed to St. Bonaventure. Modern criticism has disputed this claim, even though the work is included in the saint's *Opera Omnia*.[61] Even if the attribution is false, the writing does reflect the reality of the situation. Roggen notes that "in synthesis (the author) claims that the Order of Friars Minor did not want to compromise itself by becoming involved in a movement whose orthodoxy they were unsure of, or whose organization was insufficient and could endanger its friars if (they became) directly involved."[62]

Things, however, slowly evolved towards better relations between the friars and the penitents; the climate which we have examined before probably was an important factor. Bernard of Bessa, writing after 1278, noted that "in the beginning a friar was assigned to the penitents as minister, but today they are directed by their own ministers, in such a way, however, as to be sustained with advice and help of the Friars Minor, as we are brethren and sons of the same Father."[63]

In 1289, as we have seen, Nicholas IV established (first advising, and later decreeing) that the visitator of the penitents, now known as tertiaries, would be a Friar Minor.

From Florence we have vast documentation of a fraternity of penitents who, for a great part of the thirteenth century, had been associated with the Friars Preacher, the Dominicans, and not the Friars Minor. The case has been amply illustrated by Meersseman.[64] The birth of this fraternity in close relationship with the Dominicans can probably be attributed to the almost simultaneous arrival of the Friars Minor and Friars Preacher in the city. The Franciscans arrived around 1220 and were first received at the Hospital of San Gallo and soon spread to the urban area at Santa Croce. The Dominicans, who had arrived in 1219, gathered near the (then) small church of Santa Maria Novella.

The penitents pre-dated both groups of mendicants, and approached one or other of the orders, depending on where they lived. Soon two distinct fraternities were established. As time passed, the usual neighborhood rivalries and diverging interests made the two fraternities take different paths, sometimes openly contrasting with one another. It eventually reached the point that even the color of the penitential habit was different: the "Franciscans" kept the traditional gray habit, while the "Dominican" group adopted a black one.[65] The development of events is strictly linked with the person of "Friar Caro," and his rule.

FRIAR CARO OF AREZZO

Friar Caro of Arezzo, not to be confused with Friar Claro of Florence (documents speak of him from 1250-1261),[66] was guardian or custos of the Friars Minor in Florence around the years 1280-1284. Along with a Friar Bartolomeo he was inquisitor for Tuscany.[67]

Our main source of documentation on Caro's activity is a letter of Pope Martin IV, December 13, 1284, addressed to the bishop of Florence and to the other ecclesiastics.[68] From it we know that Caro had made a canonical visitation to the Florentine penitents, claiming to have done so under "apostolic authority."[69] In his "visit" Caro had tried to bring unity to the penitents who had been so long divided into the "black" and "gray" groups. To ensure this unity, Friar Caro considered it advisable to impose the gray habit on all Florentine penitents. Many "black" penitents refused to obey. One of them in particular, Manetto di Cambio, not only refused to obey, but protested loudly, claiming that Friar Caro's action was *contra iustitiam* and appealed to the pope. Friar Caro, ignoring the appeal (*huiusmodi appellatione contempta*), issued a sentence of excommunication against him. The pope's letter was in reply to Manetto's appeal. The letter authorizes the bishop of Florence and two ecclesiastics of Lucca to conduct an inquiry on the matter; unfortunately, we do not know the results.[70]

From the canonical visit of Friar Caro, however, was born a new edition of the *Memoriale*, the "Rule of Friar Caro." We do not know the real author of this rule, or which jurists may have helped Friar Caro. From the precision of the document, however, we must deduce that it was the work of very able jurists. This is the rule which, with some important changes, was approved by Nicholas IV, thus becoming the "Regula bullata" of the Franciscan Third Order.

THE RULE OF NICHOLAS IV (1289)

Shortly after his election to the papacy (Feb. 15, 1288) Nicholas IV, Friar Jerome Masci of Ascoli Piceno, former minister general of the Friars Minor, received requests for an official approval of the rule of the *Poenitentes b. Francisci*. These requests must have come from several parties, for we have explicit reference to at least two of them.

The first request we have comes from the documentation of a "general chapter" of the penitents held in Bologna in November of 1289, three months after the promulgation of the new rule.[71] In the minutes of the chapter all are ordered to remember in their prayers "the providential Ugolino de'Medici of Ferrara, who had worked so hard for the approval of our rule at the papal curia."[72]

The second request came from the Franciscan penitents of Toulouse who had been living in community at least since 1287 when "an illustrious benefactor..., Bartholomew Bechin or Bequin, put a large house at the disposal of these fervent tertiaries who asked Nicholas IV for an official confirmation of the rule of the Franciscan Third Order. In 1289, in answer to their appeal, they received the text of the apostolic constitution *Supra montem*, an original of which was kept in the conventual archives of Our Lady of Peace, a house rebuilt with this title in the sixteenth century on the site of the previous one."[73]

Thus we see that the approval of the rule took place with the famous bull, *Supra Montem*, of August 18, 1289.[74]

What the pope had approved, in fact, was the rule of Friar Caro, with some modifications. Matanić observed that "the texts of both are almost identical; there are a few noteworthy differences."[75] The Rule of Nicholas IV is, most of all, more "Franciscan" because it affirms that "the present way of life (of the penitents) had its beginning in blessed Francis."[76]

Consequently Nicholas IV, in contrast to the norm that the visitator could be "of any approved religious order"[77] and that, in the monthly meetings the penitents should receive the exhortation of "a religious who is informed in the word of God"[78] advised that these persons, both visitators and instructors (*visitatores et informatores*)[79] should be members of the Order of Friars Minor.

It seems, however, that there were some complaints and opposition against this norm. *Unigenitus Dei Filius* (August 8, 1290) of the same pontiff bears witness to this fact.[80] In it Nicholas IV reasserted his desire that all the penitents belonging to an order "begun by St. Francis" should have visitators and directors (*visitatores et procuratores*) of the Order of Friars Minor.

Another "Franciscan" detail included in the Rule of Nicholas IV concerns the color of the habit. The *Memoriale* made no mention of it, but the Rule of 1289 stipulates that it be neither "all black nor all white," that is, gray. It is clear that on this point the penitents, because of their association with the Minors, had been influenced by the legislation of St. Bonaventure, the Constitutions of Narbonne of the Friars Minor (1260), which prescribed that very same norm, using the same words.[81]

The Rule of Nicholas IV, accepted universally, remained the "Magna Charta" of the Franciscan movement of penance, which from that time on was commonly called "The Third Order of St. Francis." This rule, in fact, remained in effect for the Secular Franciscans until 1883; for the regular tertiaries, men and women, until 1521, and for some of them until 1927.[82]

TOWARDS A "RELIGIOUS LIFE"

Although the scope of this work has as its terminus the year 1289, the year of the approval of the Rule of Nicholas IV, we feel it necessary to present a synthesis of what happened to a part of the Third Order before and after that date, in order to give some illumination and clarification about a phenomenon that touches the hearts of hundreds of thousands of men and women living a religious life in community following the "Rule of the Third Order Regular of St. Francis." The phenomenon of the trend towards religious life on the part of the Third Order of St. Francis gave rise, throughout the centuries, to innumerable congregations of Franciscan brothers and sisters.

During the lifetime of St. Francis hermits and recluses entered the Order of Penance and were recognized by the ecclesiastical order of that day as religious. Some of these were inducted by the saint himself, such as Blessed Verdiana of Castel Fiorentino, the noblewoman Praxides of Rome, and Gherardo of Villamagna near Florence. There is also evidence of a community of penitents, that of Bartholomew Baro, instituted directly by St. Francis.[83]

From this we can see that, even during Francis' lifetime, the beginnings of a "regular religious life," both eremitical and communal forms, were to be found.

As we have also seen, the Order of Penance had an extraordinary development and good organization during the thirteenth century. The development of the religious life must have followed the same lines. The knowledge that Francis had accepted hermits and recluses and, most of all, that he had begun a community of penitents, would have encouraged the spread of this type of life. The nature of the order itself favored the spread of community life; it had been, in fact, since its beginning, not merely a pious association, with statutes, but a real "order," with a rule, habit, novitiate, profession, and privileges recognized by the ecclesiastical order. The institution therefore had a natural suitability for an evolution towards the regular state.

This occurred for the male and female branches alike. Even though the documentation that has survived is scant, mostly because of the simplicity of life and the lack of any sort of external or federational organization, we do have proof of convents of male and female tertiaries in the very same thirteenth century. The oldest convent of men is the convent of Monte Casale (1269);[84] the community of St. Clare of Montefalco, the "convent of the Holy Cross" begun by the saint's sister in 1274 seems to be the oldest one for women.[85]

The promulgation of the Rule of the Third Order by Nicholas IV was an important factor for the development of the common life among Franciscan penitents. This rule, with its more orderly and organic organization, also gave "greater emphasis to the religious nature of this order,"[86] gave it a partially new configuration in which the two pre-existing realities within it, namely, the life *in domibus propriis* and community life, could develop.[87]

There were two main ways by which a part of the Third Order set out towards a regular life: the eremitical life and the communal life in the hospitals and hospices. Some examples have come down to us from the thirteenth century. "In Tuscany, St. Margaret of Cortona (1247-1297) accepted into the Third Order in 1277 . . . some pious young women called the "Poverelle" and founded in 1278 the Home of Our Lady of Mercy to care for the sick. Likewise, St. Angela of Foligno (1249-1309) gathered under her direction a group of friars and sisters who cared for the lepers in the municipal hospital."[88]

Around the turn of the century the practice of profession of religious vows developed among those penitents living in community. This was the decisive step in the complete "regularization" of the order. Pope John XXII, with the bull *Altissimo in divinis* of November 18, 1323, approved and praised this action which represented an approval of the "regular religious life" within the Third Order.[89]

In the second half of the fourteenth century there is an increase of efforts to unify the various tertiary communities which had remained independent of one another up until that time. This phenomenon rapidly unified and centralized various congregations in national or regional confines, according to the many geographic subdivisions of that day.[90] To our knowledge, this marks the beginning of various congregations, such as that of Blessed Angelina of Marsciano (1397),[91] the male tertiaries of Holland in 1401,[92] the Grey (Hospital) Sisters in 1413,[93] the male tertiaries of Cologne in 1427, the Spanish friars in 1442,[94] and the Italian friars in 1447.[95] These all received papal bulls which generally granted them the power to elect a superior general.

In the centuries that followed there arose, under various circumstances, innumerable Franciscan congregations, especially of women, engaged in the active life, with the immediate purpose of serving the needs of the place and time. All were characterized by, and sometimes without realizing it, the presence of the two essential elements of the spirituality of the penitents who followed Francis: ongoing conversion (*poenitentia-metànoia*) and the works of mercy,[96] that is, helping to serve the spiritual or physical needs of one's neighbor, following the spirit of St. Francis.

Many of these congregations spontaneously asked to follow the Rule of the Third Order Regular of St. Francis, by whatever name it was known in that particular period. Those who did not do so, or felt uncertain about the choice, generally received from the Church the advice or an order to adopt and follow that rule. In the Franciscan context, this was the only rule possible. At the same time they could express their particular spirituality through the constitutions of their congregation.

All of these Franciscan congregations, old and new alike, should see themselves as shoots on the one large tree of the penitential movement that was renewed and enlived ("instituted," as Nicholas IV preferred to say) by St. Francis. Each one, therefore, should thirst for that vital "sap" infused into the tree by the saint of Assisi.

In the last two decades we have rediscovered much that is new in our common "historical and spiritual tradition."[97] We did not even suspect its existence. Should this, perhaps, cause us to close ourselves in and say "I don't recognize myself in this tradition or spirituality"? Who would be so foolish that, finding a precious heirloom in the attic, would throw it out, simply because he never knew it was there?

We should all be proud of the spirituality given directly by St. Francis to his penitents, our ancestors. Of course, we must learn it better, accept it with an open heart, live it actively, even accomplish it in new works, but with an "ancient spirit," with the certainty that, in this way we will become "better sons and daughters" of St. Francis.

NOTES

INTRODUCTION

1. Manselli, R. "Chi fu Francesco d'Assisi," in *Francesco d'Assisi nella storia, I: Dalle origini al 1517,* Ed. Istituto Storico dei Cappuccini, Rome, 1982, p. 353.
2. 3 *Comp.* 37, *Omnibus,* p. 925; cf. *An P.* 211, published in Isabell, D., *Workbook for Franciscan studies* (second edition), Franciscan Herald Press, Chicago, 1979, p. 102.
3. *Vita S. Francesci,* 23. *Anal. Fran. X,* 346. Cf. L. Canonici, "I Terziari francescani 'fratelli e sorelle della penitenza' " in *Quaderni di spiritualità francescana,* 18, p. 149.
4. *Sermo Il de S.P.N. Francisco,* in *Opera Omnia,* IX, 576. (cf. *Omnibus,* p. 837).
5. Recently, with the approval of the new rule by Pope Paul VI (24 June 24, 1978) the "Third Order Secular" is now called "The Order of Secular Franciscans."
6. The acts of all of them have been published:

    1) *L'Ordine della Penitenza di san Francesco d'Assisi nel secolo XIII,* O. Schmucki, ed., Istituto Storico dei Cappuccini, Rome, 1973;

    2) *I Frati Penitenti di san Francesco nella società del Due e Trecento,* M. D'Alatri, ed., Istituto Storico dei Cappuccini, Rome, 1977;

    3) *Il movimento francescano della Penitenza nella societa medioevale,* M. D'Alatri, ed., Istituto Storico dei Cappuccini, Rome, 1980;

    4) *Prime manifestazioni di vita communitaria—maschile e femminile—nel movimento francescano della Penitenza,* ed. by R. Pazzelli-L. Temperini. Commissione Storica Internazionale T.O.R., Rome, 1982.

7. "The appropriate renewal of religious life involves ... a continuous return to the sources of all Christian life and to the original inspiration behind a given community. . . . Therefore loyal recognition and safekeeping should be accorded to the spirit of founders, as also to all the particular goals and wholesome traditions which constitute the heritage of each community." Decree on the appropriate renewal of the religious life (*Perfectae Caritatis*). *The Documents of Vatican II,* Herder and Herder, New York, 1966, p. 468.

CHAPTER ONE

1. With the term "discipline" in the context of bodily mortification we mean the traditional "tool of penance, consisting ordinarily of a complex of ropes or chains, small or large, simple, or having barbs or small balls of hard substance, such as wood or metal at the tips, and used to chastise the flesh by flagellation." A. Lanz, "Disciplina" in *Enciclopedia Cattolica*, IV, 1743.

2. Cf. The Letter *Poenitemini* in *Enchiridion Vaticanum*, ed. Dehoniane, Bologna, 1977.

3. For a more thorough study, see Roland J. Faley, T.O.R., "Considerazione bibliche sulla metànoia" in *Analecta TOR* XII (1974), pp. 11-32.

For the New Testament concept of penance-conversion, cf. A. H. Dirkens, *The New Testament Concept of Metànoia*, Washington, 1932; P. A. Aubin, *Le problème de la "Conversion." Etude sur le terme commun a l'hellenisme et au christianisme des trois premiers siècles*. Paris, 1963; C. Spicq, "Benignité, mansuétude, douceur, clémence," in *Révue biblique*, LIV (1963), 321-329. *See also* R. Michiels, "La conception lucanienne de la conversion," in *Ephemerides theologicae Lovanienses*, XLI (1965), 42-78.

4. Z. Alszeghy-M. Flick, *Il Sacramento della riconciliazione*, Rome, 1976, pp. 106-107.

5. "First conversion" (or initial conversion) means the acceptance of the Christian faith by a pagan or Jew; a baptized person who changed from a lukewarm or even sinful Christian life to a life of serious Christian commitment in which God becomes the center of his or her activity and aspirations is more properly called a "second conversion." In this way, "the conversion" of Francis is rather a "second conversion."

6. Alszeghy-Flick, p. 108.

7. This "re-discovery" indicates our conviction that, as had happened previously, in the time of Francis the biblical sense of *metànoia* had been more or less forgotten.

Christian *metànoia* had developed into an emphasis on the external aspect of penance, even in ostentatious forms, but only as a cultural and cultic phenomenon. We will treat this further at a later time.

8. Kajetan Esser, *Origins of the Franciscan Order*, Franciscan Herald Press, Chicago, 1970, p. 204.

9. Esser, pp. 204-205.

"This is obvious and convincingly clear from another regulation of the same *Testament*, which is expressly intended as well for the future life of the fraternity. In it, Francis forbids his friars to request in any way letters of protection from the roman curia, either for a church or for any place, whether under the pretext of preaching or on account of bodily persecution; moreover, if they are not received anywhere, they must flee to another land "to do penance with the blessing of God." Since Francis is most deeply convinced that the will of God is manifested in all that happens and wants to subject himself to it obediently always and everywhere, he excludes here the possibility of securing oneself by human means against the will of God; it must be accepted by the friars in every case. Thus, they are to persist in the penitential attitude of their Founder. This regulation of the saint clearly shows that he sums up the whole way of life of his friars in this essential witness. This spirit of penance must prevail always and everywhere" (Esser, pp. 204-205).

10. Esser, p. 206.

11. Cf. Esser, p. 205. Cf. Regula S. Chiara, VI, *Francis and Clare: The Complete Works*, Paulist Press, 1982, p. 218; Testament of St. Clare, 8, 18, 24, *Francis and Clare*, pp. 226-232.

12. Cf. the testimony of a breviary composed before 1250, which describes the "conversio ad Deum" of the saint, and, in complete agreement with his own evidence in his *Testament*, states the following: "Subito enim in alterum virum conversus est et ad ea quae consuervat gaudere nequibat; nam et cetera quae ipsum delectaverant pridem, sibi modo taedium ingerebant" (*Testimonia minora*, 35 f.). Thus, according to the author of the breviary, after Francis' "conversion to God," he "quickly, in fact, becomes (conversus est in) another man and could not enjoy those things he would normally enjoy; in fact, the same things which first entertained him, now bring him only weariness." Esser, p. 253, note 24.

13. Esser, p. 207.

CHAPTER TWO

1. Z. Alszeghy-M. Flick, p. 109.

2. Originally the word "confession" did not indicate an individual and detailed accusation, public or private, of one's faults, but was a synonym for conversion in the sense we have used it. It was more of a public manifestation of the decision to "be converted" and was of equal value to praising God within the assembly of the Christian community, especially before the celebration of the Eucharist. This collective penitential prayer, or confession, as it is called in the Didache, did not correspond to the public request for pardon of grave sins; for that, a long and difficult period of expiation was necessary. Cf. Cyrille Vogel, *Il peccatore e la penitenza nella Chiesa antica*, ed. L.D.C., Turin, 1967, p. 13. For "Penance in the Middle Ages" see also: P. Galtier, S.J., "Pénitents et convertis" in *Rev. Hist. Eccl.* 33 (1937) 5-26, 277-305; A. Nocent, "La riconciliazione dei penitenti nella Chiesa dal VI al X secolo," in *La penitenza* (*Quaderni di rivista Liturgica*, 9), Turin-Leumann, 1968, pp. 226-240; C. Vogel, *Il peccatore e la penitenza nel Medioevo*, Turin, 1970.

3. Tertullian, *Trattato della Penitenza*, cap. IX; cf. in Vogel, *Il peccatore e la penitenza nella Chiesa antica*, p. 19.

4. Cf. Vogel, pp. 20, 24.

5. Cf. Vogel, p. 23. St. Cyprian (+258) gives us an observation worthy of note: it is church doctrine that ecclesiastical penance is required only for grave faults; yet many of the faithful, because of delicacy of conscience, requested it, even though, strictly speaking, they did not have need of it. In this particular point we can see the *first beginnings of the voluntary penitential movement*. (We may also note, although this is

not directly related to the present study, that at the time of St. Cyprian, "private sacramental penance" is still unheard of. Good works are considered sufficient for the forgiveness of lesser sins.)

6. Erma, *Il Pastore*, Prec. IV, 1, 8, in *Padri Apostolici*, Antologia Patristica. Ed., Paoline, Alba, 1967, p. 392. Two centuries later, St. Ambrose would affirm: "Sicut unum baptisma, ita una paenitentia quae tamen publice agitur." *De Poenitentia*, liber II, X, 95.

7. C. Vogel, p. 15.

8. E. Amann, "La Pénitence" in *Dictionnaire de Theologie Catholique*, XII, 1, 803.

9. Cf. C. Vogel, p. 35.

10. This position was officially reconfirmed by the Second Lateran Council (1139); Canon 22 states: "Falsa etiam fit poenitentia, cum poenitens ab officio vel curiali vel negotiali non recedit, quod sine peccato agi nulla ratione praevalet. . . ." Cf. in J.D. Mansi, *Sacrorum conciliorum nova et amplissica collectio*, Florence, 1763, 21, 532.

11. E. Amann, *La Pénitence*, c. 805.

12. As early as 538 the Third Council of Orleans decreed (cap. 24), that: "ut ne quis benedictionem poenitentiae iuvenibus credere praesumat, certe coniugatis, nisi ex consensu partium et aetate iam plena eam dare non audeat." Cf. in G.C. Meersseman, *Disciplinati e Penitenti nel Duecento*, 1962, p. 55, n. 2.

13. "From the fifth century on, the voluntary penitents appear in documents along with the involuntary or compulsory penitents." Meersseman, *Ordo Fraternitatis. Confraternite e Pietà dei laici nel Medioevo*. Herder, Rome, 1977, p. 266. "From that time on the Order of Penitents was composed above all, if not exclusively, of model Christians, while the converted sinners were a very small minority." Meersseman, c. 832.

14. Cf. Gennadius Massiliensis, *Liber de ecclesiasticis dogmatibus*, cap. 53, in *PL* 58, 994.

15. Cf. C. Vogel, pp. 38, 47-48; Alfonso Pompei, O.F.M. Conv., "Il movimento penitenziale nei sec. XII-XIII," in *AA. VV. L'Ordine della Penitenza di san Francesco d'Assisi nel secolo XIII*. Rome, 1973, pp. 14-21.

16. Cf. Bartolomé Pastor Oliver, T.O.R., *Consideraciones historico-espirituales sobre algunas expresiones de Penitencia voluntaria y de "Conversio"-"Abrenuntiatio" no monástica hasta el siglo XIII*, Vienna, 1981. Manuscript, p. 52.

17. The similarity, for example, of format and style between the murals of the rocky landscaped churches of Cappadocia in modern Turkey and those of the "Lucan" churches in southern Italy would be unexplainable if we do not admit such a connection. Cf. R. Pazzelli, T.O.R., "Sulle vie della fede. Efeso e la Cappadocia," in *Pace e Bene, Periodico Francescano TOR*, n. 140, 1979, p. 296.

18. Cf. Pastor, pp. 24-25.

19. Cf. Pastor, pp. 22-23.

20. In medieval documents the term *conversatio* indicated the whole manner of behavior, including speaking and action, but most of all,

action. We note, for example, in the Franciscan sources, the use that the *Legend of the Three Companions* makes: "Haec quoque (Franciscus) dicens addebat: 'Talis deberet esse fratrum conversatio inter gentes ut quicumque audiret vel videret eos glorificaret Patrem caelestem et devote laudaret' " (3 Comp. 58). It then added: "His great desire was that he and his brothers should abound in the good works for which men give glory and praise to God" (*Omnibus*, p. 942). And again "Multi videntes eorum humilem et sanctam conversationem" (3 Comp. 66) is translated as "When people saw the humble and saintly lives of the friars" (*Omnibus*, p. 950). "Conversatio" is therefore something that can be seen; and that which is seen most of all are one's actions. Cf. the Latin texts in the critical edition of Théophile Desbonnets, O.F.M., *Legenda trium Sociorum*. Edition critique, in *AFH* 67 (1974), pp. 38-144.

21. Cf. C. Vogel, *Il peccatore*, p. 17.

22. Nicolas Sastre Palmer, T.O.R., *La espiritualidad penitencial a través de la historia*. Manuscript. Rome, 1978, p. 46. Reconciliation "in extremis" was that penance, or absolution of sins, granted to Christians at the end of life, even to those who had refused to enter the *Ordo Poenitentium*.

23. Amann, c. 813.

24. Cf. C. Vogel, pp. 14-15.

25. C. Vogel, pp. 22 ff.

26. Cf. C. Vogel, *Il peccatore* . . . , pp. 24-25. Let us note, by way of historical curiosity, that the "redemption" or penitential commutation helped, toward the ninth century, to transform the religious state into a clerical state. The Mass became one of the most frequently used means of "redemption" of personal penance; many priests were needed to celebrate the Masses requested by the penitents, and these priests had to be free enough of other obligations. Since there were not enough parish priests to do so, the practice of ordaining male religious to the priesthood began.

27. "Quoniam comperimus per quasdam Hispaniarum Ecclesias non secundum canonem sed foedissime pro suis peccatis homines agere paenitentiam, ut quotiescumque peccare voluerint, toties a presbyteris se reconciliari expostulent, ideo pro coercenda tam exsecrabili praesumptione, id a sancto concilio jubetur, ut secundum formam canonicam antiquorum detur paenitentia, hoc est ut prius eum quem sui paenitet facti a communione suspensum faciat inter reliquos paenitentes ad manus impositionem crebro recurrere; expleto autem satisfactionis tempore, sicut sacerdotalis contemplato probaverit eum communioni restituat: his vero qui ad priora vitia vel infra paenitentiae tempus vel post reconciliationem relabuntur, secundum priorum canonum severitatem damnentur." III Council of Toledo, can. 11. *PL* 84, 353. Cf. also in Amann, c. 840.

28. "De paenitentia peccatorum, quae est medela animae, utilem hominibus esse censemus; et ut paenitentibus a sacerdotibus data confessione indicatur paenitentia, universitas sacerdotum noscitur consentire." *M G H., Leg. t. III*, 1, p. 197. Cf. also in Amann, c. 848.

29. Amann, c. 853.

30. Amann, c. 853-854.

31. Amann, c. 846.

32. In many of them we find canons related to penance, always in conformity with the ancient legislation, characterized by the necessity of entering into the *ordo poenitentium*. Cf. *Concilio VI* (638), can. 7-8 in Mansi, X, 664; *Concilio XII* (681), can. 2., Mansi XI, 1029; *Concilio XVI* (693), can. 3, Mansi, XII, 71.

33. Meersseman, *Ordo Fraternitatis*, p. 269.

34. "Real" commutation means the substitution of one penalty with another of a diverse nature, such as substituting fasting with almsgiving; the term "personal" commutation means the custom whereby the prescribed penitential practice can be done by another person.

35. They are *Sententiae*, in *PL* 83, cc. 537-737; *De ecclesiasticis officiis*, in *PL* 82, cc. 73-728.

36. Cf. Amann, c. 824.

37. J. Fontaine, "Pénitence publique et conversion personnelle: l'apport d'Isidore de Séville à l'evolution médievale de la pénitence," in *Revue de droit canonique* 28 (1978), p. 152.

38. Pastor, p. 52.

CHAPTER THREE

1. Amann, "*Pénitence*," in *Dictionnaire de Theologie Catholique*, XII, 1, c. 829. "There is no great difference between the pastoral attitude of St. Gregory the Great (590-604) and that of St. Leo the Great (440-461); the homilies given to their people, notwithstanding the distance of time and the happenings through which Rome had passed, have more than one element in common."

2. After the famous Third Council of Toledo in 589 and during the seventh century, in the space of about sixty years fourteen Councils, all of notable importance, were held in Toledo: The Fourth Council of Toledo in 633; the fifth in 636; the sixth in 638; the seventh in 646; the eighth in 653; the ninth in 655; the tenth in 656; the eleventh in 675; the twelfth in 681; the thirteenth in 683; the fourteenth in 684; the fifteenth in 688; the sixteenth in 693; and the seventeenth in 694.

3. It is well known that the methodical tables, similar to the *Hispania*, existed before this time. Cf. Amann, c. 814.

4. Cf. Amann, c. 815. See the collection *Hispania* in *PL* 84, 25-92. On this point, see also P. Fournier and G. Le Bras, *Histoire des collections canoniques en Occident*, t. I, Paris, 1931.

5. Militia enim in sensu canonum duplex est: togata et paludata. Haec arma et bella respicit; ista muneraque politica. Jean Morin, *Commentarius Historicus de disciplina in administratione Sacramenti Poenitentiae tredecim primis saeculis in Ecclesia*. Antwerp, ed. Metelen, 1682, p. 315.

Recalling this work of Morin, together with the works of Petau (*De poenitentiae veterae in Ecclesia ratione diatriba*, 1622) and that of Sirmond

(*Historia paenitentiae publicae*, Paris, 1651), Amann observed: "These works and especially (that of Morin) remain storehouses of information" (c. 844); and again "Their investigations (Petau and Morin) reconstructed in an eminent way the canonical discipline of the first seven centuries. Until the present day no notable revisions have been made to their descriptions" (c. 837).

6. "Qui [hoc] genus artis profitentur absolute a Poenitentia repellundur ut docet Innocentius II. . . . Falsa enim fit Poenitentia cum Poenitens ab officio vel Curiali vel negotiali non recedit, quod sine peccato agi nulla ratione praevalet" (Morin, *o.c.,* pp. 315-316).

"Eos qui saecularem potestatem adepti ius saeculi exercuerunt, immunes a peccato esse non posse manifestum est. Dum enim et gladius exeritur, aut iudicium confertur inustum, aut tormenta exercentur pro necessitate causarum, aut parandis exhibent voluptatibus curam, aut praeparatis intersunt, in his se quibus renuntiaverunt sociantes, disciplinam observationis traditam mutaverunt."

["Those who perform this kind of work are to be absolutely excluded as Innocent II teaches. . . . It is a false penance when the penitent does not cease from a curial or business office, which in no way can be performed without sin" (Morin, pp. 315-316).

"It is evident that those who exercise a secular power, having adopted the right of the world, cannot be free from sin. For while they use the sword or confer an unjust judgment or inflict punishment because of the necessity of the cases, or show care in preparing for unlawful delights or share in those already prepared, associating themselves in those things that they have renounced, change the discipline of observance that has been given to them" (Morin, p. 316).]

We have the impression that this phraseology reveals clearly enough, as few other passages do, what unorthodox methods the "justice" of the times used to extract false confessions.

7. "Poenitenti utilius est dispendia pati quam periculis negotiationis obstringi: Quia difficile est inter ementis vendentisque commercium non intervenire peccatum."

["It is useful for the penitent to suffer this loss rather than be exposed to the dangers of business; it is difficult that there be no sin in the business of buying and selling" (Morin, p. 315).]

8. Ideo agricolae et artifices sub "militia saeculari" prohibita comprehendi non possunt, nec trivialium mercatorum magna pars.

["Thus farmers and artisans are not included under the prohibition "secular militia," neither the greater part of small merchants" (Morin, p. 316).]

Hence we find that Omobono di Cremona (died November 13, 1197), a penitent and merchant, continued in his work "with all tranquility of conscience and was canonized fourteen months after his death" (Meeresman, Ordo Fraternitatis, p. 287). See the bull of Canonization of Innocent III, *Pietatas promissionem* (January 12, 1199 in *PL* 214, 483-485).

9. Qualitas lucri negotiantem aut excusat, aut arguit, quia est

honestus quaestus, et turpis.

["The quality of the gain either excuses the merchant or augments the guilt, because there is an honest gain and an unlawful gain" (Morin, p. 315).]

10. Unde si quis Poenitens habet causam, quam negligere forte non debeat melius expedit Ecclesiasticum quam forense iudicium.

["Whence if a penitent has a case, which perhaps he cannot neglect, it is better for him to seek an ecclesiastical judgment rather than a civil one" (Morin, p. 315).]

11. We must admit, however, that from the beginning there are contrary opinions in regard to a "just war." The first noteworthy Father in the East to admit this legitimacy is St. Basil who will be followed in turn by St. Athanasius. The greater part are commonly against any use of arms whatsoever by the penitents. "Whatsoever soldier . . . who considers himself a true penitent cannot continue . . . unless he lays down his arms, and he shall not take them up again, except on the advice of religious bishops in the defense of justice" (Morin, p. 317).

12. Morin, p. 317.

13. Apud Graecos—nota il Morin—(usus trium Quadragesimarum) in Poenitentiarum impositione celebris fuit (*o.c.*, p. 470).

["Among the Greeks the use of three lents was known to be given to the penitents (Morin, p. 470).]

14. A canon of a regional Council held under Louis the Pious in the year 821 prescribed five lents for the person who had calumniated a subdeacon, six lents for the same crime against a deacon, and twelve lents if the offended one was a priest (Morin, p. 470).

15. Cf. Pazzelli, "Digiuno, abstinence, cibo, in the *Dizionario Francescano*, Ed. Messagero, Padova, 1983, p. 358f.

16. Morin, p. 470.

17. Licet laicis poenitentias impositas pecunia et eleemosinis redimere.

["It is lawful for the laity to redeem imposed penances by money and almsgiving" (Morin, p. 472).]

18. "Qui non habet in aere, solvat in corpore."

["One who does not have money, let him pay with his body."]

The promoters of such a solution based their reasoning upon a curious interpretation of Scripture: "Dominus noster (Mt 18, 25) eum qui talenti sibi commissi fructum reddere non potest, corporaliter punit."

["Our Lord physically punished him who was not able to render fruit for the talent given to him" (Morin, p. 472).]

19. Cf. Vogel, p. 28.

20. In his commentary on Psalm 118, he has the following ideas:

"Si volueris perfecte agere Poenitentiam, segregare te debes a consortio pecatorum et fugere in alium locum, ut perfecte eam agere valeas."

["If you wish to do penance perfectly, you must separate yourself from the company of sinners and flee to another place, so that you may perfectly do this" (Morin, p. 474).]

21. Jean Leclercq, *Spiritualità del Medioevo. Da S. Gregorio a S. Bernardo*

(sec. VI-XII), ed. Dehoniane, Bologna, 1969, n. 80.

22. Leclercq, pp. 80-81.

23. St. Peter Damian has the following to say in regard to this point: "Those who are in the world as if in a puddle ... we exhort them to assume the way of exile, and to placate the terrible Judge by abandoning their home-land" in Leclercq, p. 170.

24. Cf. Dal Pino, pp. 521-522.

25. For such reason the imposed penitential pilgrimage was censured by some important persons of the time, among whom was Rabanus Maurus, a Benedictine monk (784-856) who brought the school of the Abbey of Fulda to prominence.

26. Cf. Franco Andrea dal Pino, *I Fratri Servi di S. Maria dalle origini all'approvazione* (1233 ca.-1304). Storiografia. Fonti. Storia. Louvain, 1972, pp. 462-463.

27. Leclercq, p. 123.

28. Evidence of the reform are the Councils of the region of Renana, those of the Concilium Germanicum in 743, of Leptines and of Soissons in 746.

29. Cf. Joseph Lortz, *Storia della Chiesa considerata in prospettiva di storia delle idee. Volume I, Antichita e Medioevo.* Ed. Paoline, Milano, 1980, p. 311.

30. Cf. Amann, p. 862.

31. Leclercq, p. 124.

32. Amann, p. 862.

33. There is a well-known case of an influential nobleman who, having received a penance of seven years of fasting, paid a certain number of his subjects (851, to be exact) to fast for three days each; thus, the total number of fast days corresponded to the total number of days in seven years.

34. Cf. Amann, p. 877 for the specific reasons for this impossibility.

35. Cf. Leclercq, p. 125. Rabanus Maurus, a Benedictine, (ca. 784-856) was born at Magonza and educated at the schools of Fulda and Tours; he became a priest in 814 and from 817 directed the school of the Abbey of Fulda. He was abbot of that same monastery from 822 to 842. He was elected Archbishop of Magonza in 847. Under his care Fulda was transformed into a first class intellectual center. Rabanus fostered the sciences in order to give the clergy the necessary preparation to bring Christianity to Germany. His works have the same purpose: they are practical manuals, useful instruction for a simple people. His principal works are: *De videndo Deum, de puritate cordis et modo poenitentiae. Libri tres.* (PL 112, 1397-1424). This last work is a summary of all the principal canons on penance of all the preceding Councils. Cf. G. Mollat, Rabano Mauro, in *E.C.*, X, 439.

36. Among these are: *de institutione regia* of Jonas of Orleans (PL 106, 279-306) and *De regis persona et regio ministerio* by Hincmar of Rheims (Hincmarus Archiepiscopus Rhemensis) PL 125, 833-856.

37. Cf. Leclerq, p. 127.

38. Leclercq, p. 128.

Jonas of Orleans was born in Aquitaine shortly before 780 and died in Orleans between 841 and 843. He acquired his literary and theological formation in southern France and entered the ecclesiastical state. He is one of the few ecclesiastical writers of his time who is not a monk. He was elected bishop of Orleans in 818 and remained there until his death. A zealous pastor, he fostered the monastic reform, seeking to assure monasticism a spiritual independence. He was one of the more influential prelates during the reign of Louis the Pious and represents the ecclesiastical culture and theology of Carolingian renaissance. He shows a great biblical-patristic knowledge, but is not very original.

His principal works are: *De institutione laicali* (*PL* 106, 121-278); the previously-mentioned *De institutione regia* (*PL* 106, 279-306). *De institutione laicali* is a "type of treatise on Christian morality with reference on the various states of life and contains precious information on the penitential discipline of the time" (A. Piolanti, *E.C.*, VI, 430-431. Cf. Amann, in *DTC*, VIII, 2, 1504-1508).

39. Leclercq, p. 128.
40. Leclercq, p. 145.
41. In the *Antiquitates*, Muratori states: "Quum vero plerumque poenitentes pecunia deficerent . . . cuius ope sese redimerent, praedia ac fundos lubenter offerebant, et ex his unus, aut alter, aut plures, nonnumquam in ius Ecclesiae transferebant, hoc est, aut novis ecclesiis, coenobiis, et xenodochiis constructis, aut antiquis donabantur, sed saervato sibi saepe ac saepius usufructu, dum viverent."

["Since many penitents lacked money . . . by means of which they could redeem themselves, immovable goods and possessions were freely offered and from these, one or the other or many were transferred into the use of the Church, that is, they were donated for new churches, monasteries, old and new hospices, but often and very often they kept for themselves the interest accruing from such possessions as long as they lived."] Cf. in Salvi G., "Gli oblati benedettini in Italia" Cenni storici, in *Rivista storia benedettina* 21 (1952), p. 98; Pastor, p. 48.

42. Pastor, p. 50.
43. Cf. Salvi, p. 167. "The Lombard diplomatic codex of the eighth and ninth century gives us examples of oblations with a penitential character on every page expressed according to the typical formulas of that culture. The testimony of these cases of offerings tell us that the practice was common to clerics and laity, men and women." Pastor, p. 49. Cf. also Schiaparelli L., *Codice diplomatico longobardo*. Fonti per la storia d'Italia. Rome, 1929-33, passim.

44. Cf. Carolus Magnus, capitulare aquisgranense, cap. 15, in *PL* 97, 287; cf. also Salvi, p. 103 ff.
45. Cf. Lortz, vol. 1, p. 348.
46. Cf. Leclercq, p. 167.
47. Lortz, vol. c, pp. 361 and 394.
48. Cf. Leclercq, p. 178.

49. Cf. Lortz, p. 391.
50. Cf. Amann, c. 895.
51. Leclercq, p. 168.
52. Leclercq, p. 178.
53. Leclercq, p. 179.
54. Franco Andrea dal Pino, *I frati Servi di S. Maria*, p. 459.

55. Born in Ravenna toward the middle of the tenth century, he entered the monastery of St. Apollinaris in Classe in 973; this monastery had been reformed by Cluny in 972. Notwithstanding the reform, he found the monastic life too mitigated and, after a few years, withdrew into solitude under the influence of a strong eremitical local tradition and, together with some noble Venetians, undertook "an austere eremitical life of penance, prayer, and manual labor" (Dal Pino, p. 465). Later he retired to the recesses of the Appenine mountains, establishing hermitages at Camaldoli. The Camaldolese eremitical life had a long influence in the surrounding area. He died in 1027, a recluse in an eremitical cell near the monastery of Val di Castro (Fabriano).

56. F. Dal Pino, p. 468.

57. Born near Ravenna in 1007 and having lived in a Benedictine monastery, around the year 1035, he retired to an eremitical life at Fonte Avellana (Pesaro), erecting monasteries and hermitages in the surrounding areas. He wrote at various times on the eremitical life; this life, with solitude, constant mortification, and the bare poverty that distinguished it, remained for him the most perfect imitation of Christ. A castigator of the customs and of the simony of the clergy to whom he proposed a life similar to that of the apostles, Peter Damian was in close rapport with the first reform popes, beginning with Leo IX (1049-1054). He was against the "cura animarum" undertaken by the monks, as was done by those of Vallombrosa, founded by St. John Gualbert (died 1073). St. Peter Damian died in the Monastery of St. Mary in Faenze in 1072.

St. John Gualbert permitted his monks of Vallombrosa to leave their solitude in order to perform reform activity against the simoniacs, considered the kings of heresy, and to this end he also sought the help of the people, who quickly responded (Dal Pino, p. 473). Among other things, the Vallombrosians taught "the invalidity of simoniac ordinations." There is no great difference between this affirmation and that of the Cathari and Waldensians a hundred years later.

58. Cf. F. A. Dal Pino, p. 472.
59. Cf. F. A. Dal Pino, p. 469.

60. Altopascio is an Appenine locale along the Lucca-Fucecchio Road, about sixteen km. from Lucca, in which province it is located. In the documents it is indicated as "in the Florentine territory in Lucca" or in "the diocese of Lucca, a district of Florence."

61. The road was so named, we learn from a note to the Rule of the Brothers of St. Jacobo d'Altopascio (pp. 6-7) because "it was the road which the pilgrims took going to Rome"; it was also called 'Francesca'

because most of the pilgrims were French and everybody coming from the other side of the Alps was considered to be "French." The real reason seems to be that it was one of the more widely-traveled roads connecting Rome and France. According to Fortini, the road led from Rome, following the Tiber to Orvieto, then on to Assisi and, having crossed the plains, it passed along Lake Trasimeno and then on to Arezzo, Bologna, Modena, passing through the Po Valley, and finally reaching the Great Saint Bernard and Moncenisio Passes. Cf. Arnaldo Fortini, *Nova Vita di San Francesco*, 1959, vol. III, p. 70. It must have had other branches; in Tuscany the road passed Cisa, descended through Pontremoli and reached Lucca, Altopascio, and Fucecchio. Cf. F. A. Dal Pino, p. 497.

62. Dal Pino states that this rule was that of the Hospitalers of St. John of Jerusalem of whom we shall subsequently speak (Dal Pino, p. 497). A copy of this rule exists from the fourteenth century, written in good Italian of the time: "Regola dei Frati di S. Jacopo d'Altopascio," Bologna, Commission for the texts of the language, 1968. A photographic reproduction was published by Forni of Bologna in the edition of Gaetano Romagnoli, Bologna, 1864. The Letter *"solet annuere"* of Gregory IX is found in Bertelli, *L'Ospizio e il paese di Altopascio (Dalle origini all'anno 1239)*, p. 9.

63. See the aforementioned editon of the Regola, the preface, p. 9.

64. Cf. Damien Vorreux, *The Tau, A Franciscan Symbol*. Franciscan Herald Press, Chicago, 1979, p. 16.

65. Vorreux, p. 17.

66. Near this Roman hospital which was found on Monte Celio, near St. John Lateran, "St. Francis was found by those sent by Pope Innocent III," if we are to believe the story which quickly accompanied the remembrance of the first approbation of the fraternity of Francis in 1210. The episode is told by St. Bonaventure in the Major Life (IM) III, 9a, or rather, in a "later insertion" to the work of St. Bonaventure by his successor in the office of minister general of the Friars Minor, Jerome of Ascoli, who later became Pope Nicholas IV. Jerome said that he had obtained this information from Cardinal Richard of Annibaldis, a relative of Innocent III.

The insertion reads: "The following morning the pope had his servants seek that poor one (St. Francis) throughout the city. They found him in the hospital of St. Anthony, near the Lateran and by command of the pope brought him at once to the Holy Father" (*Omnibus*, p. 1063).

67. Dal Pino, p. 523.

68. Dal Pino, p. 525.

69. Dal Pino, p. 527.

70. Dal Pino, p. 588.

71. Vorreux, pp. 1-37; cf. also Pazzelli, R., "Il segno Tau, simbolo penitenziale e francescano," in *Analecta TOR*, XIV (1980), 789-800.

72. Anonymous Benedictinus saeculi XII, *Liber de Poenitentia et tentationibus religiosorum*, in PL 213, 865-904.

73. This date of composition is taken from an examination of

the text. In fact there one reads:

"Igitur in expeditione, quae praesenti anno sub imperatore Romano Frederico, ipso duce, facta est adversus paganos" (*PL* 213, 893).

[Whence in the expedition, which in the present year, under the leadership of the Roman Emperor Frederick took place against the pagans" (*PL* 213, 893).] Frederic Barbarossa left for the Crusades in May of 1189. He died, however, a year later, June 9, 1190, drowned in the river Selef near Seleucia.

74. This new position in the sphere of monasticism was probably due to the influence of St. Bernard (1090-1153) who was the apostle and, in a certain sense, the organizer of the second Crusade (1147-1149). The teaching of the Anonymous Benedictine is instead a return to the ancient and more or less constant doctrine of monasticism, i.e., the life of the monk is prayer and work in the cloister.

75. "Fili hominis, ingredere domum et fode parietem, et vide abominationes, quas illi fecerunt hic, fode parietem, et iterum fode, et tertio fode sicut praeceptum est prophetae (Jer. VIII). Fode parietem cogitationum, parietem locutionum, fode parietem operationum, et quidquid his singulis peccaveris, vide. Cumque in his singulis te peccasse criminaliter cognoveris, accipe super te T, quod est signum gementium et dolentium. T figura crucis est, crux passio est. Imitare ergo passionem Christi, et comple ea quae desunt passionum Christi in carne tua, et vir ille indutus lineis, et atramentum in dorso suo habens, cum viderit T super te, transiens non percutiet te" (*PL* 213, 882. C).

[Son of man, go into your house and examine yourself and see the abominations which they have done there; examine yourself for the second and the third time, as the prophet prescribed (Jer. VIII). Examine your thoughts, your speech, your works and see if in these things you have sinned. And if in these things you see that you have grievously sinned, take upon yourself the T, which is the sign of those who weep and mourn. The T is the figure of the Cross, the Cross is the passion. Imitate, therefore, the passion of Christ and fulfill in your flesh those things that are lacking to the passion of Christ and that man dressed in linen and bearing the sign on his back, when he sees the T on you, passing he will not strike you (*PL* 213, 882, C).]

76. "Ubi poenitentia, ibi et indulgentia est. Poenitentia autem homini peccatori a Deo est; ab hoc et indulgentia. Quoties ergo Deus dat homini poenitentiam, toties dat et indulgentiam" (*PL* 213, 873).

77. "Si iniquitates tuas videris, et eas dimiseris, et signum super te acceperis, hoc est amaritudinem verae poenitentiae ad instar passionis Christi habueris, angelus percutiens non laedet te, hoc est, vindicta Dei non veniet super te" (*PL* 213, 882 D).

[If you shall have seen your iniquities and shall have confessed them and shall have accepted the sign upon you, this is the sadness of true penance after the passion of Christ which if you have, the punishing angel will not harm you, that is, the vengeance of God shall not come upon you (*PL* 213, 882 D).]

78. Regola dei Frati di S. Iacopo d'Altopascio, pp. 34-35.
79. Regola dei Frati di S. Iacopo d'Altopascio, pp. 62-63.
80. Cf. above, p. 23. Meeresman thus summarizes the various forms under which the penitents are presented and the terminology with which they are categorized from the fourth to the thirteenth centuries: "In regard to their relationship among each other, they are separate or associated; in regard to their control of material goods they are proprietors or communitarian penitents; according to the social class to which they belong, they are either rural or urban penitents; according to their stability of place they are donati or free penitents; according to residence, they can be eremitical, domestic, residential, and conventual; according to the vow of chastity they are continents or married penitents; according to the works of mercy that some practiced, they are called hospital, apostolic, teaching, etc.

The generic name of penitents that can be applied to all of them derives from their state of "conversion" to a voluntary "penance" which rarely reached a conventual form of life. All wore the habit, renounced certain worldly pleasures, practiced certain corporal austerities and recited psalms or their equivalent in the Lord's Prayer at the traditional hours. These obligations were more or less the same for all the various categories of penitents." Meeresman, pp. 312-313.

81. Pastor, pp. 44-47; Cf. Vogel, "La discipline penitentielle en Gaule des origines au IX siecle." Le dossier hagiographique in *Revue de sciences religieuses de l'Universite de Strassbourg*, 30 (1956), p. 175; Meersseman, p. 32.

82. Cf. Pastor, p. 32.

83. J. Leclercq, "Il monachesimo femminile nei secoli XII e XIII" in *Movimento religioso femminile e francescano nel sec. XIII*. Acts of the seventh congress of the Societa Internazionale di studi francescani. Assisi, 1980, p. 77.

84. In Assisi at the beginning of the thirteenth century there was a hospital where lepers were served by oblates. Cf. Fortini, vol. II, p. 223.

85. Cf. E. Delaruelle, L'autel romain de Saint Sernin (1095). Confreres, pelerins et penitents, in Melanges R. Crozet. Ed. Gallais, Poitiers, 1966, pp. 383-389.

86. In regard to burying the dead, cf. Pastor, p. 44, note 17. Cf. also Concilium Carthaginense IV (a. 436), can. 81, in J. Hardouin, *Acta Conciliorum et epistolae decretales ac constitutiones Summorum Pontificum*, I, Paris, 1714, col. 984; "Statuta ecclesiae antique" in *Concilia Galliae* a. 314-506, ed. C. Munier, Turnholti, 1963, can. 66, p. 169.

87. At least since the time of St. Gregory (590-604) "the faithful did not receive Holy Communion except on the three great feasts: Christmas, Easter and Pentecost. . . . The particular class of Christians who practice the evangelical counsels in the world and whom we know by the name of *conversi* ordinarily receive Holy Communion each week" (Amann, col. 831). We can also recall the instruction given by Jonas of Orleans on this subject. See above, p. 29.

88. This was defined for the first time in a pontifical document

of Gregory IX with the bull *Detestanda* of May 21, 1227 by which the penitents are permitted to make the solemn oath in four circumstances. The phraseology used by the pontiff is repeated in the *Memoriale propositi* of 1228, n. 17. Cf. in Meersseman, *Dossier*, p. 101.

89. Cf. Meersseman, *Ordo*, pp. 268-269.
90. Meersseman, *Ordo*, pp. 273-274.
91. *Decretum Gratiani*, Pars II, C. XXIII, q. L, c. 11.
92. *Decretum Gratiani*, Editio Romana, Romae 1582, col. 1572.
93. Born near Liege about the year 890, Ratherius grew up at the school of Ilduin, Abbot of Lobbes (near Charleroi, Belgium). With him Ratherius came to Italy in 926 and was elected Bishop of Verona. A strong character with reform ideas, he was not capable of compromise and impatient in the realization of his plans; he soon lost favor with Hugh of Provenza and was imprisoned in a tower in Pavia where he remained from 935-937. It was during this period that he wrote his most important work, the *Praeloquiorum libri sex*. Freed from prison, he traveled for some years, receiving various ecclesiastical offices; in 944 he was once again with his monks at Lobbes. He returned to Verona in 946. Once again opposed, this time by new enemies but for the same reasons, he had to leave his see after two years. In 953 he was elected bishop of Liege, where he remained for two years. In 961 he was brought back to Verona by Otto, where he remained until 968. From there he retired to Namur where he died in 974.

The works of Ratherius were accurately edited by the Ballerini Brothers in 1775 and re-published by Migne (*PL* 136). "They are the mirror of his soul and of his times" (G. Pavani, *E.C.* X, 542-543). Amann has noted that "it is impossible to find in all of medieval literature a work parallel to the *Praeloquia*. It represents a complete examination of conscience which the author presents to Christians of every state of life, condition, and age, together with questions capable of making them reflect on their duties; he gives each one advice to guide them in matters of conscience. Moralists will find here a most interesting description of the Christian and moral life of the tenth century; Church historians will prefer the third and fourth books that pertain to the duties of sovereigns, especially in their dealings with bishops.

"It is here that Ratherius' reform ideas are best expressed. The imprisoned bishop understands perfectly that independence of ecclesiastical power from civil authorities is the primary condition for the reform of the Church" (E. Amann, Rathier of Verona in *DTC* XIII, 2, 1682).

94. See above, p. 18.
95. It seems that either Ratherius did not know or did not take into account the ecclesiastical writers of the eighth to tenth centuries. "He prefers to follow almost exclusively the Fathers, particularly St. Isidore of Seville." (G. Tampieri, *I doveri morali di ciascun stato di vita secondo i 'Praeloquia' di Raterio Vescovo di Verona (sec. X)*, Bagnacavallo, S.T.E. 1943, p. 7).
96. Sciendum autem alium modum esse poenitentiae, quo judicio

totius Ecclesiae quis certo tempore [poenitentiam agit], alium quo nostra sponde poenitemus omni tempore: Istud nulla constringitur lege, nisi prout quisque sibi velit indicere tantum, ut pro modo aegritudinis medicinam sibi noverit adhibere salutis.

[It is known that one way of penance is that by which in the judgment of the entire Church one undertakes penance for a certain period; another way is that by which we freely do penance all the time. This latter penance does not oblige by law, unless one freely takes it upon himself to do so, as in the case of sickness one uses medicine, knowing that it will give him health (*Praeloquia*, liber VI, IID. *PL* 136, 326).]

97. Si ex toto corde ad Dominum conversi, hanc humilitatem in corde habetis quam in habitu praetenditis. . . . Nam si ex toto corde non convertamur . . . non solum in peccatis remanemus sed etiam ficto corde coram hominibus conversionem peccatorum mentimur. Ait enim Job sanctissimus: Simulatores et callidi provocant iram Dei.

[If you have converted to the Lord with all your heart, have this humility in your heart which you show with your habit. . . . But if with all your heart you do not convert to the Lord . . . not only do you remain in your sins, but you also simulate the conversion from your sins with a false heart, before men. For the most holy Job says: "Simulators and the hard of heart provoke the wrath of God" (*Sermo III* in *coena Domini*, *PL* 136, 714-715).]

98. Poenitens itaque es, aut esse vis? Considera regulam poenitendi in dictis expressam Baptistae Domini: *Facite*, inquit, *fructus dignos poenitentiae*; et paulo post: *Qui habet duas tunicas, det non habenti*; caeteraque exsequens misericordiae opera, docet perspicacissime curam aliorum necessitatibus misericorditer debere impendere.

["You are, therefore, a penitent or you wish to be! Consider the rule of penance expressed in the words of the Baptist of the Lord: *Do*, he says, *works worthy of penance*; and a little later he adds: He who has two tunics, give to the one who has none; fulfilling other works of mercy, he teaches most wisely that the care of the needs of others be mercifully undertaken" (*Praeloquia*, *PL* 136, 321. Cf. Pastor, p. 53).]

99. "Vestiat itaque necesse est nudum, qui amissam innocentiae vult recipere ornamentum. Pascat esurientem, qui mortiferam animae desiderat evadere famem. Potet sitientem, qui vult evadere aegritudinem morum. Consoletur in carcere constitutum, qui inferni non vult subire ergastulum. Confortet dolentem, qui aeternum non videre desiderat dolorem. Recipiat hospitio peregrinum, qui vult a Domino recipi in aeternum illud paradisi tabernaculum. Redimat captivum, qui a diaboli laqueis cupit liberari. Per Christum solatietur in aliquibus necessitatibus constitutum, qui de necessitatibus diversarum vult liberari angustiarum. Sepeliat mortuum, qui perditionis aeternae cupit evadere lethum. Liberet constrictum pro debitis, qui liberari a suis cupit peccatis. Eripiat eos qui ducuntur ad mortem, qui vult inferni effugere carcerem. Vincat animum impatientem, qui vult diabolum superare bacchantem. Corripiat in misericordia negligentem, qui castigantem placare vult Deum Patrem."

[Let him, therefore, clothe the naked, who having lost the garment of innocence wishes to regain it. Let him feed the hungry who wishes to avoid the deadly hunger of the soul. Let him give drink to the thirsty who wishes to avoid moral sickness. Let him console the one in prison who does not wish to suffer the torments of hell. Let him comfort the sorrowing who does not wish to see eternal sorrow. Let him receive the pilgrim as a guest who wishes to be received by the Lord in that eternal tabernacle of heaven. Let him redeem the captive who wishes to be liberated from the snares of the devil. For Christ's sake let him console the afflicted one with certain necessities if he wishes to be freed from the necessities of diverse sorrows. Let him bury the dead who wishes to avoid the death of eternal perdition. Let him free the one bound with debts if he wishes to be freed from his sins. Let him free those who are led to death if he wishes to flee the prison of hell. Let him conquer the impatient soul who wishes to overcome the fury of the devil. Let him correct the neglectful with mercy if he wishes to placate the wrath of God the Father" (*Praeloquia, PL* 136, 321-322. Cf. Pastor, p. 54).]

100. *Praeloquia, PL* 136, 321-322.

101. Hoc pertinet maxime . . ., [quod] sese a licitis caute restringat.

[It is of great importance . . . that they cautiously abstain from licit things (*Praeloquia*, 323).]

102. Sed ad hoc quis idoneus, cum nemo aliquid possit sui viribus? Unde quotidie clama, imo incessanter, etiam tacendo et aliud quodlibet agendo desiderans postula: 'Cor mundum crea in me, Deus.' Quod si nitenti tibi ipsa prava consuetudine exui difficilis occurrit effectus, ne rogo ideo deficias.

103. Magnus enim lapis difficile evehitur ad summa, cito ruit ad infima; nec a primordio quis potest esse perfectus. . . , Tunc tene te ad Christum, clama: "Trahe me mpost te' (Cant 1,4); et 'Educ de carcere animam mean' " (Ps 141, 8).

CHAPTER FOUR

1. The Roman Synod held in 1059 deserves special note. Besides re-establishing the liberty involved in the election of the bishop of Rome, it decreed a more energetic and systematic fight against the corruption of the clergy to combat simony and nicolaitism. The Nicolaites were clerics who did not observe celibacy. Cf. Rudolf M. Mainka, "I movimenti per la Chiesa povera nel XII secolo" in *AA. VV. Povertà Religiosa*. Studies under the auspices of the Institute of Theology of the Religious Life. Claretianum, Rome, 1975, pp. 141-142.

2. For example, Pompei writes: "The twelfth century presents an historical situation different from those that preceded it and its religious phenomena have their own impulses, motivations, and tendencies. Thus a religious movement of this century cannot be considered in a true continuity with those of the preceding centuries." A. Pompei, "Il

movimento penitenziale nei sec. XII-XIII," in *L'Ordine della Penitenza di San Francesco d'Assisi nel sec. XIII.* Rome, 1973, p. 22.

3. Raphael Morghen, for example, bases the motives and religious tendencies of the two centuries on a spontaneous and fundamentally unified religious sense. R. Morghen, *Medioevo cristiano*, 1962.

4. Cf. Pompei, p. 23.

5. Mansi, 19, 897. Cf. in Mainka, p. 142.

6. Pompei, p. 23, note 35.

7. Ida Magli, *Gli uomini della penitenza.* Anthropological outlines of the Italian Middle Ages. Ed. Cappelli, Bologna, 1967, p. 57.

Recently Duane Lapsanski, in his volume *Evangelical Perfection, An Historical Examination of the Concept in the Early Franciscan Sources,* (The Franciscan Institute, St. Bonaventure University, St. Bonaventure, N.Y., 1977, pp. 18-30) treated of the phenomenon of the itinerant preachers in the twelfth century. He writes: "Both men and women eagerly listened to the preachers' message and admired their ascetical lives to such an extent that many actually became members of these new communities. This certainly indicates a hunger on the part of the populace for new modes of Christian living.... Traditional monasticism, often bound to landed estates and the power structure, could not quench this hunger. In part, therefore, the movement can be considered as a reaction to the general worldliness of the Church, particularly of the monks and clerics. At a time when the rapid growth of riches blinded many a Christian heart, the itinerants' example of voluntary poverty and even physical deprivation embodied an appropriate and needed form of Christian asceticism. All these factors, together with a fresh reading of the gospel, gave birth in many Christian hearts to a burning desire to imitate the life of Christ and his apostles in a very literal fashion" (p. 29).

8. Lapsanski, pp. 18-19.

9. Cf. *Vita B. Roberti de Arbrissello*, in *PL* 162, 1046 ff.

10. Lapsanski, pp. 19-21.

11. Cf. *Vita B. Bernardi*, Author Godfrey Grosso, in *PL* 172, 1403.

12. "Habitum quidem monachi habentes, sed vilem, incultum, villosum, a caetorum habitu monachorum valde dissimilem, ovibus ipsis a sumptus fuerat valde consimilem." *Vita B. Bernardi*, 1410.

13. "Indurato in pedibus asperitate laboris callo, nudus pedes, verbum Dei spargendo regiones diversas peragaret, corpus quoque sacci asperitate edomuit." Vita B. Vitalis Saviniacensis, *Analecta Bollandiana,* I, 386.

14. Lapsanski, p. 24.

15. Cf. Vita B. Giraldi de Salis, in *Acta Sanctorum*, Oct. X, 255 ff; cf. Lapsanski, pp. 24-25.

16. He thought of his mission thusly: "Nos autem non nostris meritis, sed sola Dei super habundanti gratia imitatores eorum (Apostolorum) effecti eandem pacem vobis denunciamus." Vita Norberti Archiepiscopi Magdeburgensis. *Monumenta Germaniae Historica* (MGH) Scriptores XII, 676.

17. MGHS 675.
18. MGHS, 678.
19. Lapsanski, p. 28.
20. Cf. Meersseman, Dossier, p. 1.
21. It is not easy to explain why a "preaching" religious order did not emerge in the twelfth century. Those who try to give a reason have not been convincing. Cf. Lapsanski, p. 29 and note 118.
22. Cf. I. Magli, pp. 27-29, 38, 39.

CHAPTER FIVE

1. Hubert, Jedin, *Manual de Historia de la Iglesia.* Ed. Herder, Barcelona, 1973. Vol. IV, p. 187.

2. Honorius of Autun (Honorius Augustudunensis) was a theologian of the twelfth century. In his works he defines himself on various occasions as *solitarius, scholasticus,* and *presbyter;* there is insufficient material to allow a reconstruction of his biography, nor even to establish definite dates. He wrote between the years 1112 and 1137, predominantly between 1122-1125. Although he was born in Burgundy (Autun), he was active in Germany, probably around Ratisbonne in the religio-scientific milieu of Christian "abbas Scotorum" of St. James, to whom he dedicated some of his works. He was a strenuous defender of the papacy; he was in favor of external apostolic activity of the monks and denounced priests who lived with concubines, considering them *extra ecclesiam,* according to the dispositions of the First Lateran Council (1123). He wrote on all theological subjects. In the fourth part of his work entitled "Dogmatica et Ascetica" we notice the moral severity of Honorius of Autun and his pessimistic outlook. He is not always a good critic, nor is he a good "ratiocinator" according to modern thought, but he amply illustrates the religious situation of his times. (cf. Antonio Piolanti, "Onorio di Autun," in *Enc. Catt.;* cf. also *PL* 172, c. 846).

3. *Speculum Ecclesiae* in *PL* 172, c. 846.

4. Unde dicitur: canes muti non valentes latrare (Is 56:10). Ob conscientiam pravae vitae a verbo Dei obmutescunt, et ne redarguantur contra perverse viventes, latratus praedicationis non edunt. *Speculum, PL* 172, 846.

5. On this subject the promoters of the reform movement were more than explicit from the beginning. At the very beginning of the monastic reform, a century and a half before the Gregorian Reform, Odo of Cluny (924-932) in his famous didactic epic poem entitled "Occupatio" had insisted on the "moral incompatibility of the priestly function and concubinage." Odo did not specifically state that the concubine priests *did not have the power* to consecrate the body of Christ, but it could already be seen that the uneducated lay preachers, would first begin to doubt, and then to deny the "validity of the sacrament," as the Patarines and Arnoldists later did.

6. Ida Magli, *Gli uomini della Penitenza.* Anthropological features of

the Middle Ages in Italy. Ed. Cappelli, Bologna, 1967, p. 57.

7. It is also necessary to keep in mind the sad conditions of the papacy during this difficult period in the life of the Church. Upon the death of Honorius II in 1130, the majority of the Cardinals elected Gregory, deacon of St. Angelo, who took the name of Innocent II (1130-1143). Some Cardinals, however, in opposition elected Peter, the son of the powerful Roman citizen Leon, who took the name of Anacletus II (1130-1138). St. Bernard strenuously defended the legitimacy of Innocent II, but Anacletus, with the help of the forces of his friends and relatives, occupied St. Peter's Basilica and the other principal churches of Rome; Innocent was forced to leave the city. France, England, and Germany, however, remained faithful to Innocent. When Anacletus died in 1138, his successor, Victor IV submitted to Innocent II in May 1138 after two months.

8. Knowing the doctrinal peculiarities of the heretics really helps one better appreciate the thought and attitudes of St. Francis. For example, when we read in the Testament that "the Lord gave me such faith in the churches that I prayed simply and said, 'We adore you, Lord Jesus Christ, in all your churches throughout the world and we bless you, because through your holy cross you have redeemed the world,' " this phrase of itself says little or nothing. However, when we realize that even such simple points as the sacredness of church buildings and of the wood of the cross had been attacked by some heretics, and that these ideas still had an influence on the people, we understand how Francis, even in the simplest manifestations of his conduct, maintained an attitude of complete fidelity to the doctrine and praxis of the Church and insisted on these doctrines, inviting the Christian people to do likewise. This is repeatedly seen, even though in all of his writings, he never mentions heretics.

9. Cf. Ilarino da Milano, "Bruys Pietro," in *Enc. Catt.*

10. Peter Abelard was born in Pallat, near Nantes, in 1079; he died in the monastery of St. Marcel-sur-Saône in 1142. A great philosopher of the Middle Ages, he did, however, often commit errors in the use and application of principles. In the philosophical field his name is connected with the solutions to the questions of the universals, specific problems of the twelfth century with two main streams of thought: that of the nominalists (*vox*) headed by Roscelin, and that of the realists (*res*) headed by William of Champeaux. Abelard was first a disciple of this latter, but he later changed and defeated him in the philosophical field. He also exchanged violent polemics with Roscelin. Because of his treatise, *De unitate et trinitate divina*, he was accused of heresy; his chief adversary on this point was St. Bernard. Invited by the Council of Sens in 1141 to withdraw his doctrine, he appealed to the pope. Discovering, however, that Innocent II had already confirmed the sentence and the condemnation of the Council, he stopped at Cluny. Abbot Peter the Venerable helped effect his reconciliation with St. Bernard and with the Church. He died a pious death at Cluny.

After Abelard's well-known and stormy romance with Heloise he became a monk. Neither the habit nor the desert, however, of the monastery at Troyes were able to change his aggressive character. In the field of philosophy, there was no one of his time better at understanding or assimilating the Aristotelian doctrine of knowledge. He knew how to distinguish sensitive and imaginative perception common in man and animals from abstract perception, found only in man. Through this the intellect is able to grasp the resemblance among individuals, that is, the nature of human beings. The universal is the result of this abstraction. It is not, therefore, a thing (*res*) nor a word (*vox*), but a concept (*sermo*). Abelard was the first to consider the *ideal* value of the universals.

In his theological treatise "Know thyself" Abelard enunciates for the first time the two moral principles which were commonly accepted: that intention can make indifferent actions either good or bad; error in judgment diminishes guilt. In methodology he introduced the process of "pro and con" arguments; from this process the solution comes forth. This process was followed and further developed by Alexander of Hales and Thomas of Aquinas. (cf. Ugo Mariani, "Abelardo Pietro," in *Enc. Catt*).

11. Ilarino of Milano, "Arnaldo da Brescia," in *Enc. Catt.* I, 2001-03.

12. *Enc. Catt.* I, 2002-03.

13. In the reaction to this latter phenomenon we find some "curiosities" in the primitive Patarines, such as the custom of some of them who would force their entry into the houses of the priests and carry off the concubines.

14. Paolo Brezzi, "Catari," in *Enc. Catt.* III, 1087.

15. Raffaello Morghen, *Medioevo cristiano*, Laterza, Bari, 1958, pp. 237-252.

16. Morghen, pp. 252-255.

17. Morghen, pp. 255-272.

18. Morghen, pp. 272-281.

19. Mainka, Rudolf M., "I movimenti per la Chiesa povera nel XII secolo," in *AA.VV., La Povertà Religiosa*. Studies under the auspices of the Institute of theology of the religious life. Claretianum, Roma, 1975, pp. 149-150. Cf. Latin text of Evarino of Steinfeld in *PL* 182, 677.

20. Brezzi, 1087.

21. Mainka, p. 150. cf. *PL* 179, 938.

22. Mansi, 19, 897 f.

23. Mainka, p. 150.

24. Jedin, p. 189.

25. Mainka, p. 150.

26. Mainka, p. 151.

27. Mainka, p. 151. The text is from *Chronicon Anonimi Landunensis*, 1178. Cf. Christine Thourzellier, *Catharisme et Valdeisme en Languedoc à la fin du XIIme et au debut du XIIIme siècle*. Louvain-Paris, 1969, p. 24.

28. Cf. Thourzellier, pp. 27-30.

29. It seems, however, that the Council fathers were not unanimous

in conceding these privileges. Geoffrey d'Auzerre, who took part in the Synod of Lyons wrote: "Galliarum sedes prima Lugdunum novos creavit *apostolos* nec erubuit apostolis etiam sociare.... *Circuierunt urbes et viculos* sub praetextu *paupertatis et praedicationis* obtentu impudenter *panibus alienis sine labore manum victitantes.*" Cf. in J. Leclercq, *Analecta Monastica,* 2, Roma, 1953, 194 f; Mainka, p. 152, note 50.

30. Mainka, p. 152.
31. Cf. The Decrees of the Council of Verona in Denziger-Schonmeitzer, *Enchridion Symbolorum,* 760.
32. Ilarino da Milano, "Umiliati," in *Enc. Catt.* XII, 755.
33. Ilarino da Milano, "Umiliati," in *Enc. Catt.* XII, 755.
34. James of Vitry, Letters written in October 1216 from Genoa in *FF* 2201. Cf. the Latin text in R.B.C. Huygens, *Lettres de Jacques de Vitry, edition critique.* Leiden, 1960.
35. Ilarino da Milano, ibid.
36. Cf. the letter *Eius exemplo* in *PL* 215, 1510-1513 and in Meersseman, *Dossier,* pp. 282-284.
37. Dal Pino, pp. 567-68. The three letters are two of May 12, 1210, both beginning with the words *Cum inaestimabile (PL* 216, 274).
38. Dal Pino, p. 569. Cf. the letter *Dilectus filius Durandus* in *PL* 216, 601-602 and Meersseman, pp. 286-288.
39. Ilarino da Milano, "Poveri Lombardi," in *EC IX,* 1866.
40. Ilarino da Milano, *E.C. IX,* p. 1867.
41. Dal Pino, p. 571.
42. Dal Pino, p. 572.
43. A. Pompei, *Il movimento penitenziale,* pp. 19-20.
44. Cf. Meersseman, *Ordo fraternitatis,* pp. 297-298; *see also* J. Leclercq, "La vie et la prière des chevaliers de Santiago d'après leur règle primitive," in *Liturgia II, Scripta et documenta,* 10, Monserrat, 1958.
45. Meersseman, *Ordo Fraternitatis,* pp. 296-297.
46. Meersseman, *Ordo Fraternitatis,* p. 299.
47. Cf. Alcantara Mens, "Beghine e Begardi" in *E.C.* I, 1143-1148.
48. A. Pompei, pp. 20-21.
49. I Magli, passim.
50. I Magli, pp. 62-63.

CHAPTER SIX

1. Today a new set of documents sheds light on the local situation in the Spoleto Valley which Assisi overlooks as if from a balcony. They are the "Carte dell'Abbazia di S. Croce in Sassovivo," recently published by the Scuola Superiora per Archivisti e Bibliotecari of the University of Rome, under the sponsorship of the University for Studies of Perugia, with the collaboration of the Delegation for Historical Studies for Umbria; the documents are thus divided: Vol. I—Documents of the years 1023-1115 (Prof. Giorgio Cencetti), 1973; Vol. II—Documents, 1116-1165 (Vittorio De Donato), 1975; Vol. III—Documents,

1166-1200, (Riccardo Capasso); Vol. IV—Documents 1201-1214 (Attilio Bartoli-Langelli), 1976; Vol. V—Documents 1215-1222 (Pietro Roselli), Vol. VI—Documents, 1223-1227 (Attilio De Luca), 1976; Vol. VII— Documents 1228-1231 (Giovanni Nicolai), 1975.

One fact readily seen in these papers, which confirms our assertion concerning the support of various cities for the imperial authority or for the papacy is seen in the witness of the notaries. In stating the year, some cite the reigning pope, others the emperor. Thus, for the years 1201-1214 (Vol. IV), "the notaries of Todi, Orte and Amelia always mention the pope; those of Spoleto are inconsistent, while almost always the notaries of Camerino name the pope. Those of Montefalco and Nocera generally indicate the pope until the coronation of Henry VI" (CdS, Vol. IV, p. xxx).

Another important source for the reconstruction of life in Assisi at the time of Francis are in the documents of Assisi conserved in the two principal Archives of the city, that of the Cathedral (*Arch. Cath.*) and the other in the Archives of the city (*Arch. Com.*). Until now these have been greatly consulted only by Arnaldo Fortini (cf. *Nuova Vita di San Francesco* [FNV], S. Maria degli Angeli, 1959) who has been able to place Francis directly in the "Sitz-im-Leben" of the times. It is on him that we mainly rely. Unfortunately, perhaps because Fortini's work is too detailed and wordy, and even more so because the essential historical information is often overshadowed by the oratorical and poetic style of the author, his work has not been given the credit that it deserves from other writers of biographies of St. Francis. From our point of view, this is a great loss for each of these writers.

    2. *"Specialiter et libere ad nostram imperialem jurisdictionem pertinet."* ("It belongs in a special way and freely to our imperial jurisdiction.") cf. FNV, Vol. I, p. 79. Cf. the text of the Diploma in FNV Vol. III, p. 535.

    3. FNV Vol. I, p. 80.
    4. FNV Vol. I, p. 90.
    5. FNV Vol. I, p. 94.
    6. FNV Vol. I, p. 129.
    7. FNV Vol. I, p. 95.
    8. cf. Daniel Waley, "Le istituzioni comunali di Assisi nel passagio dal XII al XIII secolo," in *Assisi al tempo di San Francesco*. Acts of the V International Congress (Assisi, 13-16 October, 1977), Assisi, 1978, pp. 64-65.
    9. Cf. Arch. Cath., Assisi, Fasc. VIII, no. 1 and 14.
    10. Cf. FNV, Vol. I, p. 95.
    11. The medieval expression "hominicium-hominicia" indicates the relationship of dependence of a worker, farmer, upon his "lord." The free farmers, as early as the time of the barbarians were forced by necessity to place themselves under the protection of a potentate, castle-owner, or someone else who became their "lord." They then became servants, maids. Their lives and possessions were at the disposition of the "lord." They were traded, given in loan, or as payment of interest.

In this regard, see the very interesting Document 170 of Vol. II of the *Carte di Sassovivo*; in October 1154 Count Ugolino, together with his brothers Marico, Rinaldo, and Attone, sons of Count Giraldo, gave to the Monastery of Sassovivo, in the person of the prior, Rudolph, the Church of St. Mary and St. Blase in the castle of Agello, together with other goods, designating all in favor of the Church of St. Nicholas of Valle Parraria. The priest of the Church was given and ceded, together with the goods, books, and bells. "Dedimus et concedimus quoddam de re nostra proprietario iure, idest ecclesia Sanctae Marie et Sancti Blasii . . . cum dotis et libris et cum omnibus sibi pertinentibus *et cum presbitero Grimaldo* et cum omnibus suis rectibus pertinentis." Vol. II, p. 198.

12. CdS Vol. IV, p. xxix.

13. Ferrari, G., *Histoire des revolutions d'Italie*, Paris, 1856-58, vol. II, p. 90.

14. Cf. the vast documentation on "boni homines" in FNV Vol. II, passim.

15. Cf. FNV Vol. I, p. 43 ff.

16. FNV Vol. I, p. 45.

17. FNV Vol. I, p. 129.

18. There were, for example, "major" soldiers and "minor" soldiers. This division was also found among the clergy: with the increasing importance of the church of San Rufino, the canons were called "major," in contrast with the "minor" canons of St. Mary Major, which was still the Cathedral of Assisi. (cf. Luciano Canonici, "Guido II d'Assisi, il Vescovo di San Francesco" in *Studi Francescani*, 77, 1980, pp. 190 ff.) Even the merchants were divided into three groups, "majors," "sequenti," and "minors" according to their income. Pietro di Bernardone must have then belonged to the class of major merchants. When one went to battle, the majors fought with a horse, shield, lance, and sword; the "sequenti" did not use the shield, while the "minors" went on foot, armed with bow and arrow (cf. FNV Vol. I, p. 55). Francis, preparing for the journey to Apulia, went with a horse and shield (cf. 3 *Comp* 6, *Omnibus*, p. 894). "At daybreak, with great haste he directed his horse to Assisi . . ." is a further indication that he belonged to the "majors."

19. Cf. Alfonso Casini, O.F.M., "Francesità di San Francesco" in *Studi Francescani* 77, 1980, pp. 371-373. There are considerations that we accept concerning the probability of Francis' business trips to France. *See also* Salvatore Attal, *San Francesco d'Assisi*, Padua, 1947, p. 65.

20. FNV Vol. I, p. 129.

21. The following excerpts are from the letter: "Having heard of the severity of the terrible judgment which the divine hand had used over the land of Jerusalem, both we ourselves and our brothers are so confused with horror and afflicted with such sorrow, that it is not easy for us to discern how we are to act or what we are to do. . . . Whenever in such a time of grief, if not corporally and at least with his heart one does not cry, he has forgotten not only the Christian faith which teaches

that we must suffer with all those who suffer but he has forgotten our humanity itself.... Whence this is to be considered by all and moreover must be done so that, repenting our sins by voluntary punishment, we may be converted through penance and works of piety to our Lord God, and that we may amend first in ourselves what evil we have done..." (*PL* 202, col. 1539-1541).

22. Arnoldo Fortini, *Gli ultimi Crociati*, Milan, 1935, pp. 11ff.
23. FNV Vol. I, p. 130.
24. FNV Vol. I, p. 1321.
25. As to how, through marriage, he became a relative of Costanza d'Altavilla and even connected with the genealogical line of St. Clare, see Gemma Fortini, "La famiglia di S. Chiara d'Assisi" in *Analecta TOR* XIV (1981, p. 898).
26. FNV Vol. I, p. 134.
27. FNV Vol. I, p. 135.
28. FNV Vol. I, p. 118.
29. FNV Vol. I, p. 139. There were many eye-witnesses from that period who could have given precise information to Thomas of Celano for use in his *Vita Prima*. Such information, even if it was hearsay, must have reached Giotto towards the end of the century. The representation of the pre-conversion of Francis in the biographical cycle of frescoes in the upper Basilica in Assisi shows Francis, passing in front of the Church of the Minerva, "dressed in his beautiful blue garment, self-confident, radiant with youth" (FNV Vol. I, p. 139).
30. FNV Vol. I, p. 139.
31. 1 Cel 2, *Omnibus*, p. 230. The *Legend of the Three Companions* adds: "In all things Francis was lavish, and he spent much more on his clothes than was warranted by his social position. He would use only the finest materials; but sometimes his vanity took an eccentric turn, and then he would insist on the richest cloth and the commonest being sewn together in the same garment." (*Three Companions*, 2, *Omnibus*, p. 891.) It is no wonder then that the youth of today often find that they have something in common with Francis.
32. Frederick Barbarossa had long sought to unite to the imperial crown the crown of Sicily, held by the Normans. For this reason he decided on the marriage of his son Henry with Constance, the daughter of Roger II of Sicily. At that time William II ruled Sicily, but he had no heirs and had promised his courtiers that the crown would pass to Constance. Pope Urban II had supported the autonomy of the South, and the court of the Normans; he was opposed to this marriage because he did not want to see a further spread of the empire. The emperor, however, had his way and the marriage of Henry and Constance was celebrated in the Church of St. Ambrose in Milan in 1186. On this occasion the patriarch of Aquileia crowned Henry King of Italy. Urban III suspended the patriarch and the bishops who had assisted at the coronation. Henry in turn occupied "certain territories of the Church." The Norman king of Sicily, William II, died soon after.

The Norman party proclaimed the succession of Tancred of Lecce, the natural son of Roger, the duke of Apulia, and Emma of the counts of Lecce. Henry VI advanced twice toward Sicily to regain the kingdom, but both times (1190 and 1191) his armies were decimated by terrible epidemics. In 1191 Constance was taken prisoner by the people of Salerno and turned over to Tancred. In a magnificent gesture of chivalry (so admired by Francis and his contemporaries) he sent her to Henry, along with precious gifts. Tancred died in 1194; his young son, William III, succeeded him under the regency of his mother, Sibyl, the widow of Tancred. Henry VI, now aided by the fleets of Pisa, Genoa, and Venice, who were worried by the naval activity of the Normans, had no difficulty in conquering the kingdom of Sicily. At Christmas 1194 Henry united that crown to the German and imperial crown. He mistreated the heirs and relatives of Tancred, and for that reason he was despised. At his death in 1197, Queen Constance wished to remain in Sicily, putting the interests of her inherited land above those of the empire. She kept her small child, Frederick II, with her, expelled the Germans from the kingdom and, dying in 1198, confided the regency to the new pope, Innocent III.

Meanwhile, Henry VI, in the dispositions of his testament, had recognized the Kingdom of Sicily as a feudal territory of the Church and bequeathed Mathilda's riches and the ancient possessions claimed by the Church in central Italy back to the papacy. Having soon established his rights over these restored territories, Innocent III sought to re-establish the Church's authority in Sicily, also taking advantage of the expedition of Walter of Brienne, Francis' hero. Notwithstanding the death of Walter in 1205, the pontiff succeeded in his plan one year later. (For more detailed information on the delicate situation in Italy and Germany in subsequent years, particularly in regard to the relationship of the papacy to Frederick II, cf. Morghen, R. "Federico II, Imperatore" in *Encyclopedia Italiana*, Treccani, ed. 1949, vol. I, p. 148.)

33. FNV Vol. I, p. 148.

34. FNV Vol. I, p. 148.

35. We should note that Conrad, objectively viewing the situation after the death of Henry VI and the turbulent atmosphere in Umbria, responded to Innocent's first approaches, offering to the Church "his fidelity, . . . ten thousand pounds of silver, an annual contribution of a hundred pounds and two hundred soldiers who would have made a good guard for the pope" (FNV Vol. I, pp. 151-152). Innocent would have probably gladly accepted the offer, except that he was soon accused of "being in league with these Germans in Italy." It was then that he called the meeting of Narni for discussions.

36. FNV Vol. I, p. 152.

37. See the beautiful description given by Fortini in FNV Vol. I, pp. 157-160.

38. Cf. FNV Vol. I, 160-161.

39. He was the first bishop of Assisi with this name in the period

1179-1204. He is not to be confused with his more famous successor of the same name, Guido II (or di Secondo), the advisor of St. Francis, who governed the diocese of Assisi from 1204-1228. See the chronological inscription in the episcopal palace at Assisi.

40. It is conserved in the Communal Archives of Assisi, Pergamene A, I. Cf. the text in FNV Vol. III, pp. 543-545.

41. It is often stated, even in "learned circles" that the diocese of Assisi, at the time of St. Francis, was a "suffragan diocese of Rome," or "dependent directly on the Holy See." This is not exact; the diocese of Assisi was only "under the protection of the Apostolic See" by virtue of the bull of Innocent III. The Holy See often conceded this privilege to a diocese, abbey, or monastery that asked for it in times of particular danger or other circumstances. The more apparent consequence and the one stated explicitly in such documents was that henceforth any "violence, attack, or damage" done to that particular place was considered as being made directly against the Apostolic See. One can easily understand the great value of such a privilege. The other prerogatives were clearly specified in each document, and varied from case to case. Here are a few examples:

A. The bull *Religiosis desideriis* of Innocent II of May 21, 1138, conceded the "protection of the Holy See" to the monastery of the Holy Cross of Sassovivo (cf. CdS, Vol. II, doc. 97, pp. 116-121);

B. The bull *Religiosam vitam* of Adrian IV of November 7, 1156, placed the monastery of St. Apollinaris di Sambro in the diocese of Assisi under "Apostolic protection" (cf. CdS Vol. II, doc. 181, pp. 208-210;

C. the brief *Cum Nobis Sit* of Urban III of January 27, 1185, with which he places "under Apostolic protection" the abbey of St. Mary de Reno, Bologna, in *PL* 202, cc. 1355-1357.

42. This bull of Innocent III, probably issued after consultation with the bishop of Assisi who must have given the pontiff a detailed description of the properties of the diocese, contains the following main elements:

a. Placing "under the protection of the Apostolic See" possessions and goods, both actual and future, of the diocese of Assisi, the document lists the churches and monasteries of the city and its surroundings, mentioning also the possessions of the diocese; the Tiber River is twice mentioned as the boundary line for some of these;

b. It affirms the power "of orders" of the bishop over monks and nuns;

c. It renews the prohibition against ordaining clerics within the limits of the diocese without the consent of the bishop of Assisi;

d. It prohibits, under pain of excommunication, the taking by "violence, theft, or malice" any goods, lands, or possessions belonging to the diocese or churches or monasteries within the limits of the diocese.

e. It prohibits, again under pain of excommunication, any authority or minister from calling any cleric or resident dwelling in the territory of the episcopacy into judgment without the consent of the bishop. Cf. the Latin text in FNV Vol. III, pp. 543-545. The original of the document is lost, but a copy dating back to 1301 is extant. This has caused some scholars to doubt its authenticity (Cf. M. Sensi, "Monasteri benedettini in Assisi. Insediamenti sul Subasio e Abbazia di S. Pietro" in *Aspetti di vita benedettini in Assisi nella storia di Assisi*. Atti of the Accademia Properziana del Subasio, Series VI, n. 5, Assisi 1981, p. 35, note 28; G. Casagrande, "L'Abbazia di San Crispoldo del Piano di Bettona" in the same *Atti*, pp. 81-82, note 53, 59). The reasons given are rather vague, even though "an interpolation concerning the monasteries" cannot be excluded; that is, in regard to these, in the document of Assisi the situation existing in 1301 is more represented than that of 1198. Nevertheless, the privileges given in the document and mentioned above are those usually conceded by the pontiffs to bishops.

43. "The sober indication" in regard to the early youth of St. Francis given to us by Celano in the first chapter of his *Vita Prima*, and the more explicit description of some customs in regard to the youth of Assisi found in certain local documents (cf. FNV Vol. I, pp. 122-123, 167-171) invite us to say a few words about the religious environment of Assisi at the time of St. Francis. More than reconstructing the religious ambience, from the few but reliable historical data that we have on the argument, one receives the well-founded impression that the religious character of the Assisian has never changed. Believing in God, he also believes in business; devout to the point of attending religious functions, he does not disdain from time to time to participate in festivities or ceremonies that are not strictly religious; faithful to the ecclesiastical authority in all that pertains to it, he does not accept its slightest interference in civil affairs; he is slightly aloof from religious institutions, but will become rather friendly with individual ecclesiastical persons whom he esteems for their culture, behavior, or civic activity. The documents to which we refer, beyond the description already mentioned, are in the account of 1 Celano, 1, 2, *Omnibus* 229-231 and the dispute between the city and the Apostolic See in 1203-1205 concerning the first mayor of Assisi. We will treat this matter later.

44. Cf. FNV Vol. I, p. 165.

45. Cf. FNV Vol. III, pp. 173-174.

46. Cf. FNV Vol. II, p. 182.

47. Born in the second half of the twelfth century of a patrician Roman family, he was a canon regular of St. Frediano of Lucca; in 1200 he was named cardinal deacon of Sta. Lucia in Settesole and in March 1202 became titular bishop of Santa Croce di Gerusalemme. His first duty in the curia was in February 1201 when Innocent III assigned him to draw up the judgment between Bishop Benedict of Spoleto and the monastery of St. Gregory in the same city. Thus he began to learn the state of affairs in Umbria. On February 25, 1204 he was named papal legate to Hungary, Serbia, and Bulgaria. His diplomatic activity met with success on the occasion of the oath of fidelity to the Holy See by the new king of Hungary, Kalijan. The cardinal returned to Rome in the winter of 1204; the following spring he was named papal legate to

Assisi, where he favorably resolved the case between the Holy See and Assisi, and received the oath of fidelity from the new mayor. Two years later he was entrusted with a mission of great responsibility; together with Cardinal Ugolino he went repeatedly to Germany where Philip of Swabia and Otto of Brunswick were fighting to succeed Henry VI. The cardinals returned to Rome in 1209. During the following years his name appears frequently among the witnesses of pontifical documents. He is also remembered as one of the first cardinals who supported St. Francis at the curia. The saint must have had a friendly relationship with him; in fact, the *Vita Seconda* of Celano, as do other sources, recalls a visit of St. Francis to the cardinal (2 Cel. 119, *Omnibus*, p. 461; LP 92, *Omnibus*, p. 1067; *Spec. Perf.* 67, *Omnibus*, pp. 1194 ff.) *See also* Janos Bak, "Brancaleoni Leone" in *Dizionario Biografico degli Italiani*, Treccani, Roma, 1971, vol. 13, 814-817.

48. "In the future one who is excommunicated or one who is an enemy of the Church shall not knowingly be elected to rule the affairs of the city." Cf. FNV Vol. I, pp. 222-223 and Vol. II, p. 182.

49. A very eloquent witness can be found in the document, signed by a notary, of the event when, on January 18, 1200, one of the lords of Sassorosso, Gerard of Gislesio, presented himself to the consuls of Perugia, asking to be received among its citizens (cf. FNV Vol. III, p. 547).

50. FNV Vol. II, p. 165.

CHAPTER SEVEN

1. FNV Vol. I, p. 240 ff.
2. FNV Vol. I, pp. 206-207.
3. FNV Vol. II, p. 178.
4. FNV Vol. I, p. 217.
5. 3 *Comp.* 5, *Omnibus*, p. 893.
6. FNV Vol. I, p. 228.
7. 3 *Comp.* 5, *Omnibus*, pp. 893-4.
8. It is not possible to know for certain whether or not "Gentile," (which means "kind") was really the name of the knight from Assisi, as some writers have claimed (e.g., Manselli, *S. Francesco*, Balzoni ed., Rome, 1980, pp. 55 ff.) or only a descriptive adjective.
9. 3 *Comp.* 6 *Omnibus*, p. 895; Cf. also 2 *Cel.* 6, *Omnibus*, p. 366; Leg. M. I, 3, *Omnibus*, p. 637.
10. 2 *Cel.* 17, *Omnibus*, p. 377. *See also* 3 *Comp.* 51, *Omnibus*, p. 935.
11. 2 *Cel.* 17, *Omnibus*, p. 377.
12. Cf. Sophronius Clasen, O.F.M., "S. Bonaventura S. Francisci Legendae maioris compilator," in *AFH* 54 (1961), p. 265.
13. Helen Moak, "Non é mai facile," in *Pace e Bene*, Periodico Francescano T.O.R., n. 110 (1973), p. 5. Helen Moak is the translator of Fortini's *Nuova Vita di S. Francesco* into English, published as *Francis of Assisi*, Crossroads Publications, New York, 1981.
14. *Testament*, 3; *Francis and Clare*, p. 154.

CHAPTER EIGHT

1. *1 Cel.* 7, 8; *Omnibus,* pp. 235-236.
2. *1 Cel.* 8; *Omnibus,* p. 236.
3. *1 Cel.* 9, *Omnibus,* pp. 236-237.
4. A critical examination of Celano's Latin text, written in the area around Assisi, gives further proof of this meaning. Francis insisted to the priest of San Damiano "ut secum *morari pro Domino* pateretur," that he permit him to live with him in the service of the Lord." "Acquievit tandem Sacerdos de *mora* illius." According to Fortini, this word (*mora, morare,* "was the characteristic word used to designate the condition of the *oblati*. We find an example in the statutes of Assisi where, concerning the *oblati* in the hospital of the lepers, one reads: "*Oblatum* et *oblatam,* eiusdem hospitalis *moram* continuam habentes." FNV Vol. II, p. 223.
5. "The son who does not obey his mother and father on their request (will) be banished from the city and district; no one may give him anything to drink or eat or help him in any way." Book II, Rule 58 establishes that they must be jailed on the request of two close relatives and be freed only when these (relatives) are satisfied. FNV Vol. I, pp. 287-288.
6. *3 Comp.* 19; *Omnibus,* pp. 908-909.
7. "Ex quo servitium Dei est aggressus, de potestate nostra exivit." *3 Comp.* 19. Cf. in the critical edition of Théophile Desbonnets, O.F.M., *Legenda trium Sociorum. Edition critique,* in *AFH* 57, pp. 38-144. This critical edition has been translated into English under the title *We who were with him* by Salvator Butler, O.F.M., and published in Assisi in 1974.
8. We must note that there are many who admit that Francis became an *ecclesiasticus* or *clericus,* but who do not want to admit (or admit with reserve) that he became a *conversus* or penitent. (Cf. Pastor, pp. 78-79). *Ecclesiasticus* or *clericus* mean "belonging to the clerical class or order"; it is therefore a consequential qualification that presupposes that something happened to cause and indicate his passage from the lay order to the clerical. Francis became an *ecclesiasticus,* with all the rights of that state, precisely because he had become a *conversus* or penitent. Conversely, it is his having become a *conversus* or penitent that makes him an ecclesiasticus.

According to Fortini, as a *conversus* Francis was required to consider himself subject to the authority of the bishop *ratione materiae et loci.* In fact, there could no longer be any doubt since he was at the service of the Church and living in a place belonging to the bishop. The imperial decrees and papal bulls which were written one after another for more than two centuries spoke very clearly. We need only refer to the bull of Innocent III to Bishop Guido only nine years earlier: "It is not licit for any authority or minister of any authority to rashly cite clerics of your churches, or any man living on the property of the bishop without the consent of the bishop." The penalty was excommunication. "Hoc enim omnino sub pena anatematis interdicimus."

Thus, eight days passed and no messenger came to San Damiano for the second summons (FNV Vol. I, pp. 289-290). For the sources and notes concerning the complaint brought by Pietro di Bernardone before the civil authorities and the bishop of Assisi, see also FNV Vol. II, pp. 223-237.

Gemma Fortini adds that "the building of San Damiano had gone through a series of change of ownership: built by oriental monks, it was later acquired by a Lombard vassal. . . . It then passed into the hands of a Lombard consortium, who, in turn ceded it to the church of San Rufino, the Bishop of Assisi, and the canons." (Gemma Fortini, "Una nuova ioptesi sulle origini della famiglia di San Francesco" in *Analecta T.O.R.* XIII (1976), p. 836.

9. *Cronaca* of Jordan of Giano, I; *XIIIth Century Chronicles*, translated from the Latin by Placid Hermann O.F.M. (Chicago, 1961).

10. Magli, pp. 66-67 and note 15.

11. "Factum est autem, cum iam dictam ecclesiam reparasset, conversionis eius annus tertius agebatur. Quo in tempore quasi heremiticum ferens habitum, accintus corrigia et baculum manu gestans, calceatis pedibus incedebat" *1 Cel.* 21.

In the *Treatise of the Miracles*, commonly referred to as "3 Celano," after having recorded the word of the Crucifix of San Damiano and that "from then on was impressed in his heart . . . the memory of the passion of the Lord," the same Celano observes: "Just because he was interiorly conformed to the same Cross, he wore the habit of penance, made in the shape of the Cross"; "Nonne etiam in ipsa se cruce recludens, habitum poenitentiae sumpsit, crucis imaginem ferentem." *3 Cel.* 2, *Anal. Franc.* X, 273.

12. Julian of Speyer affirms: "Beatus itaque Franciscus, trium, ut dictum est, ecclesiarum opere consumato, habitum adhuc eremiticum tunc temporis habuit, baculumque manu gestans, pedibus calceatis et corrigia cinctus incessit." *Vita S. Francisci* 15, *Anal. Franc.* X, 342.

13. The *Legenda choralis Carnotensis*, for example, contained in the "leggendario" of the cathedral of Chartres and dating back to the thirteenth century states: "tandem eremitico assumpto habitu, baculo scilicet et corrigiis cum calceamentis, tres ecclesias iuxta Assisium . . . reparavit." *Anal. Franc.* X, 538.

14. Cf. *3 Comp.* 19-20, in the critical edition of Desbonnets. The *Deo servire* has the same meaning as the expression used by the Assisian Consuls in their answer: "Ex quo *servitium Dei est aggressus*." See above, note 7.

15. "Revertensque ad ecclesiam Sancti Damiani, gaudens et fervens, fecit sibi quasi hermiticum habitum." *3 Comp.* 21.

16. *3 Comp.* 25, 27; *Omnibus*, pp. 915-916.

The value of the *Legend of the Three Companions*, according to the Franciscan historians, "is in the representation of the primitive Franciscan fraternity, collecting above all the tradition of Assisi." Stanislao da Campagnola, "Francesco visto et interpretato dai biografi." Introduction to the *Fonti Francescane*, p. 250.

Concerning the historical value of the *Legend of the Three Companions*, we are pleased to point out the judgment of the Franciscan critic, Octavian Schmucki, O.F.M. Cap. "Examining the studies of Sophronius Clasen, O.F.M. and Théophile Desbonnets, O.F.M., I consider it critically certain that chapters 1-16 are the genuine work of the three companions, signers of the letter (of 1246) which, in the manuscripts usually precedes the legend." Octavian Schmucki, O.F.M. Cap., "Il T.O.R. nelle biografie di san Francesco" in *L'Ordine della Penitenza di san Francesco d'Assisi nel secolo XIII*, Rome, 1973, pp. 124-125.

Franceschini was convinced that this *Legenda* was edited between October 1244 and August 1246; he affirmed that it was a "document of highest value for the knowledge of Franciscan spirituality through the simple and candid testimony of those that were the companions of Francis and were near him until his death, the most worthy, therefore, to be faithful and authoritative interpreters of his ideals and religious life." (*La leggenda dei tre Compagni*; Preface and notes by E. Franceschini, ed. O.R. Milan, 1968, p. XVI. Among the modern writers of the same position is Duane V. Lapsanski of St. Bonvaventure University, New York. Cf. his volume *Evangelical Perfection*, pp. 119-122. See also Teodosio Lombardi, *Introduzione allo studio del Francescanesimo*, ed. Porziuncola, Assisi, 1975, p. 27.

Our personal point of view is that the *Legend of the Three Companions* has an historical value almost equal to that of the *Vita Prima* of Celano.

17. In retrospect, Celano may have referred to this situation when he wrote: "He could not delay any longer, because a deadly disease had grown up everywhere to such an extent and had so taken hold of all the limbs of many . . ." *1 Cel.* 8, *Omnibus*, p. 236.

18. On this point, cf. Ida Magli, p. 63.

19. Cf. FNV Vol. II, pp. 22-90. *See also* the summary of the study by Fortini in Pietro Chioccioni, T.O.R. "La casa paterna di san Francesco secondo la documentazione del Prof. Arnaldo Fortini," in *Analecta T.O.R.* vol. X (1964-1967), pp. 605-627.

If one accepts the theory of Fortini that the paternal house of St. Francis was situated just behind the Church of St. Nicholas (site of the present post office on the *Piazza del Comune*), it would have been adjacent to the house of the Benedictine monks of Mount Subasio that they then had in the city next to the little church of St. Paul, which still exists. It had been built "by an Abbot of Mount Subasio" around the year 1070. "The monastery (of Mount Subasio) wanted to build its house in the city following the custom of other vassals whom they emulated in power and wealth." FNV Vol. I, p. 113.

20. Fortini had alluded to this possibility: "Perhaps the knowledge of the Gospels that Francis later showed came from his having frequented, in the years of his adolescence, the monks of the Badia. Later events will give a confirmation of this old affectionate relationship." FNV Vol. I, p. 114.

21. This opinion, widely accepted during the centuries, is based in large part on the expression, "an unlettered man and the friend of true simplicity"; "unlettered" is the Latin *idiota* of Celano (*1 Cel.* 120). "In the medieval language, however, this word meant one who knows only his own vulgar language, that is, one who has little experience or fluency in Latin, the official classical literary language of the cultured and members of the courts." (G. Lauriola, "La formazione culturale di Francesco," in *L'Italiana Francescana* 56 (1981), pp. 371-372.

22. The whole question of the cultural formation of Francis has been recently raised by Giovanni Lauriola. He clearly explains the two opinions, for and against, Francis' educational background, and also notes that "both the official and less significant testimonies concerning Francis' little education, or even the total lack of it, prove, at most, that he had a literary incompetence, but not an absence of culture; he had a certain bias against learning, but did not reject culture," p. 372.

This author agrees with Lauriola's conclusions. However, we are in disagreement with the fact that he would like to shorten Francis' period of education, or even end it at 1205, "at the time of his existential crisis." In our opinion, it is in these very years, 1206-1209, that Francis refines his scriptural and theological knowledge.

23. Pasquale Tuscano, "Rassenga di testi e studi francescani (1965-1975)," in *Lettere italiane*, XXVIII (1976), p. 368.

24. V. Branca, "Francesco d'Assisi, Santo" in *Dizionario critico della letteratura italiana*, vol. II, p. 118. Cf. in Tuscano, p. 368.

25. Ignazio Baldelli, "Il cantico di Francesco" in *San Francesco nella ricerca storica degli ultimi ottanta anni*, Todi, Accademia Tudertina, 1971, p. 94.

26. Kajetan Esser, "A Forerunner of the 'Epistola ad Fideles' of St. Francis of Assisi (Codex 225 of the Biblioteca Guarnacci of Volterra)" in *Analecta T.O.R.*, XXIV, fasc. 129 (1978), p. 28.

27. Esser, p. 40.

28. Esser notes that "in such things our letter is similar to the *Epistola ad clericos*, which in its first edition belongs to the oldest Opuscula of St. Francis. It also has no address, and only a brief concluding sentence. Hence they both come from a time when Francis had not yet found his later style of letter-writing," p. 34.

29. The fact that some Franciscan critics mock the opinion—as if it were almost heretical—or even the mere suggestion of the hypothesis recently presented by Gemma Fortini concerning the possibility of Jewish origins of the family of St. Francis does not resolve the question; it still remains. See Gemma Fortini, pp. 817-841.

30. These were S. Angelo in Limigiano (1058); S. Crispoldo in Bettona (1058); S. Nicolò in Campolongo (1066); S. Pietro in Assisi (1029); the priory of St. Paul in Assisi (ca. 1071); S. Apollinare of Sambro (1058); Priory of S. Masseo (1091); S. Quirico in Bettona (1185); S. Benedetto in Satriano (1039); S. Maria in Valfabbrica (1101). Cf. Sensi, "Monasteri benedettini in Assisi" in *Aspetti di vita benedettina nella storia di Assisi*. Atti Accademia Properziana del Subasio. Series VI, n. 5.

Assisi 1981, pp. 38-48.

31. This list is reproduced by Placido T. Lugano, O.S.B. in "Le Chiese dipendenti dall'abbazia di Sassovivo" in *Riv. Stor. Benedettina*, 7 (1912), p. 56. It is almost identical to the preceding one of 1188 except for some additions. That would mean that the situation was essentially the same in the years with which we are concerned, namely, 1205-1210. Cf. Lodovico Jacobilli, *Cronica della Chiesa e Monastero di Santa Croce di Sassovivo nel territorio di Foligno*. Foligno, Altieri, 1653, p. 12.

32. Cf. CdS Vol. I, Document 167.

33. Cf. Lugano, p. 51; Jacobilli, p. 14.

34. *3 Comp.* 20, *Omnibus*, p. 910.

35. *3 Comp.* 33, *Omnibus*, p. 921.

36. *3 Comp.* 47, *Omnibus*, p. 933.

37. FNV Vol. I, p. 321.

38. FNV Vol. I, pp. 293-294.

39. *3 Comp.* 47, *Omnibus*, p. 933.

40. Francesco Salvatore Attal, *San Francesco d'Assisi*, Padua, 1947, p. 142.

Cardinal John of St. Paul was the first Cardinal of the Colonna family, which was just beginning its historical prominence; he is not to be confused, however, with John Colonna of the same name who was created cardinal in 1212 and died in 1245. Because of this confusion, some have denied that John of St. Paul was a Colonna.

As a young man he studied medicine at Salerno, then became a Benedictine monk at the monastery of St. Paul Outside-the-Walls in Rome. This is attested to by a letter of the Benedictine Chapter of Canterbury, written in 1197 to Cardinal Graziano, titular cardinal of the Basilica of Ss. Cosmas and Damian in Rome. "Joanne de S. Paulo, cardinali monacho et fratre nostro" was how he was mentioned.

He was named cardinal-priest with the titular of St. Prisca in 1193. In memory of his monastic life he chose to take the "surname" "of St. Paul." "Of great holiness, esteemed by the curia for his knowledge and integrity, he had already been appreciated by Celestine III, who had given him numerous missions and, when he was seriously ill, desired to pass the tiara to him." (C. Thouzellier, *Catharisme et Valdeisme en Languedoc a la fin du XII et au debut du XIII siecle*. Paris, 1966, p. 156).

In 1200 John of St. Paul was confessor of Innocent III. On July 25, 1208, we find him celebrating the Mass in Cassino (probably in the famous abbey) in the presence of Innocent III and fifteen cardinals. Celano mentions him with the phrase "qui inter alios Romanae Curiae principes et maiores videbatur terrena despicere et amare coelestia" (*1 Cel.* 32, *Omnibus*, p. 255).

His signature doesn't appear on any pontifical documents after April 21, 1214; neither is his name found in the list of prelates making interventions at the IV Lateran Council (November 1215). He had probably died in the interim. (Cf. M. Bihl, O.F.M., "De Iohanne de S. Paulo, Cardinali episcopo Sabinensi, primo S. Francisci in Curia Romana an. 1209 fautore" in *AFH* 19 (1926), 282-285; C. Thouzellier, p. 156; Paschini, "Il Cardinale Giovanni di S. Paolo" in Studi di *Storia e Diritto in onore di Carlo Calisse*, tome III, Milano, 1940, pp. 110-112.

41. The Passagini were heretics found in the second half of the twelfth century, mostly in Lombardy. Their main characteristic was the re-emphasis of their interpretation of the Old Testament. They understood monotheism in an anti-trinitarian sense; Jesus Christ was only an adopted Son and the first of God's creatures. They held that the Holy Spirit was not divine. They recognized Mosaic law as the only means of salvation, rejecting baptism and performing circumcision. They further rejected the Eucharist and everything that was, in their opinion, of ecclesiastical origin. Cf. Ilarino da Milano, "Passagini" in *EC* IX, 907; bibliography.

42. The identity of the Josephines is not certain. It seems, however, that this name indicates a part of the Cathari, especially if one accepts the derivation of their name from Joseph-Epaphrodite, one of the "ancestors" of southern Catharism, who lived in Armenia in the seventh century. When the Arabs occupied Armenia, he may have gone to Antioch of Pisidia, taking with him the teaching and the first community of Parlicians. Cf. Aman, "Josephists ou Josepins," in *DTC*, VIII, 2, Col. 1547.

43. The Decree carefully distinguished two groups: those who dared to preach without authorization and those who taught a doctrine contrary to the tradition of the Roman Church concerning the sacraments of Eucharist, baptism, penance, and matrimony.

"Contra ipsos haereticos, quibus diversa vocabula diversarum indidit professio falsitatum ... consurgimus et omnem haeresim condemnamus. In primo ergo Catharos et Patarinos, et eos qui se Humiliatos, vel Pauperes de Lugduno falso nomine mentiuntur, Passaginos, Josepinos, Arnaldistas, perpetuo decernimus anathemati subiacere. Et quoniam nonnulli *sub specie pietatis virtutem eius,* juxta quod ait Apostolus, *denegantes, authoritatem sibi vindicant praedicandi,* cum idem Apostolus dicat: *Quomodo praedicabunt, nisi mittantur? Omnes qui vel prohibiti,* vel *non missi, praeter auctoritatem ab apostolica sede* vel *episcopo loci susceptam, publice* vel *privatim praedicare praesumpserint;* et universos qui de sacramento corporis et sanguinis domini nostri Jesu Christi, vel de baptismate, seu peccatorum remissione, aut de matrimonio, vel de reliquis ecclesiasticis sacramentis, aliter sentire aut docere non metuunt, quam sacrosancta Romana ecclesia praedicat et observat." (Cf. in P. Fredericq, *Corpus documentorum Inquisitionis haereticae pravitatis Neerlandicae*, Gand, 1889, t. I, p. 53-55).

44. Cf. Dal Pino, p. 547.

45. *1 Cel.* 33, *Omnibus,* p. 255.

46. Dal Pino, pp. 551-552.

47. Cf. Dal Pino, pp. 559-564. For *unum propositum,* see Dal Pino, pp. 551, 553, 559; Cf. *Incumbit nobis* of June 7, 1201 in Tiraboschi, *Vetera Humiliatorum monumenta,* II, pp. 128-134; G.C. Meersseman, *Dossier,* pp. 276-282. Pope Gregory IX, with his *Propositum vestrum* of June 11, 1227,

referred to and approved a similar "propositum" for the third order (Tiraboschi, p. 164).

48. See above, p. 61.

49. See above, p. 62.

50. "Parvulis petentibus panem, juxta quod ad officium pertinet pastorale, non frangis . . . dum haeretici, absentiae tuae opportunitate captata . . . perversa dogmata publice . . . proponunt" (*PL* 215, 84 B).

51. "The example of these authentic poor, whose sincere austerity confirmed their claims, is dangerous for the simple souls who, failing to see the dangers of their false orthodoxy, would compare their poverty with the opulence of an 'omnipotent' clergy" (Thouzellier, p. 47).

52. "Doctrina vitam informet, ut hoc in eorum legatur moribus, quod sermonibus explicatur" (*PL* 215, 359 B).

53. Bishop Diego continued the chapter reforms in his diocese together with the young Dominic, who had become vice-prior of the chapter. In the spring of 1204 Dominic decided to dedicate himself to "apostolic preaching." In the winter of 1205-1206, accompanied by Dominic, Bishop Diego, on his "ad limina" visit, revealed to Innocent III his desire to renounce his diocese and dedicate himself to preaching. The pontiff did not consent. On the return trip, Diego and Dominic met with the three papal legates at Montpellier, and were surprised at their lack of success in preaching to the people, "who always brought up the subject of clerical scandals and the story of an (unworthy) metropolitan who had been pardoned by Innocent III" (Thouzellier, p. 194). They particularly mentioned two cases: the first was that of Raymond of Toulouse who, although removed from office because he was convicted of simony, retained the power of "liturgical functions" and an annuity to avoid "the shame of begging" (Cf. Thouzellier, p. 192). The second case was that of Bishop Berengarius of Narbonne, from whom the pope had accepted "apparent repentance." Most of all, it was the case of Berengarius, a "living example of greed and negligence" which was most embarrassing to the apostolic preachers, who were continually reminded of the situation. Nonetheless, Diego and Dominic joined the pontifical legates.

54. At Servian, 60 kilometers from Montpellier, the heretics William, a former deacon of Nevers, Baldwin, and Bernard of Simorre, Cathari bishop of Carcassonne, were in command. After eight days of debate, Diego's group convinced the inhabitants, who were ready to throw out the heretics. A cheering crowd accompanied the preachers when they left the city (Cf. Thouzellier, p. 195).

55. "Qui paupertatem Christi pauperis imitando, in despectu habitu et ardenti spiritu non pertinescant accedere ad despectos . . . ut, ad eosdem haereticos festinantes, per exemplum operis et documentum sermonis eos, concedente Domino, sic revocent ab errore" (*PL* 215, 1025 B).

56. Thouzellier, p. 197.

57. "Sic suo pertinaciter inherebant errori, ut nullis veridicis acquiescerent documentis, sed tamquam aspides obsurdescerent ad

voces incantantium sapienter, ne mentes dimersas tenebris penetraret audicio veritatis. Per tres itaque menses urbibus, villis et oppidis multo labore et sollicitudine peragratis, multisque periculis et insidiis appetiti, paucos revocant, paucos fideles repertos de fide cercius instruunt et confirmant." D'Auxerre, 1207. *MGH Script.* XXVI, p. 271, 35. Cf. in Thouzellier, p. 205, note 108.

58. "Ipsi tamen in reprobum sensum dati nec propositas rationes attendunt nec terrentur comminationibus, nec possunt blanditiis deliniri." Innocentius III, *Ep. IX,* 149: *PL* 215, 1247 A.

59. "Auxilium tuum . . . invocandum duximus . . . (ut) haereticae perfidiae sectatores potentiae tuae virtute contriti ad veritatis notitiam saltem inter afflictiones bellicas reducantur." *PL* 215, 1247 B-C.

60. "Viros idoneos, de quoquam ordine vel religione, ad predicationis officium exercendum vobis assumere procuretis." Teulet, p. 319 A-B; cf. in Thouzellier, p. 208, note 118.

61. Cf. Luigi Cipriani in Quacquarelli-Andreotti, *San Francesco d'Assisi —La sua gente poverella e il monachesimo Benedettino,* Rome, 1977, p. 12.

62. *3 Comp.* 47-48, *Omnibus,* p. 933.

63. One of the major personages who might have played an important role in this was Abbot Nicholas of Sassovivo, because of his connection between Rome and Umbria, and his frequent stays within the Roman curia. He became Abbot of Sassovivo, probably right after the general chapter of the independent monasteries of central Italy, which was convoked by Innocent III and held at Perugia on October 2, 1203. Langeli writes in his Preface to Vol. IV of *Le Carte di Sassovivo* that "it really fell to him to carry out the work of religious reform begun in that chapter and to gain the complete trust of Innocent III" (p. xxi). So much so, that in 1208 the pope, continuing his work of reorganization of the same monasteries, entrusted the visitation of them to a committee of three prelates, including Nicholas, Abbot of Sassovivo. The other two were the bishop of Florence and the prior of Camaldoli. The letter of appointment confirms this; see the entire document in *PL* 215, 1490. The documents of Sassovivo relative to these years bear witness to the frequency and intensity of the communication between the pope and the abbot of Sassovivo (see doc. 91) "and the even more frequent, almost regular, stays of Nicholas at Rome, at the papal curia where he personally conducted the most important discussions and had the support of the same curia in all the arguments, great and small." Langeli, p. xxii. Doc. 89 and ff. of Vol. IV of *Le Carte di Sassovivo* show the almost uninterrupted presence of Abbot Nicholas at the papal court from the second half of 1208 to April 1209 and again in July 1210.

It is in this very period that the papal curia was interested in and requested information about the young Francis. The documents of Sassovivo show that Abbot Nicholas also travelled throughout the cities of Umbria.

The following documents of Vol. IV show that Nicholas was in the various cities at these times:

No. 55 - 1205 - Trevi
No. 62 - 1206 - Amelia
No. 81 - 1208 - Todi
No. 82 - 1208 - Orte
No. 102 - 1208 - Spello.

It would seem unthinkable that the curia would not turn to such a person for information; he most certainly knew well what was going on in that small Umbrian town (Assisi) and its surrounding area.

CHAPTER NINE

1. *1 Cel.* 36, *Omnibus,* pp. 258-259.
2. *1 Cel.* 33, *Omnibus,* pp. 255-256.
3. C.G. Meersseman, *Disciplinati e Penitenti nel Duecento,* Perugia, 1962, p. 46.
4. *3 Comp.* 37, *Omnibus,* p. 925. cf. *Anon. Per.* 211, Isabell, p. 102.
5. *1 Cel.* 37, *Omnibus,* pp. 259-260. "Resonabat ubique gratiarum actio et vox laudis, ita ut multi saecularibus curis abiectis, in vita et doctrina beatissimi patris Francisci suimet reciperent notitiam et ad Creatoris amorem et reverentiam aspirarent. Coeperunt multi de populo, nobiles et ignobiles, clerici et laici, divina inspiratione compuncti, ad sanctum Franciscum accedere, cupientes sub eius disciplina et magisterio perpetuo militare. Quos omnes Sanctus Dei, velut caelestis gratiae rivus uberrimus, charismatum imbribus rigans, cordis ipsorum virtutum floribus exornabat: egregius nempe artifex, ad cuius formam, regulam et doctrinam, efferendo praeconio, in utroque sexu Christi renovatur Ecclesia et trima triumphat militia salvandorum. Omnibus quoque tribuebat normam vitae ac salutis viam in omni gradu veraciter demonstrabat" *Anal. Franc. X,* 30.
6. Meersseman, *Disciplinati,* p. 46, note 1.
7. O. Schmucki, "Il T.O.R. nelle biografie di san Francesco" in *L'Ordine della Penitenza di San Francesco d'Assisi nel secolo XIII,* 1973, p. 120.
8. For another interpretation, see *Omnibus,* p. 596, note 133.
9. Cf. *Anal. Franc. X,* 377, note 1: "trino numero hic (this is the expression used by Julian of Speyer of *Officium rhythmicum S. Francisci,* Ad I Vesperas, hymnus) subest etiam allusio ad tres Ordines a S. Francisco institutos . . . vel, si mavis, ad tres fidelium categorias, quibus tres Ordines respondent."
10. O. Schmucki, p. 120. Celano, Julian of Speyer and St. Bonaventure use the word "militia" to mean the First Order (the Order of Friars Minor). *2 Cel.* 212: "iam emeritae militiae"; *Leg. S. Clarae,* n. 8: "nova militia pauperum"; Julian of Speyer, *Vita S. Francisci,* n. 3 (*Anal. Franc. X,* 337): "novae militiae dux futurus"; St. Bonaventure, *Legenda Maior,* c. 13, n. 10 (*Anal. Franc. X,* 620): "dux in militia Christi futurus."
11. *3 Comp.* 60, *Omnibus,* 943. Feligiano Olgati observes in a note on the matter: The Franciscan Third Order "was approved by Nicholas IV in 1289. The statement (of the *Legend of the Three Companions*) creates

a serious problem; either it was inserted later, or the composition of the *Legend of the Three Companions* should be placed after" 1289. (*Fonte Francescani*, 1977 ed., note 25). Why not consider another possibility, a much more plausible one; Franciscan historiography has not yet been able to identify the document or series of documents that the biographers of the thirteenth century refer to as the official pontifical approval of the Third Order.

According to Meersseman, the pontifical approval of the three orders mentioned in the *Legend of the Three Companions* refers to "the first five bulls (1221-1227, cf. *Dossier* notes 41-47) that reconfirmed for the new penitents all the privileges already granted to the ancient penitents" (*Ordo Fraternitatis*, p. 361).

12. Meersseman, *I Disciplinati*, p. 45.

13. Meersseman, *I Disciplinati*, p. 46.

14. The *Little Flowers of St. Francis*, XVI, *Omnibus*, p. 1335. "And from that time he (St. Francis) planned to organize the Third Order of the Continent for the salvation of all people everywhere." Celano, in referring to this extraordinary event merely states: "When these men therefore saw this miracle, they were filled with the greatest admiration and said: 'Truly this man is a saint and a friend of the Most HIgh.' And they hastened with the greatest devotion to at least touch his clothing, praising and blessing God" (*1 Cel.* 59, *Omnibus*, pp. 278-279). In the *Treatise of the Miracles*, also by Celano, we read, "All those that witnessed it, with great marvel, gave glory to God" (*3 Cel.* 21). In his *Legenda Maior* St. Bonaventure uses more or less the same expression: "The onlookers were amazed and gave glory to God" (*Leg. M.* XII, 4, *Omnibus*, p. 723).

15. The *Little Flowers of St. Francis*, XVI, *Omnibus*, p. 1335.

16. Cf. Domenico Cresi, *S. Francesco e i suoi Ordini*, Florence 1955, p. 282; Fausta Casolini, "Appunti per una storia del T.O.F." in *Il Terz'Ordine Francescano nella storia, nel diritto, nella sociologia*, Rome, 1955, p. 102. Raffaele Pazzelli, *Il Terz'Ordine Regolare di S. Francesco attraverso i secoli*, Rome, 1958, p. 29.

17. Kajetan Esser, O.F.M., *Life and Rule: A Commentary on the Rule of the Third Order Regular of St. Francis.* Translated by Sr. M. Honora, O.S.F., and edited by Marion A. Habig, O.F.M., Franciscan Herald Press, Chicago, 1967.

18. Kajetan Esser, O.F.M.-Engelbert Grau, O.F.M., *Love's Reply*, translated by Ignatius Brady, O.F.M., Franciscan Herald Press, Chicago, 1963.

19. Kajetan Esser, "La lettera di san Francesco ai Fedeli," in *L'Ordine della Penitenza*, p. 14.

20. Kajetan Esser, "A Forerunner of the 'Epistola ad Fideles' of St. Francis of Assisi (Codex 225 of the Biblioteca Guarnacci of Volterra)," in *Analecta T.O.R.*, XIV, fasc. 129 (1978), pp. 11-47.

21. Esser, "Forerunner," p. 38.

22. "Modern criticism fixes the date between 1215 and 1226." Esser, *Lettera*, p. 69.

23. K. Esser, "Un documento dell'inizio del Duecento sui Penitenti"

in I *Frati Penitenti di san Francesco nella società del Due e Trecento*, Rome, 1977, p. 96.

24. Esser, *Documento*, p. 96.
25. Esser, "Forerunner," p. 34.
26. Esser, "Forerunner," p. 34.
27. Esser, "Forerunner," p. 37.
28. *3 Comp.* 57, *Omnibus*, pp. 940-941.
29. Esser, "Forerunner," p. 37.
30. Esser, "Forerunner," p. 37.
31. Esser, "Forerunner," p. 27.
32. Esser, "Forerunner," p. 45.
33. *1 Cel.* 37, *Omnibus*, pp. 259-260.
34. Schmucki, p. 120.
35. Esser, "Forerunner," p. 39.
36. Cf. in Luciano Canonici, "I Terziari francescani 'fratelli e sorelle della penitenza' " in *Quaderni di spiritualità francescana*, 18, Assisi, 1970, p. 149. We here give the Latin text of Julian of Speyer: "Omni namque ordini, conditioni, aetati et sexui congruenter documenta salutis impendit; omnibus vivendi regulam tribuit, cuius hodie felicem ducatum in utroque sexu sequentium triumphare se gaudet Ecclesia triplici militia salvandorum. Tres enim, supra tetigimus, Ordines ordinavit. . . . Tertius quoque non mediocris perfectionis Ordo Poenitentium dicitur, qui clericis et laicis, virginibus, continentibus coniugatisque communis, sexum salubriter utrumque complecitur." *Vita S. Francisci*, n. 23. *Anal Franc. X*, 346.

The *Vita S. Francisci* of Julian of Speyer is important most of all because, even though it does depend greatly on the *Vita Prima* of Celano for its material, it clarifies some vague expressions used by Celano. Julian lived for many years with Celano and knew his thought well. His explanations can therefore be said to be not subjective, personal interpretations, but representations of Celano's own meaning.

37. Schmucki, p. 124.
38. Schmucki, p. 124, note 32.
39. *Leg. Maior IV*, n. 6, *Omnibus*, p. 657. "Nam praedicationis ipsius fervore succensi, quam plurimi secundum formam a Dei viro acceptam novis se paenitentiae legibus vinciebant, quorum vivendi modum idem Christi famulus Ordinem Fratrum de Paenitentia nominari decrevit. Nimirum, sicut in caelum tendentibus paenitentiae viam omnibus constat esse communem, sic et hic status clericos et laicos, vergines et coniugatos in utroque sexu admittens, quanti sit apud Deum meriti, ex pluribus per aliquos ipsorum patratis miraculis innotescit," *Anal. Franc., X*, 573.

One could ask to whom St. Bonventure was referring when he wrote the final words of this passage. It would be difficult to give a complete answer, taking into consideration the number of holy people known by St. Bonaventure. Perhaps a probable name would have been that of Umiliana dei Cerchi, who died in Florence as a recluse penitent on

May 19, 1246. Her "vita" was composed in the same year by "an important person in the convent of Santa Croce, Brother Vito of Cortona, who had been received into the order by St. Francis himself, and was sent by (Francis) as provincial to Rumania." (Cf. A. Benvenuti-Papi, "Umiliana dei Cerchi. Nascita di un culto nella Firenze del Duecento" in *Studi Francescani*, 77 (1980), p. 101 and note 75.) Umiliana had wanted to live the idea of "penance" in the smallest detail: widowed at the age of twenty-two, she did not want to remarry; she renounced her marital inheritance, because she would have been required to swear an oath. Living in seclusion from the world as a recluse," enclosed in a tower of the family home, she later privately created an autonomous penitential form with penitent *sociae*, such as Ravenna, Gisla, and Benvenuta. In the Florentine society the *Ordo Poenitentium* had assumed vast dimensions, assuming the characteristics of a "confraternity" to answer the charitable needs of an urban society. In this phenomenon, however, there was almost exclusively male participation. Because of the juridical position of women at that time, their participation was limited. Because of this the female penitents developed other expressions of private penance, which were primarily conducted "in domibus propriis" (Cf. Benvenuti-Papi, p. 111).

40. Schmucki, p. 129.

41. "Doctrinae Francisci elucet maxime fructus in tribus ab eo statutis Ordinibus . . . Tertius Ordo est Fratrum et Sororum de Poenitentia, clericis, laicis, virginibus, viduis et coniugatis communis, cuius propositum est: in domibus propriis honeste vivere, operibus pietatis intendere, pompam saeculi fugere. . . . In regulis seu vivendi formis Ordinis istorum dictandis sanctae memoriae dominus papa Gregorius, in minore adhuc officio constitutus, beato Francisco intima familiaritate coniunctus, devote supplebat quod viro sancto iudicandi scientia deerat." Bernard of Bessa, *Liber de Laudibus b. Francisci*, c. 7, in *Anal. Franc. III*, 679, 686.

42. Schmucki, p. 132.

CHAPTER TEN

1. The earlier critical edition of the Opuscula is that of the Collegio S. Bonaventura, Ad claras aquas, third ed., (1949).

2. K. Esser, *Die Opuscula des Hl. Franziskus von Assisi*, Grottaferrata, 1976. An English translation can be found in *Francis and Clare, the Complete Works*, translation and introduction by Regis J. Armstrong, O.F.M. Cap., and Ignatius Brady, O.F.M., New York, 1982, pp. 62-65.

3. K. Esser, "Forerunner," p. 36.

4. Esser, "Forerunner," p. 37.

5. Esser, "Forerunner," pp. 37-38.

6. Cf. our entry, "Penitenza, mortificazione" in *Dizionario Francescano*, ed. Movimento Francescano, 1983, col. 1287.

7. Esser, "Forerunner," p. 36.

8. Esser, "Forerunner," p. 38.

9. Bartolomeo Pastor Oliver, T.O.R., "Un Precursor de la 'Carta a los Fieles' de san Francisco de Asis. Comparacion con otros textos anteriores," in *Analecta T.O.R.*, XIV (1980), pp. 751-770.

10. Richardus S. Victoris, "Explicatio in 'Cantica Canticorum,' " c. 8, *PL* 196, 426 c.

11. Esser, "Forerunner," p. 38.

12. It is our opinion that it was this last expression "to conserve these words . . . because they are spirit and life," which led the copyist of the Volterra document, or the document from which it was copied, to entitle the work *"Haec sunt verba vitae et salutis, quae, si quis legerit et fecerit, inveniet vitam et hauriet salutem a Domino. Amen."* The illustrious Paul Sabatier considered this the title of the work, and used it when he published the *Recensio prior* in 1900 in "an appendix to the second volume of his *Collection d'études et de documents sur l'histoire religieuse du Moyen Age*" (Esser, "Precursor," pp. 11-12).

It should be noted that the "part (of the codex of the Volterra document) that contains this Opuscula was, according to the experts, written around the middle of the thirteenth century; . . . one should, therefore, recognize in this (*Vo*) a special importance of the textual history of the works (Esser, p. 12, note 1). The copyist of *Codex 4* in the Vatican Library, which is very close to, and possibly dependent on the Volterra manuscript (cf. Esser, Oliger, *La tradition manuscrite des Opuscules de saint François d'Assise*, Rome, 1972, p. 92) decided to copy the Admonitions, but not what came after it in the Volterra codex, namely, *1 Lf.* Since there was no division in *Vo* between the Admonitions and *1 Lf*, the V4 copyist took the title of *1 Lf* (*Haec sunt . . .*) as the conclusion of the Admonitions. Thus many scholars were led to believe that *Haec sunt* was an integral part of the Admonitions. Esser himself claimed this in 1974 when he wrote: "That which Paul Sabatier used as a title (of the *Recensio prior*) is in reality the concluding sentence of the Admonitions and is found both in Codex *Vo* and in many other texts, and was included in the *editio princeps* of the Opuscula of Wadding" ("Precursor," pp. 11-12). However, in the critical edition of the Opuscula he recognized this "concluding sentence of the Admonitions" as "an adjunct" and did not include it in the critical text. (Cf. *Opuscula sancti Patris Francisci Assisiensis.* Editiones Collegii S. Bonaventurae Ad Claras Aquas, Grottaferrata 1978, p. 82, note 6, and p. 107). (Cf. "THE TITLE OF THE 'RECENSIO PRIOR OF THE LETTER OF THE FAITHFUL': Clarifications Regarding Codex 225 of Volterra," (*cod Vo*), by Raffaele Pazzelli, trans. by Sr. Nancy Celashi, O.F.S., *Anal. T.O.R.*, Vol. XIX, Fasc. 142, Rome, 1987).

13. Esser, *Opuscula*, p. 107.

14. *Omnibus*, p. 91, note 1.

15. K. Esser, *La lettera di san Francesco ai fedeli*, p. 71. It should be noted that Esser, even though in his various studies concerning the *Letter to All the Faithful* he changed his opinions, or clarified those previously expressed, accepted the elimination of an important comma in the critical edition so that the *Letter* is directed to *Universis cristianis religiosis,*

that is exclusively to those who, in a more or less perfect way were considered "religious," that is, to the penitents. Thus, in the latest *Allegato alle Fonti Francescane*, in the outline of the presentation of la *Regola dei fratelli e delle sorelle dell'Ordine dei Frati della penitenza* of Nicholas IV (1289) there is a reference to this work as the Letter to all the Faithful Religious. (Cf. *Regola dell'Ordine di Santa Chiara di Papa Urbano IV—Regola dei fratelli e delle sorelle dell'Ordine dei Frati della penitenza di Papa Nicholas IV*. Appendix to the Fonti Francescane, ed. Movimento Francescano, Assisi, 1978, p. 36.

17. *Omnibus*, p. 91.

18. Pastor, "Precursor," p. 755. Cf. D. Zorzi, *Valori religiosi, nella letteratura provenzale. La spiritualità trinitaria*, Milan, 1954, pp. 27-33.

19. "When the sweetest melody of spirit would bubble up in him, he would give exterior expression to it in French, and the breath of the divine whisper which his ear perceived in secret would burst forth in French in a song of joy" (2 *Cel.* 127, *Omnibus*, p. 467). The *Legend of the Three Companions* attests that Francis often spoke French, "a language he delighted to speak, though he did not know it very well" 3 *Comp.* 10, *Omnibus*, p. 899. Cf. also 1 *Cel.* 16, *Omnibus*, 242; 2 *Cel.* 13, *Omnibus*, 373; 3 *Comp.* 24, *Omnibus*, 913.

On the topic of the influence of the Provençal culture on Francis' upbringing, see Cheriapattaparambil, *The influence of Troubadours in the life and writings of St. Francis*, (Manuscript) Pont. Ateneo Antonianum, Rome, 1982.

CHAPTER ELEVEN

The reader should note that the present study is essentially historical, and does not try to treat the penitential spirituality "ex professo." This will have to be done in another work. The purpose of this work is to clarify only some ideas present in the documents concerned, ideas that will have to be elaborated and developed.

1. "Seipsum per proprium sanguinem suum sacrificium et hostiam in ara crucis offerret" (v. 11).

2. We should note that the *Memoriale* here prescribes more than what was prescribed for the "faithful"; Lateran Council IV reduced the duty or obligation of receiving Holy Communion to only once a year. This gives us an examplle of how the thought of Francis expressed in the *Letter to All the Faithful* that "religious especially are bound to do more and greater things" (v. 36) was elaborated on in this legislative text.

3. Esser, *La Lettera*, p. 73.

4. Cf. Magli, pp. 77-78.

5. Magli, p. 78.

6. Esser, "Precursor," p. 36.

7. Esser, *La Lettera*, p. 73.

8. Esser, *La Lettera*, pp. 73-75.

9. Temperini, T.O.R. *"La spiritualità,"* p. 552.

10. The first "stream" is identified today with the three families of

the First Order (Conventuals, Minors, and Capuchins); the second with the Poor Clares (second Order) and the third with the Third Order, also known as the Franciscan Order of Penance, which includes friars, all Franciscan sisters (except the Poor Clares) and the Secular Franciscan Order.

11. Temperini, L. "La tradizione spirituale" in Pazzelli-Temperini, *La Tradizione storica e spirituale del nostro movimento*, ed. CSI-TOR, Rome, 1980, p. 18.

12. *3 Comp.* 37, *Omnibus*, p. 925; cf. *An P* 19, Isabell, p. 102.

13. Cf. Lemmens, *Testimonia minora*, p. 17; *Omnibus*, p. 1605.

14. *Testimonia minora*, p. 79; *Omnibus*, p. 1608.

15. *Reg n. B.*, V; *Francis and Clare*, p. 114.

16. Schmucki, O., "Linee fondamentali della 'Forma vitae' nell'esperienza di san Francesco" in *Lettura biblico-teologica delle Fonti Francescane* by G. Cardaropoli and M. Conti Ed., Antonianum, Rome, 1979, p. 211.

17. "For he wrote in the Rule 'and let them be as lesser brothers,' and when these words were spoken, indeed, in that same hour, he said, 'I wish that this fraternity should be called the Order of Friars Minor.' "

18. It is evident that the expression of the earlier Rule is a paraphrase of Mt 20:25-26 and Lk 22:26.

19. Cf. *Letter to the entire Order*, v. 51, *Francis and Clare*, p. 61.

20. Lapsanski, *Evangelical Perfection*, p. 100.

21. *1 Cel.* 24, *Omnibus*, p. 248.

22. *1 Cel.* 24, *Omnibus*, p. 249.

23. "*Sacrum Commercium Sancti Francisci cum domina Paupertate*," Florence-Quaracchi, 1929. By an unknown author and uncertain date of origin; many scholars propose accepting 1227 as the year of its composition. Concerning this work, K. Esser noted that, "unfortunately, this precious record, which bears such eloquent witness to the spirituality of the Order, still in its infancy, later underwent certain misinterpretations which earned it the mistrust of historians, mainly in regard to the time of its origin. Today, this work may be seen as a very faithful interpretation of the mind and intention of St. Francis. As such it must be carefully considered next to the sources of the early life of the Order already familiar to us. In certain critical points it can even correct them" (Origins, p. 8).

24. Lapsanski, pp. 77-78.

25. Lapsanski, p. 78. Poverty, in the meaning of the anonymous author of the *Sacrum Commercium*, requires as its first constructive element "freely renouncing earthly goods." The second element is the inclination toward spiritual goods and the third "the desire for eternal goods."

CHAPTER TWELVE

1. Esser, *Origins*, p. 37.
2. Esser, *Origins*, p. 37.

3. Cf. Fredegando da Anversa, O.F.M. Cap., *Il Terz'Ordine Secolare di San Francesco* 1221-1921. Saggio storico, Rome, Marietti, 1921, p. 78.

4. This, for example, was the single most important element for the rise and flourishing of the Order of the Umiliati.

5. It would be sufficient to recall the description that Jacques de Vitry gave of his trip through Lombardy in the spring of 1216. He called Milan a "haven for heretics."

6. See above, p. 105.

7. Philip, Duke of Swabia, was the brother of Henry VI, son of Frederick Barbarossa, who succeeded Frederick as emperor in 1191. Upon Henry's death in Sicily in 1197, Philip was elected King of Germany (March 6, 1198). The Guelf party, however, elected Otto IV of Brunswick, son of Henry, King of Bavaria (July 19, 1198). Both claimed the throne until 1208. Pope Innocent III wanted a rapid solution to the problem so that he could devote more energy to the IV Crusade, which had begun in 1202.

8. Burchard of Ursberg provides very interesting reading on the problems of Ugolino's mission and the feelings in Germany about Innocent III and the Roman Church in general. Like most of Germany, the writer considered the Staufen as the legitimate lords of the country, and therefore did not approve of the pope's initial opposition to Philip. (Cf. Burchardi et Cuonradi Urspergensium Chronicon in *MGH. Script.* tom. XXIII.)

9. Cf. above, pp. 94-96.

10. *1 Cel.* 75, *Omnibus*, p. 291. Cf. Esser, *Origins*, p. 38.

11. Cf. above, p. 93, note 40.

12. *3 Comp.* 61 *Omnibus*, p. 944. It is also necessary to bear in mind the beautiful presentation that the *Legend* itself makes of Cardinal Ugolino to establish the solidity of his relationship with Francis and to evaluate objectively the great role that the cardinal had in the shaping of the Franciscan movement.

13. Paul Sabatier, *Vita di San Francesco d'Assisi*, Italian translation by Giuseppe Zanichelli, 1978, p. 171. Sabatier also notes that "the bull *Litterae tuae* (Aug. 27, 1218) shows a similar intention to favor the Poor Clares" (p. 337, note 11).

14. Cf. Esser, *Origins*, p. 143.

15. Bernardo da Bessa, p. 686. See above, p. 107.

16. *Vita Gregorii IX, papae*, in *Vitae Romanorum Pontificum* (ed. Muratori); in Lemmens, pp. 11-14. "This work was written around 1240 by an employee of the papal curia, possibly Giovanni della Campania." (T. Lombardi, *Introduzione allo studio del Francescanismo*, Assisi, 1975, p. 47.

17. *Vita Gregorii IX, papae*, in Lemmens, p. 12.

18. There are some who dispute this; however, in the same text the anonymous author affirms that to the same sisters (*domnabus eisdem*) the pope granted a monastery in the city, that of St. Cosmas. This monastery had, in fact, been given by Gregory IX to the Poor Clares on July 5, 1233, with the brief *Quia illos vere diligimus*. Cf. in *Bull. Franc.* I, 112.

Cf. also the brief *Quoties nobis* of August 3, 1238 in *Bull. Franc.* I, 249.

It should also be noted that in the papal documents of this period the word *inclusae* was used only to refer to the Poor Clares; only later was it extended to include Augustinians and Dominicans. (Cf. Omaechevarria, *Escritos de Santa Clara y Documentos contemporaneos*, Madrid, 1970, p. 213). Gregory IX used this same name (*sororum inclusarum*) in his letter to Agnes of Prague (May 9, 1238) to refer to the Poor Clares. (Cf. Meersseman, *Dossier*, p. 53). He later noted that they, unlike the others "ut gratum praestent Deo famulatum, perpetuo sunt *inclusae*" (Feb. 21, 1241). (Cf. Omaechevarria, p. 213).

19. In order to understand the whole question better, it would be useful to summarize the formulation of the legislation of the Poor Clares: Clare and her first followers were guided by the few precepts given them by Francis; these were probably not very different from those given to the brothers (cf. Omaechevarria, p. 208). When the Fourth Lateran Council (1215) required (Canon 13) Clare to choose one of the approved rules, she took that of St. Benedict. Consequently, she had to accept the title of Abbess (cf. Omaechevarria, "La 'Regola' dell'Ordine di S. Chiara" in *Forma Sororum*, XIV (1977), no. 5, p. 174, note 10). Cardinal Ugolino, who had come in contact with various communities of Poor Ladies during his travels as papal legate (1216-1219) reported to Pope Honorius, proposing various measures to put them under the protection of the Holy See. With the bull *Littere tue nobis* of Aug. 27, 1218 (the first in *Bullarium Franciscanum*) Honorius authorized Ugolino to give some organization to the movement. Ugolino codified and adapted the regulations, thus compiling the document which would come to be known as the "Rule of Cardinal Ugolino"; it gave them the *forma vivendi* that they were to observe with the formal profession of the Rule of St. Benedict (cf. Omaechevarria, *Escritos*, p. 211).

This rule remained in effect in practice for all new monasteries of the Poor Ladies until the Rule of St. Clare, confirmed by Innocent IV in 1253 and the Second Rule promulgated by Urban IV in 1263. When, therefore, one speaks of the "Rule of St. Clare" up until 1247 (Rule of Innocent IV), one is referring to the Rule of Cardinal Ugolino. Naturally, however, there is a great difference between writing a rule and founding an order; thus the expression of the anonymous author of the life of Gregory is exaggerated. Nonetheless, he must have called him the "institutor" of the order because he had given the Poor Ladies the Rule.

20. In the *formulario* prepared by Cardinal Ugolino himself and contained in his *Registri*, by which a diocesan bishop could give his permission for the erection of a new monastery for the Poor Ladies in his diocese, there is no other rule acknowledged than that of Ugolino. The main part is presented here: "Nos ... Dei gratia ... episcopus ... in tali loco plenam facultatem monasterium constituendi, vel talem locum cum omnibus pertinentiis suis ad construendum ibidem monasterium in honore gloriose virginis Mariae, in quo virgines Deo dicatae et alie ancille Christi in paupertate Domino famulentur iuxta formam vite vel

religionis pauperum dominarum de Valle Spoleti sive Tuscia per dominum Hugonem venerabilem episcopum Hostiensem auctoritate domini papae eisdem sororibus traditam...." From *Registri dei Cardinali Ugolino d'Ostia e Ottaviano degli Ubaldini*, published by Guido Levi, Rome, 1890, doc. CXXV, pp. 153-154).

21. The esteem of Honorius for Ugolino is expressly shown by his letter *Cum is qui secundum* (March 4, 1221), addressed to the patriarchs of Aquileia and Grado, to the Archbishops and bishops of Milan, Ravenna, Genoa and Pisa and to the "ecclesiarum prelatis per Lombardiam, Marchiam, Romaniolam et Tusciam constitutis" which delegates Ugolino as Legate of the Apostolic See, "licet ipsius presentia cara nobis valde careremus inviti: ... ecce a dextris est vir dextera venerabilis frater noster ... episcopus Hostiensis qui dextera divina tanquam cedrus Libani prelatus in Ecclesie paradiso, altitudine contemplationis erectus, virtutum odore suavis, fame sinceritate penitus imputribilis, non solum sua fortitudine ad sustentationem domus Domini operatur, verum etiam honestatis candore ipsius superficiem convenustat" (*Registri*, doc. CXI, p. 139). Cf. also *Arch. Vat. Honorii Regesta*, an. V, ep. 460, c. 91.

Emperor Frederick II, in his letter, *Iocunde fame felicitas* (Feb. 10, 1221) written from Salerno to congratulate Ugolino on the news he had heard from the bishop of Reggio, namely, that Honorius had appointed his "friend" legate, calls him "vir fama integer, religione perspicuus, vita purus, facundia eloquentissimus et claris virtutum et scientie titulis circumspectus" (*Registri*, doc. CXXII, pp. 150-152).

22. Levi, Preface to *Registri*, p. x.

23. Gratian, canonist and theologian, was certainly born in Tuscany, although various cities claim the honor, and the precise dates of his birth and death are obscure. It is certain, however, that his main work, the *Decretum*, was written in the years 1140-1150. The Bologna tradition, contained in an epigraph in the Basilica of St. Petronius gives 1151 as the year of the *Decretum's* composition. Gratian's work took place within the territories of Tuscany, Emilia, and Romagna, especially in Bologna where he lived in the monastery of SS. Narbor and Felix (thus the opinion that he was Camaldolese or Cluniac), wrote his *Decretum* and was the first to teach canon law in that European judicial and cultural center; this earned Gratian the title of "founder" of canon law. The books of the *Decretum* were very successful, but were also disdained at times. Today, taking a more critical viewpoint, we can say that they are an effort towards a synthesis, which is more often better as the work of several people rather than only one; his errors are the errors common to the culture of his time. (Cf. Forchielli, "Graziano" in *E.C.*, VI, 1028-29). In some codices the work of Gratian has the title *Concordia discordantium canonum*, which better expresses its contents.

The *Decretum* is divided into three parts: prima pars de *Distinctionibus*; secuda pars de *Causis*; tertia pars de *Consecratione*. Part I contains 101 *distinctiones*. Part II has 36 *causae*, divided into *quaestiones*. The third part is also divided into five *distinctiones*. The *distinctiones* of Parts I and III, and the *quaestiones* of Part II are divided into *canones;* numeration begins at one in each part.

The material concerning penitence (in the broad sense of the word) is treated in *Causa* 33 (Part II), *Questio* III, divided (the only one in Part II) into 7 *distinctiones*. This constitutes the *Tractatus de Poenitentia* that is sometimes cited as a separate work. For example, the famous *Margarita Decreti seu Tabula Martiniana* that accompanies many sixteenth century editions of the *Decretum* and was composed by the Premonstratensian Friar Martin, Sacred Penitentiary, always and only cites "De Poenitentia," indicating the relevant "distinctio" and the first words of the paragraph. He refers thereby to the third *Questio,* of *Causa* 33, subdivided into "*distinctiones.*"

24. The reference is always to the *Memoriale propositum* already mentioned, pp. 59-62.

25. Sabatier attributed part of the merit of his discovery to a reference he found in the very precise description of the contents of those codices by Prof. Vincenzo de Bartholomais in "Ricerche Abruzzesi: communicazioni all'Istituto Storico Italiano" in *Bulletini dell'Istituto Storico Italiano* 1889, pp. 101, ff.

26. Sabatier, *Opuscules,* tom I, pp. 17-30.

27. After the text of Capistrano other texts of the same rule were discovered. The first was in a codex of Koenigsberg (Rothomagensis 1159) studied by Lemmens in "Regula antiqua Ordinis de Poenitentia iuxta novum codicem" in *AFH* VI (1913), pp. 242-250; the codex dates from the middle of the fourteenth century. A third text was found by Bughetti in the Florentine Landau Library, in codex 225, 226. It was published by him with the title "Prima Regula Tertii Ordinis iuxta novum codicem" in *AFH* XIV (1921), pp. 109-121. "According to some historians, it may be older than the other two, because it is not divided into chapters and offers a purer text of the Rule without the additions of local constitutions which the others contain in part. Therefore it should be dated before 1228. This codex is also called the Veneto Codex, because it was known through a description in a codex of the Dominican library of St. Zanipolo in Venice (eighteenth century)" (L. Temperini, "La Regola degli Ordini Francescani," in *Analecta T.O.R.,* Vol. XI, 1968, p. 37). A fourth text, transmitted in the vernacular by Friar Marianus of Florence, conserved in the "Nazionale" Library in Florence (Cod. Pal. n. 147) and also discovered by Sabatier, was studied, reconstructed, and dated by Wyngaert, "De Tertio Ordine S. Francisci iuxta Marianum Florentinum" in *AFH* XII (1920), pp. 1-77. A fifth text was described by Chiappini in *AFH* XVIII (1925), pp. 348 ff. It is contained in cod. S 73 from the fifteenth century in the Provincial Library of the Friars Minor in Aquila, where it is followed by the *Acts of a Provincial Chapter* of Bologna of November 1289. The text of the *Memoriale* is identical to that of the Capistran codex.

28. Our interpretation of the title is justified by the following considerations: 1) The word *memoriale* in documents of this period meant "charter," "basic document," in the way that "Charta Caritatis" of Citeaux

is the basic document of the Cistercians. (Cf. Meersseman, *Dossier*, p. 92, note on title). 2) *Propositum* is the biblical expression in use since Christian antiquity to indicate a public profession or a consecration to God. In the texts immediately prior to the *Memoriale propositi*, that is in the texts of the Umiliati, the Poor Catholics, and Poor Lombards, *Propositum* clearly has the meaning of "rule of life on which one makes one's profession." The same is valid for the writers of the time. Thus, in the *Decretum Gratiani*, I, D, c. 15 we find: "Si quis virorum putaverit sancto proposito, idest continentiae, convenire, etc." In regard to the first Umiliati, the Cronaca di Laon (*MGH Script.* 26, 49) says that in the year 1178 "Hi accedentes ad papam petierunt hoc eorum propositum confirmari" (cf. Meersseman, *Dossier*, p. 92).

29. Some scholars (Mandonnet, Little, Sabatier, and Meersseman) have attempted a reconstruction of the primitive text with relative success (cf. Temperini, p. 35).

30. "Omnes a iuramentis solemnibus abstineant, nisi necessitate cogente in casibus a summo pontifice exceptis in sua indulgentia, videlicet pace, fide, calumnia, et testimonio" (cf. Meersseman, *Dossier*, pp. 92-112).

31. Cf. Meersseman, *Dossier*, p. 45, note 4.

32. On this subject, see Francesco Mattesini, O.F.M., *Le origini del Terz'Ordine francescano—Regola antica e Vita del Beato Lucchese*. Ed. Vita e Pensiero, Milan, 1964, pp. 11-16.

33. Mattesini, p. 17.

34. *3 Comp.* 60, *Omnibus*, p. 943.

35. *An. P.* 41, Isabell, p. 112.

36. Atanasio G. Matanić, O.F.M. "Problematica delle origini del Terz'Ordine Francescano, in *Frate Francesco*, XXXVIII (1971), p. 245. Cf. there authors of the same opinion.

37. "Sane felicis recordationis Honorius papa predecessor noster attendens vos fructus penitentie facientes, ab huius seculi filiis angustiis inexquisitis affligi, ac propter hoc favendos esse in tam laudabili actione, religionem vestram amplexans in visceribus Iesu Christi prosecutus est gratia speciali, mandans universis archiepiscopis et episcopis per Italiam constitutis, ut vos servarent immunes a iuramentis etc." (Cf. in Meersseman, *Dossier*, p. 44, n. 2).

38. Cf. Meersseman, *Dossier*, p. 83. For example the *Propositum* of the Poor Catholics contained in the bull *Eius exemplo* of Innocent III begins: ". . . Propositum quoque conversationis eorum presenti pagine duxumus adnotandum, cuius tenor *talis est.*" Cf. in Meersseman, *Dossier*, p. 282. The second *Propositum* of the Poor Lombards (1212), contained in the bull *Ne quis de caetero* of the same pontiff says: "Conversationis ergo vestrum propositum *tale est.*" Cf. in Meersseman, *Dossier*, p. 288.

39. Meersseman, *Dossier*, p. 84.

40. Meersseman, *Dossier*, p. 84.

41. The opinion that the *Memoriale propositi* may have originally been included in a bull of Gregory IX should not be underestimated.

It is possible that the few introductory phrases were omitted by the copyists who were more concerned with copying the text of the rule as the fraternities had requested. Only a thorough archival research, combined with a bit of good luck, could substantiate such an opinion.

CHAPTER THIRTEEN

1. All reference to these papal documents is according to the numeration used by Meersseman in his *Dossier*, pp. 41-47.

2. Meersseman, *Dossier*, p. 41.

3. Meerseman, *Dossier*, p. 42.

4. Meersseman, *Dossier*, pp. 42-43.

5. Meersseman, *Dossier*, pp. 43-45.

6. Meersseman, *Dossier*, pp. 46-47.

7. Odoardi, G., "L'Ordine della Penitenza di san Francesco nei documenti pontifici del secolo XIII" in *L'Ordine della Penitenza*, pp. 83, 86.

8. Cf. Odoardi, p. 82 f.

9. See Esser's study of this in *Origins*.

10. *MGH Script.* tome XXIII. Passages of this work are found in the *Omnibus*, pp. 1604 ff. We do not know the exact year of Burchard's birth, but he said that in 1198 he was in Rome "in minore aetate et saeculari vita constitutus adhuc" (p. 366). In 1202 he was ordained a priest by the bishop of Costanza and then entered the Premonstratensian monastery "Sorethanum" where he was professed in 1207. In 1209 he was elected abbot (*praepositus*) of that same monastery. In the following year he went to Rome to ask for privileges for his monastery; these were granted by Innocent III on Feb. 13, 1211. In 1215 he was elected "ab Urspergensibus" and held that "prepositura" for eleven years. He died around the end of 1226. He is, therefore, a writer quite contemporary with St. Francis. He is considered to be "informed" because of his friendship with men who had arranged the meetings between Innocent III and Philip of Germany. He was a friend of Abbot Martin of the monastery "Parisius" (near Speyer) who, in 1204 was present at the taking of Constantinople. The editors Abel and Weiland affirm of him: "Urspergensis fide dignissimum se exhibet." In regard to Innocent III, who was initially against Philip, Burchard writes in "acri stilo" but "fidem et veritatem in rebus tradendis numquam videtur laesisse" (p. 336). Burchard's chronicle ends in 1222; Conrad, also Abbot of Ursberg, continued the chronicle till 1229.

11. Cf. Huygens, *Lettres de Jacques de Vitry*, edition critique, Leiden, 1960. *See also* Lemmens, pp. 79-84. Some passages are in *Omnibus*, pp. 1606-1614.

Jacques de Vitry is considered one of the most noteworthy personalities of the thirteenth century. Born between 1160 and 1170, probably at Rheims, he studied in Paris. From 1211 to 1216 he was a canon regular at Saint Nicholas d'Oignies, in the diocese of Liege. Here he met Marie d'Oignies, whom he venerated as a saint and considered "his mother."

In 1213 he preached against the Albigensians and in favor of the Crusades. Elected bishop of St. John of Acre, the most important port of arrival for the Crusaders, he came to Italy in the spring of 1216. In his first letter he tells of the events of his trip, calling Milan a "haven of heretics" and speaking well of the Umiliati. He arrived at Perugia on the day after the death of Innocent III (therefore on July 17, 1216); he tells how, during the night, thieves had robbed the dead pontiff of his precious vestments, leaving him in the church "fere nudum et fetidum"; that in the papal curia he found many things "spiritui meo contraria" and that his only consolation was the existence of the Friars Minor and Minor Sisters (Vitry's most famous passage). Mens (*Begijnen*, 245, note 78) as cited by Esser (*Origins*, p. 14, n. 27) "states with good reason that James of Vitry may have met Francis personally in the summer of 1216 in Perugia." In that case the prelate would have probably told him about Maria d'Oignies (+1213), supporter of the Beghines and of Eucharistic devotion in France. Perhaps from this meeting arose Francis' idea of going to France the following year; he was, however, dissuaded by Cardinal Ugolino. (G.O. Asseldonk, "Nexus S. Francisci cum motu universali paenitentiae" in *Tertius Ordo* XXXIII (1972), pp. 168-169, and notes 11 and 12). After the election of Honorius III (who received him several times most amicably and granted him some privileges, but not that of the exemption from taxes for the Crusades as he had hoped), Jacques de Vitry left for Genoa where he spent the month of September. He left for Acre in the beginning of October (his second letter states that the trip took five weeks, and he reached St. John on Nov. 4). From June 1218 to September 1221 he participated in the Crusade campaign in Egypt. After the success at Damietta, Nov. 5, 1219, the campaign seems to have ended in real disaster. Damietta fell on Sept. 8, 1221. Towards the end of 1225 de Vitry returned to Europe; three years later he renounced the difficult see of St. John of Acre. In July 1229 he is cardinal bishop of Frascati. From this period we have some very interesting sermons to the Friars Minor; in them one can see a profound knowledge of St. Francis. (The *Sermones* are edited by Ilarino Felder in *Analecta Ordinis Minorum Capucinorum* 19 (1903), pp. 22-24; 114-122; 149-158). Schreiber calls de Vitry "one of the most sensitive observers of the canonical and monastic life of the world around him" who "goes to work in thorough fashion" so that he gives "an excellent and most varied account of the religious life as he observed it" (Esser, *Origins*, p. 15, note 31). The cardinal died at Frascati on May 1, 1240; a year later his body was taken to Oignies and buried there (cf. Huygens, Introduction, p. 1).

    12. Esser, *Origins*, p. 39.
    13. Esser, *Origins*, p. 52, note 87.
    14. Meersseman, *Disciplinati*, p. 46.
    15. Meersseman, *Dossier*, pp. 88-90.
    16. Cf. Meersseman, *Dossier*, p. 6; *Disciplinati*, p. 45.
    17. Meersseman, *Dossier*, p. 83.

18. Meersseman, *Dossier*, p. 7.

19. This position had been generally accepted until the results of the recent meetings on penance.

20. Roggen seems to support this when he writes: "A narrative or legislative document capable of ascertaining sufficiently that St. Francis had really 'founded' an order for laymen as he had founded for the 'Poor Ladies' has yet to be found." (H. Roggen, "Les relations du premiere ordre franciscaine avec le Tiers Ordre au XIIIe in *L'Ordine della Penitenza*, p. 200). Julian of Speyer makes no distinction between the Third Order and the other two.

21. Even if, juridically speaking, we do not have a Franciscan Order *per se* until 1289, there is the whole reality of the penitents of the Franciscan inspiration quite evident before that date.

22. Zanoni, p. 121.

23. Burns, "Frati della Penitenza di Gesu Christi" in *DIP* VI (1980), 1398-1404.

24. Cf. Dal Pino, p. 663.

25. Cf. Meersseman, *Ordo Fraternitatis*, passim.

26. See the *Prime manifestazioni di vita comunitaria*.

27. For example, see Alberzoni in *Prime Manifestazioni*, pp. 212-214.

28. "He (Francis) founded three orders . . . the third is called Order of the Penitents; common to the clergy and to laity, to virgins, to the continent, and to the married, it embraces either sex" (Julian of Speyer, *Vita*, n. 23, *Anal. Franc.* X, 345). "(Francis) instituted then a third order, which is called the Order of Penitents or the Brothers of Penance." (St. Bonaventure, "Sermon II de S.P.N. Francisco" in *Op. Om.* IX, p. 576. *Omnibus*, p. 837). This statement immediately follows and explains his previous statement that "moreover, he founded three orders."

29. There are more thorough discussions of this topic and others to be treated in this chapter. We refer the reader particularly to the various Acts of the various Congresses of the Studi Francescani on the penitents. Here we are giving only a brief synthesis, providing a linear vision of the same arguments. On the topic of the "Franciscan evolution" of the confraternities and penitents of the XIII century, cf. Gieben, in *Francescanismo e vita religiosa dei laici nel 200*, pp. 169-201.

30. Meersseman, *Ordo*, p. 316. This took place according to the explicit instructions of the same *Memoriale*: "Omnes fratres et sorores, cuiusque civitatis aut loci, quolibet mense, quando viderit ministris, conveniant apud ecclesiam, quam ministri nuntiaverint, ibique audiant divina," n. 19; cf. Meersseman, *Dossier*, p. 102.

31. Landini, *The causes of the clericalization of the Order of Friars Minor, 1209-1260, in the light of early Franciscan sources*, Chicago, 1968, p. 61.

32. Cf. Landini, p. 70, note 57.

33. Cf. bull *Si Ordinis Fratrum*, February 1, 1230, *Bull. Franc.* I, 58, n. 46.

34. Recall the bull *Etsi nostra navicula* of March 28, 1208; see above, chapter eight, note 60.

35. Cf. Landini, pp. 62-63. *Constitutio 10*, in *Conciliorum Oecumenicorum Decreta*, 215.

36. Cf. *Nimis iniqua* of August 21, 1231 in *Bull. Franc.* I, n. 65; *Nimis prava* of August 22, 1231 in *Bull. Franc.*, n. 64.

37. Bull *Cum qui recipit Prophetam* of June 12, 1234, *Bull. Franc.* I, n. 131.

38. *Quoniam abundavit iniquitas*, of April 6, 1237. *Bull. Franc.* I, n. 224. In it the pontiff expressly stated that "God has raised up the Friars Minor to seek the cause of Christ, the extirpation, that is, of heresy and other fatal vices. To carry out this goal, the friars have dedicated themselves to the preaching of the word of God by living in voluntary poverty. Quite clearly, the pope is defining the Order of Friars Minor in terms of the existing needs of the Church" (Landini, p. 65).

39. Landini, p. 65.

40. ". . . et dicti Fratres per cooperationem vestram suscepti ministerii sui fructum felicius consequantur." Cf. in Landini, p. 65.

41. Landini, p. 67.

42. See above, p. 143.

43. "Ea propter, dilecti in Domini filii, vestris justis postulationibus grato concurrentes assensu Sepulturam Ecclesiarum vestrarum liberam esse decernimus, ut eorum devotioni, et extremae voluntati, qui se illic sepeliri desideraverint, nullus obsistat: salva, tamen, justitia illarum Ecclesiarum, a quibus mortuorum corpora assumentur." From the bull *Cum a nobis petitur*, of Feb. 25, 1250. *Bull. Franc.* I, 537, n. 316.

44. Cf. Landini, p. 69.

45. "Et tunc, si comode possunt, habeant unum virum religiosum, in Dei verbo instructum, qui eos moneat et confortet ad poenitentiae perseverantiam et opera misericordiae facienda," n. 21, *Dossier*, p. 103. Cf. *Omnibus*, p. 172.

46. See above, pp. 41-42.

47. The Secular Third Order kept the Rule of Nicholas IV until 1883. In that year Pope Leo XIII gave them a new rule with the bull *Misericors Dei* of May 30. This, in turn, remained in effect until the new rule approved by Paul VI with the Letter *Seraphicus Patriarca* of June 24, 1978.

Until 1521 the Rule of Nicholas IV was the only one for both secular tertiaries and those who desired a more strictly religious life. During the period 1298-1521 many congregations of male and female regular tertiaries arose and were approved by the Holy See.

In 1521 Pope Leo X gave the Tertiaries Regular (men and women living in community with religious vows) a distinct rule. This rule remained in effect until 1927 when Pius XI gave a new rule adapted to serve the ancient congregations and the numerous congregations of sisters (and several groups of men) that had arisen since 1521.

For a complete study, we must also note that the Rule of Leo X of 1521 presupposed the "submission to the major superiors and to the visitators of the Minors of Observance." Those friars and sisters who did not depend on the Observants (for example the male Third Order Regular in Italy) did not follow this Rule of Leo X that would have placed them under the jurisdiction of the Friars Minor; they continued to observe that of Nicholas IV (1289) with particular statutes prepared by them and approved by the Holy See, up until 1927.

For questions relative to the Rule of Leo X see Pazzelli, *Il Terz'Ordine*, pp. 161-166.

There is now the new Rule of the Third Order Regular, approved by John Paul II with the Letter *Franciscanum vitae*, of Dec. 8, 1982.

48. Matanić, in *L'Ordine della Penitenza*, p. 56.

49. Meersseman observes that "the bishop had the indisputable right and duty to control the penitents of his diocese. None of them, neither individuals nor those belonging to a fraternity, would have been exempt from his jurisdiction. Wearing the habit of penance precluded the profession of a perpetual vow recognized by the Church, and leading the life of reconciled public sinners: it was the bishop's job to see that they continued to live according to their state" *Ordo*, p. 314.

50. Articles 4, 30, 35, 35.2, 36, 37, and 39 speak of it. We shall summarize the contents of each of these:

art. 4: "other vain adornments they shall lay aside at the bidding of the visitor.

art. 30: and that (the candidate) will, when called upon by the ministers, render satisfaction as the visitor shall ordain if he has done anything contrary to (the *Propositum*).

art. 35: The ministers of any city or place shall report public faults of the brothers and sisters to the visitor for punishment.

art. 35.2: And if anyone proves incorrigible, after consultation with some of the discreet brothers, he should be denounced to the visitor, to be expelled by him from the brotherhood. . . .

art. 36: If anyone learns that scandal is occurring relative to brothers and sisters, he shall report it to the ministers and shall have opportunity to report it to the visitor.

art. 37: The visitor has the power to dispense all the brothers and sisters in any of these points if he finds it advisable.

art. 39: Yet . . . if after being admonished twice by the ministers (the brother) should fail to discharge the penalty imposed or to be imposed on him by the visitor, he shall be obligated under guilt as contumacious.

51. "Quia presens vivendi forma institutionem a beato Francisco suscepit (art. 54.2)." See Meersseman, *Dossier*, p. 156.

Throughout the history of the penitential movement the figure of the visitator seems to appear for the first time, in the Rule of the Knights of Santiago of 1175 ("Eligantur et tunc *visitatores* idonei, qui domos fratrum, per anni circulum fideliter visitent et quae digna correctione invenerint, aut ipsi corrigant aut ad generale capitulum deferant corrigenda." *PL* 200, 1028; this norm was repeated in the bull of 1206, *PL* 216, 209.

It appeared again the *Propositum* of the penitents directed by the Poor Catholics (bull *Dilectus filius*, May 26, 1212—*PL* 216, 601-602). This last document clearly states that the purpose of such a "visitator" is the care of the "wholesome teaching and ecclesiastical honesty." The institution of the visitator was generalized by Canon 12 of the Fourth Lateran Council (cf. Mansi, 22, 1002). Meersseman is of the opinion that in the

Order of the Penitents the right of correction "was taken from the local ministers and given to the regional visitor in the period in which several local fraternities, grouping themselves in regional (provincial) federations, adopted a common set of statutes that had already been in use in some local fraternity of the region" (in Romagna). *Dossier*, p. 111, note 35.

52. Meersseman, *Ordo*, p. 314.

53. A Pompei in *"Prime Manifestazione,"* cited in *Analecta T.O.R.* XV, 1982, pp. 134-135.

54. Meersseman, *Ordo*, p. 290.

54a. "Necnon etiam juramentum in quolibat articulo sub Ecclesiae forma factum peccatum esse mortale dogmatizasse dicantur." *PL* 216, 293. See above, p. 62.

55. Meersseman, *Ordo*, pp. 429-433.

56. Meersseman thus summarizes three possible reasons: "This juridical situation, on the one hand and, on the other hand, the growing hostility of the secular clergy, of the professors of the university in Paris, and the partiality of Frederick II towards the mendicant orders, induced the leaders of the Franciscan Order to adopt a certain reserve towards the penitents" (*Dossier*, p. 84).

57. Cf. the bull *Vota devotorum* in *Dossier*, p. 57, n. 22; *Bull. Franc.* I, 464.

58. Cf. in *Dossier*, p. 58, n. 23; *Bull. Franc.* I, 467.

59. Cf. in *Dossier*, pp. 58-59, n. 25. From this bull we also know that the penitents of northern Italy had already constituted a "province."

60. It is this "apostolic authority" which Friar Caro claims when in 1280 he is assigned by the bishop of Florence to act as visitator of the penitents.

61. Cf. St. Bonaventure, *Opera Omnia*, VIII, Ad Claras Aquas, Quaracchi, 1898, pp. 368-369. The complete title is: *Determinationes quaestionum circa Regulam Fratrum Minorum*, p. II, q. 16: Cur Fratres non promoveant Ordinem Poenitentium. "The second part of the work, also called *Libellus apologeticus*, is of an author other than St. Bonaventure and was written after his death, between 1274 and 1290." (M. D'Alatri in *Prime Manifestazione*, p. 73, note 26.) Cf. B. Distelbrink, *Bonaventurae scripta autentica, dubia vel spura critice recensita*, Rome, 1975, p. 34 f.

62. H. Roggen in *L'Ordine della Penitenza*, p. 205.

63. "Istis a principio frater assignabatur Minister, sed nunc suis in terra dimittuntur Ministris ut tamen a fratribus tamquam confratres et eodem patre geniti consiliis et auxiliis foventur." *Liber de Laudibus*, in *Anal. Franc.* 3, p. 686.

64. We should, in reality say that the case in Florence has been "exaggerated" by the author who assumed and presented it as an example of a widespread situation. This assumption has not been supported by the documents studied up until now.

65. Cf. Meersseman, *Ordo*, pp. 365-371.

66. In his study "Claire de Florence, O.F.M., Canoniste et Penitentier

Pontifical vers le milieu du XIIIe siècle" in *AFH* 32 (1939), pp. 3-48, Henquinet presents the most probable biographical material about Friar Chiaro of Florence. A Friar Minor who was well-known in the middle of the twelfth century, his date of birth as well as entry into the order are not known. He was born in or near Florence and studied law, probably in Bologna. Towards the middle of the century he was a papal penitentiary in residence at the papal curia; he definitely served in this capacity during the papacy of Alexander IV (+ Dec. 12, 1254) and possibly under his successor, Innocent IV. His title was *Capellani Papae et apostolicae Sedis auditores causarum sacri Palatii apostolici*; such chaplains often received assignments of diplomatic missions, canonical visitations, and the task of rendering judgment in important conflicts. However, we do not know of any important assignment given to him. Friar Chiaro must have also been a lector; it seems that that was the capacity in which he was serving when he participated in the Synod of Ravenna where all the lectors of the Province of Bologna met. Salimbene of Parma calls him "unus dei maioribus clericis de mundo," which means that he was "a very well-educated man who has published many works." There is no evidence of his involvement in the preparation of a rule for penitents.

67. He is mentioned twice by Wadding, for the years 1277 and 1289. Cf. Wadding, *Annales*, ad a. 1277, n. 17; ad a. 1289, n. 18.

68. Cf. *Dossier*, p. 69-70. An authenticated copy exists in the archives of the General Curia of the T.O.R. in Rome.

69. Since we do not possess any apostolic letter addressed to Friar Caro, we would have to assume—as Meersseman did—that Caro claimed this "authority" because he had been named visitator, by strength of and according to the letter of Innocent IV (1251) which granted the bishop of Florence the task of fulfilling the duty of visitator for the penitents by "apostolic authority." (Cf. the letter of Innocent IV, Oct. 13, 1251, in Meersseman, *Dossier*, p. 60, n. 28. Cf. above, p. 209, note 60). Meersseman is of the opinion that Caro must have been named visitator of the Florentine penitents by the bishop of Fiesole, the Franciscan, Philip of Perugia (1282-1289) since he was probably administrator of the diocese of Florence, whose see had been vacant since 1275 (Cf. Meersseman, *Ordo*, p. 372).

70. We do know, however, how the matter of the "black" penitents ended. After the promulgation of the Rule of Nicholas IV, "a large part of the brothers ("black" penitents) once again put on their old habit, adopting this rule in conformity with the requirement of the *Memoriale*." From the letter of Nicholas IV to the bishop of Florence, Sept. 20, 1291. Cf. in Meersseman, *Dossier*, pp. 77-79). The bishop of Florence, Andrea de'Mozzi (1286-1295), who was well known "for his sympathy for the 'black' penitents, among whom were many members of his family" (Meersseman, *Dossier*, p. 28) did not look too favorably on such a move and hid the chest that held the rule, the privileges, the account books, and other belongings of the penitents. An appeal was made to the pope,

who commanded the bishop to give everything back to them and to change his attitude towards them. The pope wrote that "these brothers, returning to their primitive habit, and adopting our rule, have not changed their status, and must not, therefore, be deprived of enjoying their rights and privileges. . . . With this we order you therefore to show yourself friendly towards them and to return the chest with its contents, as well as the administration and possession of their goods." (Cf. Meersseman, *Ordo*, p. 383). The bishop obeyed, but in reality the disagreements between the "black" and "gray" penitents continued until Pope Boniface VIII transferred the bishop to Vicenza in September of 1295. The two segments of penitents in Florence were definitively united in 1298. The papal legate, Matthew D'Acquasparta, cardinal and Friar Minor, approved the statutes of the union in a letter of April 8, 1298 (Cf. *Dossier*, p. 263, n. 17).

71. The Acts of this chapter were published by Golubovich "Acta et Statuta Generalis Capituli Tertii Ordinis Poenitentium D. Francisci, Bononiae celebrati an. 1289" in *AFH* 2 (1909), pp. 63-71. Thirty-one delegates participated in the chapter, some of whom, having vicariate authority, represented two or three provinces; a total of twenty-four provinces were represented. The delegates elected twelve definitors who began to compose the general statutes, which were later approved by the assembly. From the minutes we learn that another chapter had been held some time before, perhaps a regional one at Piacenza (cf. *Ibid.*, p. 66). Meersseman believes that the gathering at Piacenza was convoked to solicit the approval of the rule by the pontiff (cf. *Ordo*, pp. 412-413).

72. Art. 17: "Ordinamus, volumus et sanctimus, quod providus et discretus vir Ugolinus de Medicis de Ferrara qui pro confirmatione Regulae nostrae in Curia summo, studio, et multa sollicitudine laboravit, in nostris habeatur orationibus specialter commendatus" (p. 70).

73. Péano in *Prime manifestazione*, p. 126. This had already been stated by Elzear de Dombres in his work during the middle of the seventeenth century. (*La Règle de Pénitence du Seraphic Père S. Francois approuvée et confirmée par le Pape Nicolas IV et reformée par Leon X en Concile de Lateran*. Paris, 1664, pp. 29-30. "In the same archives (of the Tertiaries of Toulouse) was preserved the bull of Clement V, August 30, 1309, confirming the legislative document of his predecessor and containing it entirely, after having seen and compared it with the original of Toulouse" (Péano, p. 120).

74. Cf. the bull and the text of the rule in *Seraphicae legislationis textus originales*. Quaracchi, 1897, pp. 76-94. Meersseman, *Dossier*, p. 156.

75. Matanić, p. 48.

76. Art. 54:2. Cf. *Dossier*, p. 156. Friar Caro "avoids speaking expressly of the connection between the first Franciscan order and the penitents" (Matanić, p. 48).

77. Art. 54 of the Rule of Friar Caro. Cf. in Meersseman, *Dossier*, p. 136.

78. Art. 45 of the Rule of Friar Caro. Cf. in *Dossier*, p. 135. "virum

religiosum et in verbo Dei competenter instructum... qui eos ad poenitentiam et misericordiae opera exercenda hortetur sollicite, moneat, et inducat."

79. The term *informator* also means "one who instructs." Cf. Georges-Calonghi, *Dizionario della linga latina*.

80. Cf. the bull in Meersseman, *Dossier*, pp. 76-77.

81. Cf. Matanić, p. 49.

82. Cf. above, p. 207, note 47.

83. Cf. the entire treatment of the topic in R. Pazzelli, *Il Terz'Ordine Regola*, pp. 42-59. For Bartolomeo Baro see the results of the latest research in Andreozzi, in *Prime Manifestazioni*, pp. 507-541.

84. Andreozzi, "Montecasale nei Fioretti e nella nostra storia" in *Analecta TOR*, V (1951), pp. 914-924; R. Pazzelli, *Il Terz'Ordine*, pp. 78-80.

85. Andreozzi, "S. Rocco in Montefalco, la 'Porziuncola' dell Terz'Ordine Regolare" in *Analecta TOR*, IV (1949), pp. 208-221.

86. Matanić, "Legislazione propria dei Penitenti francescani dal 1289 a tutto il sec. XIV" in *I Frati Penitenti*, p. 57.

87. Cf. Pazzelli, *Il Terz'Ordine*, pp. 64-67.

88. Pierre Péano, *Le religiose francescane. Origini, storia e valori costanti*. Movimento Francescano, Rome, 1983, p. 17.

89. Cf. the bull in Bordoni, *De antiquitate Religionis Tertii Ordinis*. Bononiae 1644, pp. 9-10 and in R. Pazzelli, *Il Terz'Ordine*, pp. 98-99, note 2.

90. "Outside of Italy the movement in favor of 'congregations' of Franciscan sisters began toward the end of the XIVth century, particularly in the areas where the convents of the Beghines flourished, that is, the north of France, Belgium, and Holland. Thus, in the latter country, the 'Chapter of Utrecht,' had existed at least since 1399, numbered around 70 communities in 1433, and approximately sixty in 1500. Péano, pp. 26-27.

91. Raniero Luconi, T.O.R., *Il Terzo Ordine Regolare di S. Francesco*. Macerata, Bisson, and Leopardi, 1935, pp. 100-105.

92. Cf. Luconi, p. 31.

93. From this there arose many other congregations of Franciscan sisters in France, Belgium, Germany and, centuries later, in Scotland and the United States. The original congregation of Gray Sisters was approved by John XXIII (Pisa) with the bull *Personas vacantes* of Aug. 26, 1413. Cf. Lemaitre, "Statuts des Religieuses du Tiers Ordre Franciscan dites Soeurs Crises Hospitalières" in *AFH* 4 (1911), 713-731; Hulst C. Van, "Grigie Suore," in *DIP*, 4, 1427-1428; Moncla, S., "The Franciscan Missionaries of Our Lady" in *Analecta TOR*, XIV (1981), pp. 1005-1086.

94. Cf. R. Pazzelli, *Il Terz'Ordine*, p. 305.

95. Cf. Pazzelli, pp. 120-125.

96. See above, pp. 144-145.

97. Cf. Pazzelli-Temperini.

BIBLIOGRAPHY

PRIMARY SOURCES

Adrianus, PP, IV, "Religiosam vitam" (7 November, 1156) in *Carte di Sassovivo*, vol. II, doc. 181,pp. 208-210.

Ambrosius (s.), *De Poenitentia contra Novatianos, Liber secundus, in S. Ambrosii Opera* t. IV, Parisiis 1614, 401-416.

Anonymus Benedectinus Saeculi XII, *Liber de Poenitentia et tentationibus religiosorum*, in *PL* 213, 865-904.

Baldricus Episcopus Dolensis, *Vita B. Robert de Arbrissello*, in *PL* 162, 1043-1078.

Bernardus de Bessa, *Liber de Laudibus beati Francisci*, in *Anal. Franc.* III, Quaracchi, 1897, 666-692.

Bonaventura (s), *Legenda Maior S. Francisci*, in *Anal. Franc.* X, Quaracchi 1926-1941, 555-652. English text in *Omnibus of Sources*, pp. 631-787.

Bonaventura (s), "Sermo II de S.P.N. Francisco," in *Opera Omnia*, IX, Quaracchi, 1882-1902, pp. 576-592.

Bughetti, B., O.F.M., "Prima Regula Tertii Ordinis iuxta novum codicem," in *AFH* 14 (1921), 109-121.

Burchardi et Cuonradi Urspergensium Chronicon, in *MGH Script.*, t. XXIII, ed. G. H. Pertz, Hannoverae, 1874.

Carolus Magnus, *Capitulare Aquisgranense* (805 A.D.), in *PL* 97, 281-292.

Carte (Le) dell'Abbazia di S. Croce in Sassovivo. Published by the Scuola Speciale per Archivisti e Bibliotecari of the University of Rome. First series, 7 volumes. Florence, Olsckhi, 1973-1976.

Codice diplomatico Longobardo, 2 vol. Ed. L. Schiapparelli, in *Fonti per la Storia d'Italia*, Rome, 1929-1933.

Concilium Agathense (506 A.D.), in *Mansi*, 8, 319-346.

Concilium Aurelianense III (538 A.D.), in *Mansi*, 9, 9-24.

Concilium Carthaginense IV (436 A.D.), in Hardouin, J., *Acta Conciliorum*, I, 975-986.

Concilium Toletanum III (589 A.D.), in *Vives*, 107-145.

Concilium Toletanum IV (633 A.D.), in *Mansi*, 10, 611-650.

Concilium Toletanum VI (638 A.D.), in *Mansi*, 10, 659-679; *Vives*, 233-248.

Concilium Toletanum XII (681 A.D.), in *Vives*, 380-410.
Concilium Toletanum XVI (693 A.D.), in *Vives*, 582-521.
Decretum Gratiani emendatum et notationibus illustratum. Ed. Romana, Rome, 1582.
Desbonnets, T., O.F.M., *Legenda Trium Sociorum*. Edition critique, in *AFH* 67 (1974), 38-144.
Determinationes quaestionum circa Regulam Fratrum Minorum in *S. Bonaventurae Opera Omnia*, VIII, Quaracchi, 1898, 368 pp.
Erma, *Il Pastore*, ed. by O. Soffritti, in *Padri Apostolici. Antologia*, ed. Paeoline, Alba, 1967, pp. 333-423.
Esser, K., *Opuscula sancti Patris Francisci Assisiensis*. Ed. Colegii S. Bonaventurae. Ad Claras Aquas-Grottaferrata (Rome), 1978.
Frédericq, P., *Corpus documentorum Inquisitionis haereticae pravitatis Neerlandicae*, t. I, Gand, 1889.
Friedberg, Ae., *Corpus Iuris Canonici*. Pars prior, *Decretum Magistri Gratiani*. Pars Secunda, *Decretalium Collectiones*, Graz, 1959.
Gaufridus Grossus, *Vita B. Bernardi*, in *PL* 172, 1363-1446.
Gennadius Massiliensis, *De Scriptoribus ecclesiasticis*, in *PL* 58, 1053-1120.
Gennadius Massiliensis, *Liber de ecclesiasticis dogmatibus*, in *PL* 58, 979-1000.
Golubovich, G., O.F.M., *Acta et Statua Generalis Capituli Tertii Ordinis Poenitentium D. Francisci, Bononiae celebrati an. 1289*, in *AFH* 2, (1909), 63-71.
Gregorius, PP. VIII, *Audita tremendi* (Oct. 29, 1187), in *PL* 202, 1539-1542.
Gregorius, PP. IX, *Detestanda* (May 21, 1227), in Meersseman, *Dossier* pp. 43-45.
Gregorius, PP. IX, *Nimis patentur* (May 26, 1227), in *Dossier*, 46-47.
Hardouin, J., *Acta conciliorum et epistulae decretales ac constitutiones Summorum Pontificum*, I, Parisiis, 1714.
Hispana (seu) *Excerpta Canonum decem libris comprehensa*, in *PL* 84, 25-92.
Honorius Augustudunensis (Honorius of Autun), *Elucidarium, sive Dialogus de summa totius christianae Theologiae*, in *PL* 172, 1109-1176.
Honorius Augustudunensis, *Gemma animae*, in *PL* 172, 541-738.
Honorius Augustudunensis, *Sacramentarium*, in *PL* 172, 737-806.
Honorius Augustudunensis, *Speculum Ecclesiae*, in *PL* 172, 807-1080.
Honorius, PP. III *Ad audientiam nostram* (1226-27), in *Dossier*, 42-43.
Honorius, PP. III, *Cum illorum* (Dec. 1, 1225), in *Dossier*, 42.
Honorius, PP. III, *Significatum est* (Dec. 16, 1221), in *Dossier*, 42.
Huygens, R.B.C., *Lettres de Jacques de Vitry*, edition critique, Leiden, 1960.
Incmarus, Archiepiscopus Rhemensis (Hinckmar of Rheims), *De regis persona et regio ministerio*, in *PL* 125, 833-856.
Innocentius, PP. II, *Religiosis desideriis* (May 21, 1138), in *Carte (Le) di Sassovivo*, vol. II, doc. 97, pp. 116-121.
Innocentius, PP. III, *Cum a nobis* (May 13, 1210), in *PL* 216, 274.
Innocentius, PP. III, *Cum inaestimabile* (June 14, 1210), in *Dossier*, 284-286; *PL* 216, 289-293.
Innocentius, PP. III, *Dilectus filis Durandus* (May 26, 1212), in *Dossier*, 286-288; *PL* 216, 601-602.

Innocentius, PP. III, *Eius exemplo* (Dec. 18, 1208), in *Dossier*, 282-284; *PL* 215, 1510-1513.

Innocentius, PP. III *Etsi nostra navicula* (May 31, 1204), in *PL* 215, 358-360.

Innocentius, PP. III, *Excursus saeculi* (Nov. 17, 1206), in *PL* 215, 1024-1125.

Innocentius, PP. III, *Incumbit nobis* (June 7, 1201), in Tiraboschi, *Vetera Humiliatorum Monumenta*, II, 128-134.

Innocentius, PP. III, *In eminenti Apostolicae Sedis* (May 28, 1198), Archivio Communale di Assisi, Pergament, A. I, in *FNV*, Vol. III, 543-545.

Innocentius, PP. III, *Ne quis de caetero* (July 23, 1212), in *Dossier*, 288-289; *PL* 216, 648-650.

Innocentius, PP. III, *Pietas promissionem* (Jan. 12, 1199), in *PL* 214, 483-485.

Innocentius, PP. IV, *Dilecti filii* (Oct. 13, 1251), in *Dossier*, 60.

Innocentius, PP. IV, *Licet vos* (Nov. 10, 1248), in *Dossier*, 58-59.

Innocentius, PP. IV, *Vota devotorum* (June 13, 1247), in *Dossier*, 57.

Iona Aurelianensis (Jonah of Orleans), *De institutione laicali*, in *PL* 106, 121-278.

Iona Aurelianensis, *De institutione regia*, in *PL* 106, 279-306.

Iordanus a Iano (Jordan of Giano), *Chronica*, in *Anal. Franc.* I, Quaracchi, 1885, 1-19. English text in *XIIIth Century Chronicles*.

Isidorus Hispaliensis (Isidore of Seville) (s.), *De officiis ecclesiasticis*, in *PL* 83, 737-826.

Isidorus Hispaliensis, *Etimologiae*, in *PL* 82, 9-728.

Isidorus Hispaliensis, *Sententiae*, in *PL* 83, 537-738.

Isidorus Hispaliensis, *Synonima*, in *PL* 83, 825-868.

Iulianus de Spira (Julian of Speyer), *Vita Sancti Francisci*, in *Anal. Franc.* X, 335-371.

Legenda choralis Carnotensis, in *Anal. Franc.* X, 538-540.

Leggenda dell' *Anonimo Perugino*, in Isabell, *Workbook*, pp. 94-115.

Legend of the Three Companions, in *Omnibus*, pp. 853-955.

Lemmens, L., O.F.M., *Regula antiqua Ordinis de Poenitentia (1221) iuxta novum codicem*, in *AFH* 6 (1913), 242-250.

Lemmens, L., *Testimonia minora saeculi XII de S. Francisco Assisiensis*. Quaracchi, 1926. Some excerpts in *Omnibus*, pp. 1597-1615.

Martinus, PP. IV, *Exposuit nobis* (Dec. 13, 1284), in *Dossier*, 69-70.

Meersseman, G. G., *Dossier de l'Ordre de la Penitence au XIII siècle*. Ed. Universitaires, Fribourg (Switzerland), 1961.

Memoriale Propositi fratrum et sororum de Penitentia in domibus propriis existentium, inceptum anno domini MCCXXI, in *Dossier*, 92-112.

Muratori, L. A., *Antiquitates Italicae Medii Aevi*. Milan, 1738-1742.

Nicholaus, PP. IV, *Ad audientam nostram* (Sept. 20, 1291), in *Dossier*, 77-79.

Nicholaus, PP. IV, *Supra montem* (Aug. 18, 1289), in *Seraphicae Legislationis*, 76-94; *Dossier*, 156.

Nicholaus, PP. IV, *Unigenitus Dei Filius* (Aug. 8, 1290), in *Dossier*, 76-77.

Petrus Damianus (s) *Epistolarum libri octo*, in *PL* 205-498.

Petrus Damianus (s) *Sanctorum Historiae*, in *PL* 144, 925-1036.

Petrus Damianus (s) *Sermones*, in *PL* 144, 501-924.

Potthast, A., *Regesta Pontificum Romanorum inde ab a. post Christum natum*

MCXCVIII ad a. MCCCIV. 2 vol. Berlin, 1874-1875, reprinted Graz, 1957.

Rabanus Maurus, *De videndo Deum, de puritate cordis et modo Poenitentiae libri tres,* in PL 112, 1261-1332.

Rabanus Maurus, *De vitiis et virtutibus et peccatorum satisfactione,* in PL 112, 1335-1398.

Rabanus Maurus, *Poenitentium liber,* in PL 112, 1397-1424.

Ratherius Veronensis (Ratherius of Verona), *Epistolae,* in PL 136, 643-688.

Ratherius Veronensis, *Sermones,* in PL 136, 689-758.

Ratherius Veronensis, *Praeloquiroum libri sex,* in PL 136, 145-344.

Registri dei Cardinali Ugolino d'Ostia e Ottaviano degli Ubaldini, Guido Levi, ed. Rome, Ins. Stor. Ital., 1890.

Regola dei Frati di S. Iacopo d'Altopascio, Bologna, Commission for language texts, 1968. Reprinted by Ed. Forni, ed. by Gaetano Romagnoli, Bologna, 1864.

Regola dell'Ordine di Santa Chiara di Papa Urbano IV—Regola dei fratelli e delle sorelle dell'Ordine dei Frati della Penitenza di Papa Niccolò IV, in FF, ed. by Movimento Francescano, Assisi, 1978.

Richardus S. Victoris (Richard of St. Victor), *Explicatio in Cantica Canticorum,* in PL 196, 405-424.

Robert D'Auxerre, *Chronicon* in MGH Script. XXVI.

Sabatier, P., *Regula antiqua Fratrum et Sororum de Paenitentia seu Tertii Ordinis sancti Francisci,* in *Opuscules de critique historique,* t. I, Paris, 1903, 17-30.

Sacrorum Conciliorum nova et amplissima collectio, ed. J. D. Mansi et al. Florence, 1759-1827.

Saint Francis of Assisi, *Writings and Early Biographies. English Omnibus of the Sources for the Life of St. Francis,* edited by M. A. Habig. Franciscan Herald Press, Chicago, Ill., 1972.

Seraphicae Legislationis textus originales. Quaracchi, 1897.

Statuta Ecclesiae antiqua, in *Concilia Galliae aa. 314-506,* ed. C. Munier (CCh. SL 148), Turnholti, 1963.

Tertullianus, *Liber de Poenitentia,* in PL 1, 1335-1360.

Teulet, A., *Layettes de Tresor des chartes,* t. I, Paris, 1863.

Thomas de Celano, *Vita prima S. Francisci,* in Anal. Franc. X, 1-117. English text in *Omnibus,* pp. 213-355.

Thomas de Celano, *Vita secunda S. Francisci,* in Anal. Franc. X, pp. 127-268. English text in *Omnibus,* pp. 359-611.

Tiraboschi, H., *Vetera Humiliatorum Monumenta,* 3 vol. Mediolani, 1766-1768.

Urbanus, PP. III, *Cum nobis sit* (Jan. 27, 1185), in PL 202, 1355-1357.

Vita B. Giraldi de Salis, in Acta Sanctorum, oct. X, 249-267.

Vita Gregorii IX papae, in Lemmens, *Testimonia minora,* 11-14.

Vita Norberti Archiepiscopi Magdeburgensis, in MGH Script. XII, 663-703.

Vita B. Vitalis Saviniacensis, in Analecta Bollandiana, I, 357-390.

Vives, J. *Concilios Visigòticos e hispano-romanos,* Barcelona, 1963.

Wyngaert, A., Van Den, O.F.M., *De Tertio Ordine S. Francisci iuxta Marianum Florentinum,* in AFH 13 (1920), 1-77.

STUDIES

AA.VV. *L'Ordine della Penitenza di san Francesco d'Assisi nel sec. XIII.* Acts of the First Congress of Franciscan Studies (Assisi, July 3-5, 1972). O. Schmucki, ed., Istituto Storico dei Cappuccini, Rome, 1973.

AA.VV. *I Frati Penitenti di san Francesco nella societa del Due e Trecento.* Acts of the Second Congress of Franciscan Studies (Rome, Oct. 12-14, 1976). M. D'Alatri, ed., Istituto Storico dei Cappuccini, Rome, 1977.

AA.VV. *Il movimento francescano della Penitenza nella società medioevale.* Acts of the Third Congress of Franciscan Studies (Padua, Sept. 25-27, 1979). M. D'Alatri, ed., Istituto Storico dei Cappucini, Rome, 1980.

AA.VV. *Prime manifestazioni di vita comunitaria, maschile e femminile, nel movimento francescano della Penitenza* (1215-1447). Acts of the Fourth Congress of Franciscan Studies (Assisi, June 30-July 2, 1981). R. Pazelli and L. Temperini, ed., Commissione Storico Internazionale T.O.R., Rome, 1982 and *Analecta TOR*, XV (1982).

Alszgheny, Z. and Flick, M., *Il Sacramento della Riconciliazione.* Rome, 1976.

Amann, E., "Josephists ou Josépins," in *DTC* VIII 2, 1547-48.

Amann, E., "La Pénitence. Pénitence-repentir. Penitence-sacrament," in *DTC* XII, 1, 722-948.

Amann, E., "Rathier de Verona," in *DTC* XIII, 2, 1679-1688.

Andreozzi, G., t.o.r., "Il B. Bartolomeo Baro nelle fonti storiche e nella tradizione," in AA.VV. *Prime manifestazioni*, 507-541.

Asseldonk, O. van., O.F.M. Cap. "Nexus S. Francisci cum motu universali paenitentiae seu conversionis evangelicae antecedenti et coetaneo," in *Tertius Ordo* 33 (1972), 165-170.

Attal, F. S., *San Francesco d'Assisi.* Padua, 1947.

Aubin, P. A., *Le probleme de la "Conversion." Etude sur le terme commun à l'hellenisme et au christianisme des trois premiers siècles.* Paris, 1963.

Bak, J. M., "Brancaleoni Leone" in *Dizionario Biografico degli Italiani*, vol. 13, Treccani, Rome, 1971, 814-817.

Baldelli, I., *Il Cantico di Francesco in San Francesco nella ricerca storica degli ultimi ottanta anni.* Congress of the Center for Studies of medieval spirituality, IX (Oct. 13-16, 1968), Todi, 1971, 75-94.

Bartoli, Langeli A.,*Premessa* of Vol. IV of *(Le) Carte di Sassovivo*, Florence, 1976, pp. V-XLV.

Beer, F. de, *La conversion de saint François selon Thomas de Celano*, Paris, 1963.

Benvenuti Papi, A., "Umiliana dei Cerchi. Nascita di un culto nella Firenza del Duecento," in *Studi Francescani* 77 (1980), 87-117.

Bihl, M., O.F.M., "De Iohanne de S. Paulo, Cardinali episcopo Sabiniensi, primo S. Francisci in Curia Romana an. 1209 fautore," in *AFH* 19 (1926), 282-285.

Bonduelle J., "Convers," in *Dictionnaire de droit canonique IV* (1949), 562-588.

Brezzi, P., "Catari," in *E.C.* III, 1087-1090.

Burns, R.I., "Frati della Penitenza di Gesu Cristo," in *DIP* VI (1980), 1398-1404.

Canonici, L., O.F.M., "Guido II d'Assisi, il vescovo di san Francesco," in *Studi Francescani* 77 (1980), 187-206.

Canonici, L., O.F.M., "I Terziari francescani 'fratelli e sorelle della penitenza,' " in *Quaderni di spiritualità francescana*, 18, Porziuncola ed., Santa Maria degli Angeli (Assisi), 1970, 148-171.

Capitani, O., *La concezione della povertà nel Medioevo*. Anthology of works, Bologna, Pàtron, 1974.

Capitani, *L'eresia medioevale*. Bologna, Il Mulino, 1971.

Carpaneto, C., O.F.M. Cap., "San Francesco, penitente" in *L'Italia francescana* 58 (1978), 417-426.

Carpaneto, C., O.F.M. Cap., "Lo stato dei Penitenti nel 'Corpus iuris canonici,' " in AA.VV., *I Frati Penitenti*, 9-19.

Casini, A., O.F.M., Francesità di san Francesco d'Assisi, in *Studi Francescani* 77 (1980), 371-373.

Casolini, F., "Appunti per una storia del T.O.F." in *Il Terz'Ordine Francescano nella spiritualità, nella storia, nel diritto, nella sociologia*, Rome, 1955, 75-174.

Cheriapattaparambil, F.X., Cap., *The influence of Troubadours in the life and writings of St. Francis* (Manuscript-form), Pontificio Ateneo Antonianum, Rome, 1982.

Chiesa e riforma nella spiritualità del sec. XI. Congress of the Center for Studies of medieval spirituality (Oct. 13-16, 1963), Todi, 1968.

Chioccioni, P., T.O.R., "La casa paterna di S. Francesco secondo la documentazione del Prof. Arnaldo Fortini," in *Analecta T.O.R.*, X (1966), 605-627.

Cristiani, L., *Heresies and Heretics*. New York, 1959.

D'Alatri, M., O.F.M. Cap., "L'Ordine della Penitenza nella Leggenda di Margherita da Cortona" in AA.VV., *Prime manifestazioni*, 67-80.

Dal Pino, F.A., *I Frati Servi di S. Maria dalle origini all'approvazione* (1233 ca-1204). 3 vol. Historiography—Sources—History, Louvain, 1972.

De Dombes, E., T.O.R., *La Règle de Pénitence du Serpahic Père S. François approuvée et confirmée par le Pape Nicolas IV et reformée par Leon X en Concile de Lateran*. Paris, 1664.

Delaruelle, E., *La piété populaire au Moyen Age*. Turin, 1975.

Delaruelle E., "L'autel romain de Saint Sernin (1095). Confrères, pèlerins et pénitents," in *Mélanges R. Crozet I*, ed. Gallais, Poitiers, 1966, 383-389.

Delaruelle, E., La vie commune des clercs et la spiritualité populaire," in *Vita (La) commune del clero*, 142-185.

Delaruelle, E., "Le ermites et la spiritualité populaire," in *Eremitismo (L') in Occidente*, 212-247.

Dirkens, A.H., *The New Testament concept of metanoia*. Washington, 1932.

Dubois, J., O.S.B. "Les Ordres religieux au XIIe siècle selon la curie romaine," in *Revue Bénédictine* LXXVIII (1968), 238-309.

Eremitismo (L') in Occidente nei secoli XI e XII. Acts of the International Study week (Mendola, Aug. 30-Sept. 6, 1962). Miscellanea del Centro di Studi Medievali, IV, Milan, Vita e Pensiero, 1965.

Esser, K., O.F.M., *La Lettera di san Francesco ai Fedeli*, in AA.VV., *L'Ordine della Penitenza*, 65-78.

Esser, K., *Life and Rule. A Commentary on the Rule of the Third Order Regular of St. Francis.* Chicago, 1967.
Esser, K., *Origins of the Franciscan Order.* Chicago, 1970.
Esser, K., "Un documento dell'inizio del Duecento sui Penitenti," in AA.VV. *I Frati Penitenti,* 87-99.
Esser, K., "Un (Documento) precursore della 'Epistola ad Fideles' di San Francesco d'Assisi" (Il codice 225 della Biblioteca Guarnacci di Volterra), in *Analecta TOR,* XIV (1978), 11-47.
Esser, K.-Grau, E., *Love's Reply.* Chicago, 1963.
Esser, K.-Oliger, R., *La tradition manuscrite des Opuscules de saint François d'Assisise.* Rome, 1972.
Faley, R.J., T.O.R., "Considerazioni bibliche sulla metànoia," in *Analecta T.O.R.,* XIII (1974), 11-32.
Fanfani, P., *Preface to La Regola dei Frati di S. Iacopo d'Altopascio,* (see Sources).
Fliche, A., "La riforma gregoriana e la riconquista cristiana (1057-1123)." *Storia della Chiesa,* vol. VII, Turin, 1972.
Fliche, A.,-Thouzellier Ch.-Azaïs Y., "La cristianità romana (1198-1274)." *Storia della Chiesa,* vol. X. Turin, 1969.
Fontaine, J., "Pénitence publique et conversion personelle: l'apport d'Isidore de Séville a l'evolution médievale de la pénitence," in *Revue de droit canonique* 28 (1978), 141-156.
Forchielli, G., "Graziano," in *E.C.* VI, 1028-29.
Fortini, A., *Nova Vita di San Francesco.* 5 vol., ed. Assisi, Santa Maria degli Angeli (Assisi), 1959.
Fortini, A., *Assisi nel Medio Evo,* ed. Roma, Rome, 1940.
Fortini, A., *Gli ultimi Crociati.* Milan, 1935.
Fortini, G., "La famiglia di S. Chiara d'Assisi," in *Analecta TOR,* XIV (1981), 881-910.
Fortini, G., "Una nuova ipotesi sulle origini della famiglia di san Francesco," in *Analecta TOR,* XIII (1976), 817-841.
Francescanismo e vita religiosa dei laici nel '200. Acts of the Eighth International Congress of S.I.S.F. (Assisi, Oct. 16-18, 1980), Assisi, 1981.
Fredegando da Anversa, Cap., *Il Terz'Ordine Secolare di S. Francesco, 1221-1921. Saggio storico.* Rome, Marietti, 1921.
Galtier, P., "Pénitents et convertis," in *Revue Hist. Eccl.* 33 (1937).
Giacomozzi, G. M., *L'Ordine della Penitenza di Gesù Cristo.* Rome, *Studi Storici O.S.M.,* 1962.
Gieben, S., O.F.M. Cap., "Confraternite e Penitenti dell'area francescana," in *Francescanesimo e vita religiosa dei laici nel '200,* pp. 168-201.
Grundmann, H., "Eresie e nuovi Ordini religiosi nel secolo XII," in *Movimenti religiosi popolari ed eresie, 357-402.*
Hamilton, B., *The Albigensian Crusade.* London, 1974.
Henquinet, F.M., O.F.M., "Clair de Florence, O.F.M., Canoniste et Pénitentier Pontifical vers le milieu du XIII siècle," in *AFH* 32 (1939), 3-48.
Ilarino da Milano, Cap., "La spiritualità dei laici nei 'Praeloquia' di Raterio di Verona," in *Raterio di Verona.* Conference of the Center of studies

of mediaeval spirituality, X (Oct. 12-15, 1969), Todi, 1973, 35-93.
Ilarino da Milano, Cap., "Arnaldo da Brescia," in *E.C.* I, 2001-2030.
Ilarino da Milano, Cap., "Bruys Pietro," in *E.C.* III, 161-162.
Ilarino da Milano, Cap., "Passagini," in *E.C.* IX, 907-908.
Ilarino da Milano, "Poveri Lombardi," in *E.C.* IX, 1866-67.
Ilarino da Milano, "Umiliati," in *E.C.* XII, 754-56.
Jacobilli, L., *Cronica della chiesa e monastero di Santa Croce di Sassovivo nel territorio di Foligno.* Foligno, Alteri, 1653.
Karpp, H., *La Penitenza.* Fonti sull'origine della Penitenza nella Chiesa antica, ed. Torino, 1975.
Laici (I) nella "societas christiana" dei secoli XI e XII. Acts of the Third International Week of studies (Mendola, Aug. 21-27, 1965), Miscellanea del Centro di studi medioevali, V, Milan, *Vita e Pensiero,* 1968.
Landini, L. C., O.F.M., *The Causes of the Clericalization of the Order of Friars Minor, 1209-1260, in the Light of Early Franciscan Sources.* Chicago, 1968.
Lanz, A., "Disciplina," in E.C. IV, 1743-44.
Lapsanski, D., *Evangelical Perfection. An Historical Examination of the Concept in the Early Franciscan Sources.* The Franciscan Institute, St. Bonaventure University, N.Y., 1977.
Lapsanski, D., *The First Franciscans and the Gospel.* Chicago, 1976.
Lauriola, G., "La formazione culturale di Francesco" in *L'Italia Francescana* 56 (1981), 363-384.
Leclercq, J., "Il monachesimo femminile nei secoli XII e XIII," in *Movimento religioso femminile e Francescanismo nel secolo XIII.* Acts of the Seventh International Congress S.I.S.F. (Assisi, Oct. 11-13, 1979), Assisi, 1980, 61-99.
Leclercq, J., "Penitenza," in *DIP* VI (1980), 1383-1392.
Leclercq, J., *San Pier Damiano, eremita e uoma di chiesa.* Brescia, Morcelliana, 1972.
Leclercq, J., *Spiritualità del Medioeva. Da S. Gregorio a S. Bernardo (sec. VI-XII).* Bologna, ed. Dehoniane, 1969.
Leclercq, J., "La vie et la prière des chevaliers de Santiago d'après leur règle primitive," in *Liturgia, II, Scripta et documenta,* 10, Monserrat, 1958.
Leff, G., "The Apostolic Ideal in Later Medieval Ecclesiology" in *Journal of Theological Studies* 18 (1967), 58-82.
Leicht, P. S., *Operai artigiani, agricoltori in Italia dal sec. VI al sec. XVI.* Milan, 1959.
Lombardi, T., O.F.M., *Introduzione allo studio del Francescanesimo.* Ed. Porziuncola, Assisi, 1975.
Lortz, J., *Storia della Chiesa considerata in prospettiva di storia delle idee.* Vol. I, *Antichità e Medioevo,* ed. Paoline, Milan, 1980.
Lugano, P. T., O.S.B., "Le chiese dipendenti dall'abbazia di Sassovivo" in *Riv. Stor. Benedettina,* 7 (1912), 47-94.
Maccarrone, M., "Studi su Innocenzo III." *Italia Sacra* 17, ed. Antenore, Padua, 1972.
Magli, I., *Gli uomini della Penitenza. Lineamenti antropologici del medioevo italiano.* Bologna, Cappelli, 1967.

Mainka, R. M., "I movementi per la Chiesa povera nel XII secolo," in *Povertà religiosa*. Studi a cura dell'Istituto di Teologia della vita religiosa "Claretianum," Rome, 1975, 141-155.

Manselli, R., *San Francesco*. Bulzoni ed., Rome, 1980.

Mariani, U., "Abelardo Pietro" in *E.C.* I, 61-65.

Matanić, A., O.F.M., "I Penitenti francescani dal 1221 (Memoriale) al 1289 (Regola bollata) principalmente attraverso i lori Statuti e le Regole," in AA.VV., *L'Ordine della Penitenza*, 41-63.

Matanić, A., O.F.M., "Problematica delle origini del Terz'Ordine Francescano," in *Frate Francesco* 38 (1971), 241-246.

Mattesini, F., O.F.M., *Le origini del Terz'Ordine Francescano. Regola antica e Vita del Beato Lucchese*, ed. Vita e Pensiero, Milan, 1964.

Meersseman, G. G., "Disciplinati e Penitenti nel Duecento," in *Il Movimento dei Disciplinati nel settimo centenario dal suo inizio* (Perugia, 1260), Perugia, 1962, 43-72.

Meersseman, G. G., *Chiesa e 'Ordo laicorum' nel sec. XI* in *Chiesa e riforma nella spiritualità del sec. XI*, 37-74.

Meersseman, G. G., *Ordo Fraternitatis. Confraternite e pieta dei laici nel Medioevo*, in collaboration with G. P. Pacini. 3 vols. Italia Sacra, 24-26, Herder ed., Rome, 1977.

Meersseman, G. G., "I Penitenti nei secoli XI e XII," in *Laici (I) nella 'societas christiana,'* 306-339.

Melia, P., *The Origin, Persecutions, and Doctrine of the Waldenses*. New York, 1978.

Mens, A., Cap., "Beghine e Begardi," in *E.C.* I, 1143-1148.

Mens, A., "Humilies," in *DS* VII (1969), 1129-1136.

Miccoli, G., *Chiesa Gregoriana. Ricerche sulla riforma del secolo XI*. Florence, La nuova Italia, 1966.

Michiels, R., "La conception lucanienne de la conversion," in *Ephemerides theologicae Lovaniense*, XLI (1965), 42-78.

Moore, R. I., *The Birth of Popular Hersey*. New York, 1975.

Moorman, J. R. H., *The Sources for the Life of St. Francis of Assisi*, Manchester, 1940.

Morghen, R., "Federico I, detto il Barbarossa, Imperatore," in *Encicl. Italiana* XIV, Rome, 1951, 942-44.

Morghen, R., "Federico II, Imperatore," in *Encicl. Italiana*, XIV, 944-949.

Morghen, R., *Medioevo cristiano*, Bari, Laterza, 1958.

Morinus Joannes (Jean Morin) *Commentarius historicus de disciplina in administratione sacramenti paenitentiae tredecim primis saeculis in Ecclesia occidentali et hucusque in orientali observata*. Antwerp, ed. Metelen, 1682.

"Movimenti religiosi popolari ed eresie nel medioevo," in *Reliazioni III. Storia del Medioevo*, Tenth International Congress of Historical Science (Rome, Sept. 4-11, 1955), Florence, 1955, 305-541.

Nocent, A., "La riconciliazione dei penitenti nella Chiesa dal VI al X secolo," in *La Penitenza (Quaderni di Rivista Liturgica, 9)*, ed. L.D.C., Turin, 1968, 226-240.

Odoardi, G., Conv. "L'Ordine della Penitenza di san Francesco nei

Documenti pontifici del secolo XIII," in AA.VV., *L'Ordine della Penitenza*, 79-115.

Oliger, L., O.F.M., "Expositio brevis Regulae antiquae III Ordinis S. Francisci," in *AFH* 14 (1921), 122-129.

Omaechevarría, I., O.F.M., *Escritos de Santa Clara y Documentos contemporaneos*. Madrid, B.A.C., 1970.

Omaechevarría, I., "La 'Regola' e le Regole dell'Ordine di S. Chiara," in *Forma Sororum*, XIV (1977), 165-175; 213-222, XV (1978), 10-19.

Orlandis, J., "Traditio corporis et animae. La 'Familiaritas' en las iglesias y monasterios españoles de la Alta Edad Media" in *Anuario de historia del Derecho Español* 24 (1954), 95-279.

Paschini, P., "Il Card. Giovanni di S. Paolo," in *Studi di Storia e Diritto in onore di Carlo Calisse*, t. III, Milan, 1940.

Pastor, Oliver B., T.O.R., *Consideraciones historico-espirituales sobre alcunas expresiones de Penitentia voluntaria y de "Conversio-Abrenuntiatio" no monástica hasta el siglo XIII*. Pro-Manuscript, Universidad de Vienna, Vienna, 1981.

Pastor, Oliver B., "Lo 'stato della penitenza' (status penitentiae) e gli inizi dell'Ordine dei fratelli e sorelle della penitenza (ordo fratrum et sororum de paenitentia)" in *Analecta TOR*, XIII (1974), 33-72.

Pastor, Oliver B., "Un precursor de la 'Carta a los Fieles' de san Francisco de Asisi. Comparación con otros textos precedentes" in *Analecta TOR*, XIV (1980), 751-770.

Pazzelli, R., T.O.R., *Il Terz'Ordine Regolare di S. Francesco attraverso i secoli*. Rome, 1958.

Pazzelli, R., T.O.R., "Il segno TAU, simbolo penitenziale e francescano," in *Analecta TOR*, XIV (1980), 789-800.

Pazzelli, R.,-Temperini, L., *La tradizione storica e spirituale del nostro movimento*, ed. CSI-TOR, Rome, 1980.

Péano, P., O.F.M., "Manifestations de la vie en commun parmi les Tertiaires franciscains de la France méridionale," in AA.VV., *Prime manifestazione*, 113-131.

Pellegrinaggi e culto dei santi in Europa fino alla I Crociata. Congress of the Center of Studies on mediaeval spirituality, IV (Oct. 8-11, 1961), Todi, 1963.

Penco, G., O.S.B., *Storia del monachesimo in Italia dalle origini alla fine del medio evo*, Rome, 1961.

Pompei, A., O.F.M. Conv., "Il movimento penitenziale nei secoli XII-XIII," in AA.VV., *L'Ordine della Penitenza*, 9-40.

Povertà e ricchezza nella spiritualità dei secoli XI e XII. Congress of the Center for Studies of mediaeval spirituality, VIII (Oct. 15-18, 1967), Todi, 1969.

Quacquarelli, A.,-Andreotti, S., *San Francesco d'Assisi-La sua gente poverella e il monachesimo benedettino*, S. Francesco a Ripa, Rome, 1977.

Roggen, H., O.F.M., "Les relations du premier Ordre franciscan avec le Tiers Ordre au XIIIe siècle," in AA.VV., *L'Ordine della Penitenza*, 199-209.

Russell, J. B., *Dissent and Reform in the Early Middle Ages*. Berkeley, 1965.
Sabatier, P., "Quelques mots a propos de l'ancienne regle du Tiers Ordre," in *Opuscules de critique historique*, t. I, Paris, 1903, 1-16.
Sabatier, P., *Vita di San Francesco d'Assisi*. Trad. G. Zanichelli, ed. Mondadori, Milan, 1978.
Salvi, G., "Gli oblati benedettini in Italia. Cenni storici," in *Rivista stor. benedettina* 21 (1952), 89-169.
Sastre Palmer, N., T.O.R., *La espiritualidad penitencial a traves de la historia*. Pro-Manuscript, Antonianum, Rome, 1978.
Schiapparelli, L., *Codice diplomatico Longobardo*; see Codes in *Sources*.
Schmucki, O., Cap., "Il T.O.F. nella biografie di san Francesco," in AA.VV., *L'Ordine della Penitenza*, 117-143.
Sensi, M., "Monasteri benedettini in Assisi. Insediamenti sul Subasio e abbazia di S. Pietro," in *Aspetti di vita benedettina nella storia di Assisi*. Acts of the Accademia Properziana del Subasio. Series VI, n. 5, Assisi, 1981, 27-50.
Spicq, C., "Benignité, mansuétude, douceur, clemence," in *Revue biblique* LIV (1963), 321-329.
Stanislao da Campagnola, *Francesco d'Assisi nei suoi scritti e nelle sue biografie dei secoli XIII-XIV*, ed. Porziuncola, S.M. degli Angeli, Assisi, 1981.
Tampieri, G., *I doveri morali di ciascun stato di vita secondo i "Praeloquia" di Raterio vescovo di Verona (sec. X)*. Bagnacavallo, S.T.E., 1943.
Temperini, L., T.O.R., "La 'Regola' degli Ordini Francescani," in *Analecta T.O.R.*, XI (1968), 28-59.
*Temperini, L., T.O.R., "La spiritualità penitenziale nelle Fonti Francescane," in *Analecta T.O.R.*, XIV (1980), 543-589.
Thouzellier, Ch., *Catharisme e Valdeisme en Languedoc a la fin du XIIe et au debut du XIIIe siècle. Politique pontificale, Controverses*. Louvain-Paris, 1966.
Tuscano, P., "Rassegna di testi e studi francescani" (1965-1975), in *Lettere Italiane*, XXVIII (1976), 345-384.
Vicaire, M. H., *The Apostolic Life*. Chicago, 1966.
Vita (La) comune del clero nei secoli XI e XII. Acts of the First International Week of Study (Mendola, Sept. 1959), Miscellanea del Centro di Studi Medievali III, Milan, Vita e Pensiero, 1962.
Vogel, C., "La discipline pénitentielle en Gaule des origines au IX siècle. Le dossier hagiographique," in *Revue de sciences religieuses de l'Université de Strassbourg* 30 (1956), 1-26; 157-186.
Vogel, C., *Il peccatore e la penitenza nella Chiesa antica*, ed. L.D.C. Turin, 1967.
Vogel, C., *Il peccatore e la penitenza nel Medioevo*, ed. L.D.C., Turin, 1970.
Vogel, C., "Le pélerinage pénitentiel," in *Pellegrinagi e culto dei santi*, 37-94.
Vorreux, D., O.F.M., *A Franciscan symbol, the Tau, History, Theology, and Iconography*, The Tau Series, Chicago, 1979.

---

*English translation available from the Franciscan Federation of Brothers and Sisters of the U.S.

Wakefield, W. L., *Heresy, Crusade, and Inquisition in Southern France,* 1100-1250, Berkeley, 1974.

Waley, D., "Le istituzione communali di Assisi nel passaggio dal XII al XIII secolo," in *Assisi al tempo di san Francesco.* Acts of the Fifth International Congress S.I.S.F. (Assisi, Oct. 13-16, 1977) Assisi, 1978, 53-70.

Warner, H. L., *Albigensian Heresy,* 2 vol., London, 1822, 1928.

Wolf, P. H., *Storia e cultura del Medio Evo, dal secolo IX al XII.* Bari, Laterza, 1969.

Zanoni, L., *Gli Umiliati nei rapporti con l'eresia, l'industria della lana ed i Comuni nei secoli XII e XIII sulla scorta di documenti inediti.* (Biblioteca di storia economica, 3), Milan, 1911.

Zorzi, D., *Valori religiosi nella letteratura provenzale. La spiritualità trinitaria.* Milan, 1954.

INDEX OF PERSONS AND PLACES

(Abbreviations: ab. abbot; b. blessed; bibl. Biblioteca (library); can. canon; card. cardinal; conv. convent; emp. emperor; jur. jurist; inq. inquisitor; mon. monastery; osp. hospital; pen. penitent or belonging to the order of penitents; s. saint; bish. bishop.
Religious orders: clar. Poor Clare; cap. Friar Minor Capuchin; cist. Cistercian; conv. Friar Minor Conventual; min. Friar Minor (until 1517); obs. Friar Minor of the Observance; ofm. Friar Minor (after 1517); op. Dominican; osb. Benedictine; tof. Third Order Franciscan; tor. Third Order Regular.)

A

Abel, C., 204
Abelard, P., 53, 54, 174-175, 221
Adge (Council), 10, 21
Adrian IV (pope), 54, 213
  Religiosam vitam (Nov. 7, 1156), 181, 213
Agnes of Prague, clar., 200
Alberzoni, M. P., 206
Albi, 54
Albigensians, 55, 96, 97, 98
Albiria (daughter of Tancred), 81, 83
Alexander II (pope), 43
Alexander III (pope), 58, 63
Alexander IV (pope), 210
Alexander of Hales, min., 175
Alexis (s.), 58
Alexandria of Egypt, 12
Altopascio (osp.), 35, 165, 216, 219
  Rule: 165, 166

Alszgheny, 156, 157, 217
Alviano, 103
Amalfi, 35
Amann, 158, 159, 160, 161, 163, 164, 165, 168, 169, 189, 217
Ambrose, 158, 213
Amelia, 174, 192
Anacletus II (antipope), 174
Anagni, 130
Andrew de Mozzi (bish. of Florence), 210
Andreozzi, G., tor., 212, 217
Andreotti, S., 191, 222
Angela of Foligno (s.), 153
Angelina of Marsciano (b.), 154
Anonymous Benedictine of the XII century, 36-37, 166, 167, 213
Anthony the Abbot (s.), 12
Antioch, 142
Antonines (monks), 35
Aquileia, 179, 201
Arles, 53

Armstrong, R., cap., 195
Arnold, cist., 96, 98
Arnold of Brescia, 46, 54, 175, 219, 220
Arnoldists, 53, 54, 55, 59, 129, 173, 189
Asseldonk, O., Van, cap., 205, 217
Assisi, 67-79; passim: 68, 69, 71, 177
  Church of St. Nicholas, 186
  Monastery of Monte Subasio, 91, 186
  Benedictine Monasteries, 91-92
Athanasius, 12, 162
Attal, F. S., 93, 178, 188, 217
Aubin, 156, 217
Augustine (s.), 18, 49
Azais, 219

B

Bak, 183, 217
Baldelli, 91, 187, 217
Baldric (bish. of Dol), 213
Baldwin (Cathari heretic), 190
Ballerini (brothers), 169
Barletta, 83
Bartholomais, Vincenzo de, 202
Bartholomew (inq.), 150
Bartholomew Baro, pen., 152, 212, 217
Bartholomew Bechin (or Bequin), tof., 151
Bartoli Langeli, A., 177, 191, 212
Basil, 162
Bassano, Church of St. Donatus, 142
Beer, F. de, 213
Beghards, 64, 176, 221
Beguines, 39, 64, 176, 205, 212, 221
Benedict (bish. of Spoleto), 182
Benedict of Nursia (s.), 11, 12, 48
  Rule: 48, 136, 200
Benvenuta (pen.), 195
Benvenuti Papi, A., 195, 217
Berengarius (bish. of Narbonne), 96, 190
Bernard (s.), 54, 56, 167, 174

Bernard of Bessa, min., 106, 107, 108, 114, 132, 149, 195, 199, 213
Bernard Primus, 62, 95
Bernard of Quintavalle, min., 126
Bernard of Simorre (Cathari bish. of Carcasson), 190
Bernard of Thiron, 48, 172
Bertelli, 166
Bihl, M., ofm, 188, 217
Bobbio, 17
Boehmer, 104
Bologna, 132, 181, 201, 210
  General chapter of the penitents, 151
  Provincial chapter, 202
  University, 130
Bonaventure (s.), min., xii, 83, 102, 106, 107, 141, 149, 152, 166, 192, 194, 213
Bonduelle, 217
Boniface (s.), 28, 33
Boniface VIII (pope), 211
Bordoni, F., tor, 212
Bovara (monk), 92
Brady, I., ofm, 193, 195
Branca, V., 91, 187
Brezzi, P., 175, 217
Brindisi, 83, 132
Brothers of Penitence of Jesus Christ (Frati della Penitenza), 133
Brothers of St. James of Altopascio (Frati di S. Jacopo d'Altopascio), 216, 219
Brothers Servants of Mary (Frati Servi di Maria), 141
Bughetti, B., ofm, 202, 213
Burchard of Ursberg, 126, 129, 139, 199, 204, 213
Burns, R. I., 206, 217
Butler, S., 184

C

Calisse, C., 189
Camaldolese (mon.), 165
Camerino, 91, 177

Canonici, L., ofm, 178, 194, 217-218
Capasso, R., 177
Capistrano, 134, 202
Capitani, O., 218
Capua, 74
Carcasson, 54
Cardaropoli, G., ofm, 198
Caro (Friar) of Arezzo, min., 145, 150, 209, 210, 211
Carpaneto, 218
Carte (LE) de Sassovivo, 213, 214
Cassagrande, G., 182
Casini, A., ofm, 178, 218
Casolini, 193, 218
Cassiano, 12
Cathari, 46, 53, 55-57, 60, 78, 90, 94, 95, 96, 97, 118, 119, 128, 129, 131, 165, 175, 189
Celashi, N., 196
Celestine III (pope), 76, 188
Cencetti, G., 176
Cencio Savelli (Pope Honorius III), 131
Cesar of Arles (s.) (bish.), 13
Chalon-sur-Saeone (Council), 16
Chapter of Utrecht, 212
Charlemagne (emp.), 27, 28, 30, 213
Charles the Fat, 30
Charles the Great (emp.), 27, 213
Charles Martel, 27
Charleroi, 169
Charta Caritatis of Citeaux, 202
Chartres, 185
Cheriapattaparambil, F. X., cap., 197, 218
Chiappini, A., ofm, 202
Chioccioni, P., tor, 186, 218
Christian of Magonza (archbish.), 69
Cipriani, L., ofm, 191
Citeaux, 72, 202
Clare of Assisi, ix, x, 6, 179, 219
  Rule: 200
Claro (Friar) of Florence, 150, 209, 210, 219

Clasen, S., ofm, 183, 186
Clement II (pope), 43
Clement III (pope), 74
Clement V (pope), 211
Cluny (mon.), 32, 33, 34, 43, 72, 174
Collestrada, 68, 79, 81
Cologne, 55, 56
Colombanus (s.), 14, 15, 17
Colonna (family), 188
Como, 60
Conrad of Lutzenfeld, 74, 75, 76, 180
Conrad of Ursberg (ab.), 204, 213
Constantine of Orvieto, 84
Constantinople, 204
Constance, Peace of, 70
Constance, daughter of Tancred, 81, 83
Constance, wife of Henry VI, 74, 75, 179, 180
Constance of Altavilla, 179
Constitutions of Narbonne, 152
Conti, M., ofm, 198
Cremona, 69
Crescenzi (family), 31
Cresi, D., ofm, 193
Cristiani, L., 218
Cristianus (abbas Scotorum) of S. Giacomo, 173
Cyprian (s.), 7, 157-158

D

D'Alatri, M., cap. 155, 209, 217, 218
Dal Pino, F. A., 27, 95, 163, 165, 166, 176, 189, 206, 218
Damietta, 205
Dante Alighieri, 81, 91
De Bartholomais, V., 202
De Dombes, E., tor, 211, 218
De Donato, V., 176
Delaruelle, E., 168, 218
De Luca, A., 177
Denziger-Schonmeitzer, 176
Desbonnets, Th., ofm, 159, 184, 185, 186, 214
Desiderius (s.) Penitents of, 64

Diego de Acebes (bish. of Osma), 97, 190
Dionysius of Alexandria, 13
Diepold of Vohburg, 84
Dirkens, A. H., 156, 218
Distelbrink, 209
Dominic of Calaruega (s.), 64, 84, 97, 190
Dubois, J., osb, 218
Durandus of Huesca, 61, 95

E

Eckbert of Schönau, 55
Elias (Friar) (min.), 148
Elne, 61
Emma dei Conti di Lecce, 180
Esser, K., 91, 103, 104, 105, 106, 109, 111, 112, 113, 119, 122, 124, 129, 139, 156, 157, 187, 193, 194, 195, 196, 197, 198, 199, 204, 205, 214, 218, 219
Evarino of Steinfield, 56, 175

F

Faenza (penitents), 138, 165
Faley, R. J., tor, 156, 219
Fanfani, P., 219
Felder, H., cap, 205
Ferrari, G., 70, 178
Fliche, A., 219
Flick, M., 156, 157, 217
Florence, 51, 148-150, 165
   Bibl. Landau, 202
   Bibl. National, 202
   Church of S. Croce, 142, 149
   Church of S. Maria Novella, 149
   Hospital of S. Gallo, 149
Foligno, 74, 87, 91, 92, 188, 220
Fontaine, J., 160, 219
Fonte Avellana (mon.), 165
Forchielli, G., 201, 219
Fortini, A., 71, 93, 98, 166, 168, 177, 179, 180, 183, 184, 186, 218, 219
Fortini, G., 179, 185, 187, 219

Fossalto, 60
Fournier, P., 160
Franceschini, E., ofm, 186
Francis of Assisi (s.), 67-84
Frascati, 205
Fredegand of Anvers, cap., 199, 219
Frederick II (emp.), 75, 133, 146, 148, 167, 180, 199, 201, 209, 221
Frederick Barbarossa (emp.), 54, 68, 69, 70, 74, 167, 179, 199, 221
Frederick of Lorena, 43
Frédericq, P., 189, 214
Friedberg Ae., 214
Fulda (abbey), 163

G

Galtier, P., 157, 219
Gelasius II (pope), 49
Gennadius of Marseilles, 11, 158, 214
Genoa, 126, 176, 180, 201, 205
Gentile (count), 83, 183
Geoffrey of Auxerre, 176
Georges-Calonghi, 212
Gerard of Filibert (mayor of Assisi), 78
Gerard of Salles (bish.), 48, 192, 216
Gerard of Villamagna, pen., 152
Giacomozzi, 219
Gieben, S., cap., 206, 219
Giotto, 179
Gerard of Gislesio (Lord of Sassorosso), 183
Gisella, pen., 195
Godfrey the Great, 172, 214
Goetz, W., 104
Golubovich, G., ofm, 211, 214
Gorze (mon.), 32, 33
Grado, 201
Grau, E., 193, 219
Gray Sisters (Hospital Sisters), 154, 212
Gratian (titular cardinal of SS Cosmas and Damian), 188

Gratian (jur.), 40, 201
  Decretum Gratiani, 133, 201, 203, 214
Gregory VII (pope), 43
Gregory VIII (pope), 73, 74
  Bull: Audita tremendi (Oct. 29, 1187), 73, 214
Gregory IX (pope), 35, 132, 134, 136, 142, 143, 199, 200, 203, 216
  Bulls:
    Cum qui recepit (June 12, 1234), 207
    Detestanda (May 21, 1227), 134, 136, 138, 169, 214
    Nimis iniqua (August 21, 1231), 142, 143, 207
    Nimis patenter (May 26, 1227), 138, 214
    Nimis prava (August 22, 1231), 142, 207
    Propositum vestrum (June 11, 1227), 189
    Quoniam abundavit (April 6, 1237), 143, 207
    Quoniam ut ait (March 17, 1240), 142
    Si ordinis fratrum (February 1, 1230), 206
    Solet annuere (April 5, 1239), 35, 166
Gregory (card. deacon of S. Angelo, later Pope Innocent II), 174
Gregory the Great (s.) (pope), 18, 160, 168
Grundmann, H., 219
Guido I (bish. of Assisi), 77
Guido II (bish. of Assisi), 89, 90, 92-94, 98, 99, 181, 184, 217
Guido (can. of Assisi), 75

H

Habig, M. A., ofm, 193, 216
Hamilton, B., 219
Hardouin, J., 168, 213, 214
Henquinet, F. M., ofm, 210, 219

Henry VI (emp.), 74, 76, 177, 179, 180, 183, 199
Henry, King of Bavaria, 199
Henry the Deacon (or of Lousanne), 54
Henri de Marcy (card.), 58
Hermann, P., 185
Hilary of Milan, cap., 174, 175, 176, 188, 219, 220
Hildebrand (monk, later Pope Gregory VII), 43
Hilduin, 169
Hinckmar of Rheims, 163, 214
Hispana (Collectio Canonum), 160, 214
Hoemburg, 76
Honora, 193
Honorius II (pope), 174
Honorius III (pope), 131, 133, 136, 205
  Bulls:
    Ad audientiam nostram (1226-1227), 138 214
    Cum illorum (December 1, 1225), 138, 214
    Cum is qui secundum (March 4, 1221), 201
    Litterae tuae (August 27, 1218), 199, 200
    Significatum est (December 16, 1221), 138, 214
Honorius of Autun, 52, 173, 214
Hospitalers of S. John of Jerusalem, 35, 166
Hospitalers of the Holy Spirit, 36
Hugh of Digne, min., 141
Hugh of Provenza (King of Italy), 169
Humiliati, 55, 59, 60, 61, 62, 64, 94, 132, 140, 176, 189, 199, 202, 205, 220
Huygens, R. B. C., 176, 204, 205, 214
Hulst, C. Van, 212

I

Iesi, 75

Innocent II (pope), 174
    Bull: *Religiosis desideriis* (May 21, 1138), 181, 214
Innocent III (pope), 5, 60, 61, 62, 76, 77, 78, 83, 84, 93, 94, 95, 100, 130, 131, 133, 142, 166, 180, 181, 182, 184, 188, 190, 191, 199, 204, 205
    Bulls:
        Cum a nobis (May 13, 1210), 214
        Cum inaestimabile (June 14, 1210), 62, 146, 176, 214
        Dilectus filius Durandus (May 26, 1212), 61, 176, 215
        Ejus exemplo (December 18, 1208), 61, 176, 203, 214
        Etsi nostra navicula (May 31, 1204), 96, 215
        Etsi nostra navicula (march 28, 1208), 98, 206
        Excursus saeculi (November 17, 1206), 97, 98, 215
        Incumbit nobis (June 7, 1201), 189, 215
        In eminenti apostolicae (May 28, 1198), 77, 215
        Ne quis de caetero (July 23, 1212), 203, 215
        Pietas promissionem (January 12, 1199), 161, 215
Innocent IV (Pope), 142, 143, 200, 210
    Bulls:
        Cum a nobis (February 25, 1250), 143, 207
        Dilecti filii (October 13, 1251), 210, 215
        Etsi animarum (November 12, 1254), 143
        Licet vos (November 10, 1248), 148, 214
        Vota devotorum (June 13, 1247), 147, 148, 209
Isabell, D., 192, 198, 203, 215
Isidore of Seville (s.), 18, 41, 169, 215, 219

J

Jacobilli, L., 188, 220
Jacques de Vitry (card.), 60, 126, 139, 176, 199, 205
Jedin, H., 173, 175
Jerome (s.), 24
Jerome Masci da Ascoli Piceno, min., (later Pope Nicholas IV), 150, 166
Jerusalem, 182
John XXII (pope), 212
    Bull: *Altissimo in divinis* (November 18, 1323), 153
John XXIII (Pisan pope), 212
    Bull: *Personas vacantes* (August 26, 1413), 212
John of Campania, 199
John Capistrano (s.), min., 131, 134
John Colonna (card.), 188
John Gualbert (s.), 43, 165
John Paul II (pope), ix, 208
John of Poitiers (bish. of Lyons), 59
John of St. Paul (card.), 93, 94, 98, 99, 131, 188, 217, 222
John of Sasso, 75
Jonah of Orleans, 29, 163, 164, 168, 214
Jordan of Giano, min., 88, 185, 215
Josephines or Josephists, 94, 189, 217
Joseph-Epaphrodite, 189
Judith (second wife of Louis the Pious), 29
Julian of Speyer, min., 89, 102, 106, 107, 141, 185, 192, 194, 206, 215

K

Kalijan (King of Hungary), 182
Knights Templar, 36, 40
Karpp, H., 220
Königsberg, 202

L

Landini, L. C., ofm, 206, 207, 220

Landolph the Elder, 55
Lanz, A., 220
Laon (Chronicle of), 203
Lapsanski, D., 172, 173, 186, 198, 220
L'Aquila, bibl. Provincial, ofm, 202
Lauriola, G., 187, 220
Le Bras, G., 160
Lecce, 83
Leclercq, J., osb, 28, 162, 163, 164, 165, 168, 176, 220
Leff, G., 220
Leicht, P., 220
Lemaitre, H., 212
Lemmens, L., ofm, 104, 198, 199, 202, 204, 215, 216
Leo IX (pope), 43, 168
Leo X (pope), 10, 207, 208, 211, 218
Leo XIII (pope), 207
   Bull: *Misericors Dei* (May 30, 1883), 207
Leo Brancaleoni (card.), 78
Leo Great (s.) (pope), 10, 160
Leptines (Council of), 163
Levi, G., 133, 201, 216
Liège, 56, 169, 204
Lione, 58
Little, A. G., 203
Lobbes (abbey), 169
Lombardi, T., ofm, 186, 199, 220
Lortz, J., 163, 164, 165, 220
Lothario dei Conti di Segni (later Pope Innocent III), 76
Louis the Pious (emp.), 28, 29, 162, 164
Lucius II (pope), 56
Lucius III (pope), 94
Luconi, R., tor, 212
Lugano, P. T., osb, 188, 220
Luxeil (mon.), 17
Lyons, 58

M

Maccarrone, M., 220
Macon (Council of), 21
Madonia (daughter of Tancred), 81, 83
Madonna Pica (mother of St. Francis), 67, 73
Megli, I., 53, 65, 88, 172, 173, 176, 185, 186, 197, 220
Mainka, R. M., 172, 175, 176, 221
Mandonnet, P., op, 203
Manetto de Cambio, pen., 150
Manselli, R., xii, 155, 183, 221
Mansi, J., 158, 160, 172, 175, 208, 213, 216
Map, W., 58
Margaret of Cortona (s.), pen., 153, 218
Maria d'Oignies, 204, 205
Mariani, U., 175, 221
Marianus of Florence, obs., 88, 202
Markwald, 81
Martin IV (pope), 150
   Bull: *Exposuit nobis* (December 13, 1284), 215
Martin (ab.), 204
Martin (friar), Premonstratensian, 202
Matanić, A., ofm, 144, 151, 203, 208, 211, 221
Matthew of Aquasparta, min., (card.), 211
Mattesini, F., ofm, 203, 221
Meersseman, G. G., op, 100, 102, 139, 140, 147, 149, 158, 160, 161, 168, 173, 189, 192, 193, 200, 203, 204, 205, 206, 208, 209, 210, 211, 212, 214, 215, 221
Melia, 221
Mens, A., cap., 176, 205, 221
Messina, 76
Miccoli, G., 221
Michiels, R., 156, 221
Migne, J. P., xv, 169
Milan, 60, 201, 205
Moak, H., 85, 183
Mollat, G., 163
Moncla, S., 212
Monforte, 55
Monte Casale, (conv.), 153
Monte Cassino (abbey), 32, 188
Montefalco, 177
   Convent of S. Croce, 153

Monte Rodone, 74
Montpellier, 190
Moore, R. I., 221
Moorman, J. R. H., 221
Morghen, R., 44, 56, 172, 175, 180, 221
Morin, J., 160, 161, 162, 221
Munier, C., 168, 216
Muratori, L., 169, 199, 215

N

Namur, 169
Narbonne, 53, 61, 152
Narni, 76, 180
Nicholas II (pope), 43
Nicholas IV (pope), 140, 141, 144, 145, 150, 153, 154, 166, 192, 197, 207, 210, 216, 218
   Bulls:
      Supra montem (August 8, 1289), 151, 215
      Unigenitus Dei Filius (August 8, 1290), 151, 215
      Ad audientiam nostram (September 20, 1291), 215
Nicholas, Abbot of Sassovivo, 191
Nicolai, G., 177
Nocent, A., 157, 221
Nocera Umbra, 74, 91, 177
Norbert of Xanten (archbish. of Magdeburg), 45, 48, 49, 51, 172

O

Octavian of the Ubaldini (card.), 201, 216
Odilio (abbot of Cluny), 33
Odo (abbot of Cluny), 33, 173
Odoardi, G., 204, 221
Oignies, 204, 205
Olgati, F., ofm, 192
Oliger, R., ofm, 196, 219, 222
Omaechevarria, I., ofm, 200, 222
Omobono of Cremona (s.), pen., 161
Order of S. James (or of Santiago), 63, 208

Orlandis, J., 222
Orleans (Council of), 10
Orte, 91, 177, 192
Orvieto, 52, 166
Ospedalicchio, 68
Ostia, 130, 131, 132, 133
Otranto, 83
Otto I (emp.), 31, 169
Otto IV of Brunswick (King of Germany), 130, 183, 199

P

Pacini, 221
Pamiers, 61
Paris, 130, 204
Paschini, P., 189, 222
Pasqual II (pope), 48
Passagini, 94, 189, 220
Pastor Oliver, B., tor, 112, 158, 164, 168, 170, 184, 196, 197, 222
Patarines, 53, 55, 60, 94, 129, 173, 175, 189
Paul VI (pope), ix
   Letter: *Seraphicus Patriarca* (June 24, 1978), 207
Pavani, G., 169
Pavia, 60, 169
Pazzelli, R., tor, ix, x, xi, 155, 158, 166, 193, 196, 198, 208, 212, 217, 222
Péano, P., ofm, 211, 212, 222
Pelliccia, G., xv
Penco, G., 222
Penitents (groups of), 63ff
Penitents of the Order of Knights of S. James, 63, 208
Penitents of S. Desiderius of Vicenza, 64
Penitents of Toulouse, 151
Penitentials (books), 14, 15, 17, 18, 28
Pertz, G. H., 213
Perugia, 68, 78, 79, 80, 82, 91, 92, 131, 205
Petau, 160, 161
Peter Damian (s.), 33, 43, 163, 165, 215, 220

Peter of Castelnau, cist., 96
Peter di Bernardone, 67, 71, 73, 77, 81, 82, 83, 88, 89, 95, 178, 185
Peter of Bruys, 46, 51, 53, 54, 220
Peter of Leone (later antipope Anacletus II), 174
Peter Waldo, 57, 58, 59, 61, 62, 94, 97
Peter the Venerable (abbot of Cluny), 53, 174
Philip Augustus (King of France), 81, 98
Philip of Perugia, min., (bish. of Fiesole), 210
Philip of Swabia (King of Germany), 130, 183, 199, 204
Pius V (s.) (pope), 61
Piolanti, A., 164, 173
Pisa, 180, 210
Pompei, A., conv., 158, 171, 172, 176, 209, 222
Poor Catholics, 61, 132, 202, 203
Poor Lombards, 60, 62, 95, 129, 132, 146, 202, 203, 220
Potthast, 215
Praxedes of Rome, pen., 152
Pseudo-Theodore, 15

Q

Quacquarelli, A., 191, 222

R

Rabanus Maurus, 29, 163, 216
Ratherius of Verona (bish.), 41, 42, 144, 169, 216, 217
Ratisbonne, 173
Raul, cist., 96, 97
Raymond of Toulouse (bish.), 190
Ravenna, 165, 210
Ravenna, pen., 195
Recadero (Visigoth king), 21
Reggio, 201
Rheims, 204
Richard of Annibaldis (card.), 166
Richard of S. Victor, 112, 196, 216
Rieti, 74

Rimini, 138
Robert d'Auxerre, 97, 190-191, 216
Robert of Arbrissel, 47, 48, 172, 213
Robert of Flamesbury, 24
Rocca, G., xv
Rocco di Montpellier (s.), pen., 26
Roggen, H., ofm, 206, 209, 222
Romagnoli, G., 166, 216
Rome, 85, 92, 93, 100
   Hospital of S. Anthony Abbot, 35, 166
Romuald (s.), 33, 43
Roscellino, 174
Roselli, P., 177
Rudolph (prior of Sassovivo), 178
Ruggero (Duke of Apulia), 180
Roger II (King of Sicily), 179
Russel, J. B., 223

S

Sabatier, P., 104, 131, 133, 134, 139, 196, 199, 202, 203, 216, 223
Salerno, 74, 76, 180
Salimbene de Adam of Parma, min., 210
Salvi, G., 164, 223
Saint John of Acre, 205
Saint Mary of Reno (abbey), 181
Saint Apollinaris in Classe (mon.), 165
Saint Apollinaris of Sambro, 181, 187
Sarno, 84
Sassovivo (abbey-congregation), 91, 92, 176, 178, 181, 188, 220
Sastre Palmer, N., tor, 159, 223
Schiapparelli, L., 164, 213, 223
Schmucki, C., cap., 101, 102, 126, 155, 186, 192, 194, 198, 217, 223
Schreiber, 205
Selucia, 74, 167
Sens (Council of), 174
Sensi, M., 182, 187, 223
Servian, 190
Sibyl (wife of Tancred), 76, 81, 83, 180
Siena, 69, 141

Sirmond, J., 160
Soffritti, O., 214
Soisson (Council of), 163
Spello, 77, 192
Spicq, C., 156, 223
Speyer, 194
Spoleto (city and duchy), 68, 69, 74, 76, 78, 80, 83, 84, 91, 176, 177
Stanislao di Campagnola, cap., 185, 223
Staufen (family), 199
Stephen IX (pope), 43

T

Tampieri, G., 169, 223
Tanchelmo, 51
Tancred (King of Sicily), 74, 75, 180
Taranto (principality), 81
Tarragon, 61
Temperini, L., tor, 197, 198, 202, 203, 212, 217, 222, 223
Teofilatto (family), 31
Terni, 69
Tertullian, 7, 8, 157, 216
Teulet, A., 191, 216
Theodore the Greek, 23
Thomas Aquinas (s.), op, 175
Thomas of Celano, min., 5, 65, 75, 83, 84, 87, 88, 89, 94, 100, 101, 102, 106, 126, 129, 179, 182, 183, 184, 185, 187, 188, 192, 193, 194, 216
Thouzellier, Ch., 97, 175, 188, 189, 190, 191, 219, 223
Tiraboschi, H., 189, 190, 214, 216
Todi, 177, 192
Toledo (Council of), 17, 21, 40, 160, 213
Toul (Synod of), 94
Toulouse, 53, 54, 98
 Penitents of, 151, 211
 Convent of Our Lady of Peace, 151
Trevi, 92, 192
Treviri (diocese), 52

Tribur (Diet), 30
Troyes (mon.), 175
Tuscano, P., 90, 187, 223
Tuscolo (family), 31

U

Ugolino (count), 178
Ugolino of Conti of Segni (card.) (later Pope Gregory IX), 107, 114, 129, 130, 131-133, 183, 199, 200, 205, 216
Ugolino de Medici of Ferrara, tof, 151, 211
Umberto of Silva Candida, 43
Umiliana dei Cerchi, tof, 194, 195, 217
Urban II (pope), 47, 179
Urban III (pope), 73, 94, 179
 Bulls: *Cum nobis* (January 27, 1185), 181, 216
 Religiosam vitam eligentibus (April 29, 1186), 94
Urban IV (pope), 197, 200, 216

V

Val di Castro, mon., 165
Valle Parraria, Church of S. Nicholas, 178
Vallombrosa, mon., 165
Venice, 202
 Bibl. of S. Zanipolo, 202
Verdiana of Castel Florentino (b.), 152
Verona, 41, 169
 Council of, 55, 59, 60, 94, 95
Via Romea or Via Francesca, 35
Viboldone, 60, 94
 Church of S. Peter, 94
Vicaire, M. H., 223
Vicenza, 211
 Penitents of S. Desiderius, 64
Vitalis of Savigny (b.), 48, 172, 216
Vito of Cortona, min., 195
Victor IV (antipope), 174
Vives, J., 213, 214, 216

Vogel, C., 157, 158, 159, 162, 168, 223
Volterra, Guarnacci Library, 104, 187, 193, 196, 219
Vorreux, D., ofm, 166, 223

W

Wadding, L., obs., 196, 210
Wakefield, W. L., 224
Waldo, P., 57, 58, 62, 94, 97, 119
Waldensians, 46, 53, 55, 59, 60, 61, 62, 94, 95, 96, 97, 105, 106, 118, 119, 128, 129, 131, 165
Waley, D., 177, 224
Walter Map (can.), 58
Walter III of Brienne, 81, 83, 84, 180
Warner, H. L., 224
Weiland, L., 204
William II (King of Sicily), 179
William III (son of Tancred), 180
William Arnald, 62
William of Champeaux, 174
William of Nevers, 190
Wolf, Ph., 224
Wyngaert, A., Van Den, ofm, 202, 216

Z

Zanichelli, G., 199, 223
Zanoni, L., 206, 224
Zorzi, D., 116, 197, 224

Franciscan Gift Shop
503 So. Brown's Lake Dr.
Burlington, WI 53105